NEVILLE CHAMBERLAIN'S WAR

Neville Chamberlain's War:

How Great Britain Opposed Hitler, 1939-1940

Frederic Seager

Neville Chamberlain's War

ISBN: 9798548548795

Contents

Introduction   **7**

1 Unfinished Business   14

2 Appeasement and Its Discontents   38

3 A Change of Tactics   66

4 Limited Liability   104

5 War Aims   141

6 Dénouement, 1940   173

7 Winston Churchill's War   208

Epilogue: Yalta and Beyond   241

Bibliography   260

Index   281

Introduction

The Second World War was the last opportunity for great powers to settle their differences through armed force. The frustrations engendered by today's many unresolved conflicts have resulted in nostalgia for a period when, as is widely believed, good triumphed over evil. A visit to almost any airport bookshop will reveal a history section devoted largely to the war. The curiosity of the reading public appears to be insatiable. Over one hundred thousand titles on the subject have been published so far, and there seems to be no end in sight. It is always comforting to recall a period when the choice between democracy and dictatorship, freedom and tyranny, was so clear-cut.

In this context, no historic figure is more reassuring than Winston Churchill. When all seemed lost in June of 1940, and many members of his own party favoured a compromise peace, he vowed to continue the struggle against Nazi Germany. Churchill's address to the House of Commons on taking office as prime minister leaves no room for doubt: he promised victory, whatever the cost may be. Just how he would achieve this goal was left in abeyance, but at least he stood up to Hitler. What could be more noble, more meritorious than to oppose this brutal dictator? The atrocities committed by the Nazi regime, nearly all of which took place once the war had begun, condemn Hitler to all eternity as the very epitome of evil. Present-day tyrants may not be quite as bad, but any political leader who opposes them (Israeli Premier Netanyahu, for example) is soon enshrined as a new Churchill. For every villain there must be a hero.

This wave of adulation, now consecrated in numerous films, was not altogether spontaneous. It had been carefully prepared during the Second World War by Churchill himself, a prolific author. The story goes that at the Casablanca conference of January 1943,

Roosevelt asked him: "Do you think that history will be kind to us?" Churchill replied confidently in the affirmative, "because I intend to write it!" And so he did. His detailed, highly politicized history of the war, the first volumes of which appeared just before he was awarded the Nobel Prize for literature in 1953, is focused largely on himself, with Roosevelt playing second fiddle.

The memoirs of any political leader naturally tend toward self-aggrandizement, and one can hardly blame Churchill for wanting to be judged favourably by posterity. There remains a problem, however, for the historian if not for the movie-going public: Churchill did not initiate the war against Nazi Germany. That was the work of his predecessor, Neville Chamberlain. Now Chamberlain is chiefly remembered, in so far as he is remembered for anything at all, as having negotiated the Munich accords of 30 September 1938, by which Czechoslovakia was dismembered, in the vain hope of appeasing Hitler. Soon thereafter, "appeasement" was rejected (at least officially) and has since become a dirty word. Yet it was Chamberlain, the arch-appeaser, who announced to a tense House of Commons on 3 September 1939 – more than two full days after the Nazi invasion of Poland – that Britain was at war with Germany. He brought Churchill into the cabinet in order to lend some credibility to his newly-found bellicosity.

Chamberlain was a most reluctant warrior. Far more than the protagonists of 1914, he was the quintessential sleepwalker, leading his country and France into a war he neither wanted nor understood. Ostensibly, Britain went to war over Poland, which had been invaded by Hitler's *Wehrmacht* on 1 September 1939, but it undertook no military action to relieve that hapless country. France made only a token gesture of support. In the weeks and months that followed there were some naval engagements between Britain and Germany, but almost no fighting on land. Soon the British people and press referred to the daily inactivity as the "twilight war" (an expression that seems to have originated with Chamberlain) or the "bore war". In France, it is known as "*la Drôle de Guerre,*" which does not mean "amusing war," as two American writers claim,[1] but "strange" or even "bizarre" war.[2] The French know better than most that war is never amusing.

The American expression, "phoney war," is probably the most apt. It was phoney from the start, and that is exactly what Chamberlain wanted. His strategy, if such it can be called, was to put pressure on Germany through an economic blockade and wait for the German home front to crumble. Meanwhile, he expected the French army, fully mobilized behind the Maginot Line, to convince the Germans that they could not possibly win. This turned out to be a tragic error. Since then, the allied defeat of May-June 1940 has been laid conveniently on France's doorstep. It was all France's fault. The French army, which Churchill had praised in 1933 and again in 1938 as the finest in the world, failed to deliver. As an island, Britain avoided Nazi occupation and was thus exonerated of any blame. Better still, if we are to believe an Australian historian, it "saved the West" in 1940.[3] So all's well that ends well.

In reality, Britain barely managed to save itself, and then only with the help of its far-flung Dominions, especially Canada. The entry of the United States into the war assured Churchill, as he had long hoped, of an honoured place among the victors. But Britain certainly did not save the West. Chamberlain's ill-considered guarantee to Poland in March 1939 committed Britain and France to a war that they had little chance of winning and thus condemned not only France, but most other democratic states in Western Europe to more than four years of Nazi occupation. The Dutch who had to eat tulip bulbs during the "hunger winter" of 1944-45 can attest to the privations imposed by Germany.[4] French historians tend to view the war of waiting as merely

[1] William Manchester and Paul Reid, *The Last Lion: Winston Spencer Churchill, Defender of the Realm, 1940-1945* (Boston: Little, Brown, 2012), 36.

[2] See Roland Dorgelès, *La Drôle de Guerre, 1939-1940* (Paris: Albin Michel, 1957), 9. Dorgelès a war correspondent, coined the term in a newspaper article of October 1939.

[3] Robin Prior, *When Britain Saved the West: The Story of 1940* (New Haven, CT: Yale University Press, 2015).

[4] Antony Beevor, *The Battle of Arnhem: The Deadliest Airborne Operation of*

a prelude to their country's humiliating defeat.[5] Yet the fall of France was also a British defeat, since it laid bare the failure of Chamberlain's entire European policy. He was more accomplished at appeasement than at war.

Neville Chamberlain's war was not what he had planned. He had expected victory on the cheap: the good German people would overthrow Hitler and replace him with a more compliant regime. Instead, Britain soon found itself involved in a titanic struggle against a more powerful enemy – indeed a coalition of enemies, including Japan. By 1945, Britain emerged victorious, but at what cost? In the immediate postwar period, it had to rely on American and Canadian loans in order to stay afloat financially. Meat rationing, including the roast beef of old England, did not end until the summer of 1954. The British Empire, upon which the sun had never set, quickly disintegrated. This was not all Chamberlain's fault. He had been pushed into war by Parliament, and in particular by those, such as Churchill, who felt that Britain had to take up the challenge of Nazism in order to save its honour and maintain its standing as a great power.

Was it worth the effort? The world is certainly a better place with Hitler out of the way. But was it necessary to confront him in 1939 when Britain and France together were weaker than Nazi Germany? Would it not have been preferable to let him get embroiled in war with the Soviet Union before throwing their weight into the balance? The consensus among historians, and even more so among amateur history buffs, is that Hitler had to be stopped sometime. But he was not stopped then. On the contrary, the Phoney War, which Chamberlain initiated without due consideration for Germany's military strength, led to a decisive German victory and actually reinforced Hitler's position. Sometimes the best course of action is to do nothing and wait on events. Alas, great powers typically feel compelled to act, whatever the

---

World War II (New York: Viking, 2018), 364 ff.

[5] See, for example, Henri Michel, *La défaite de la France* (Paris: Presses Universitaires de France, 1980).

circumstances may be, in order to prove to the world, and to themselves, that they are still great powers.

The great power syndrome is still reflected in British historiography, which has produced a spate of books purporting to explain the origins of the Second World War. In one typical example, the author asks rhetorically: "Why did a general European war break out in September 1939?" He goes on to assert: "When Hitler attacked Poland, Britain and France duly honoured their pledge to defend Poland's independence and war resulted."[6] Actually, of course, they did not defend Poland's independence – nor could they. What resulted, so far as Britain and France were concerned, was not war, but make-believe war, which lasted until the spring of 1940, when Hitler launched a series of spectacular offensives in Norway, the Low Countries and France. Only after Germany invaded the Soviet Union a year later was there general war in Europe. As an island, Britain remained in the fight, bravely resisting German aggression on the sea and in the air. Until September 1943, the British war effort on land was conducted mainly against Italy.

Books about the Second World War fall into two general categories: works about its origins, which are devoted primarily to the frenzied diplomacy that preceded Britain's formal declaration of war, followed by those recounting the military saga that began in 1940. In the former, the narrative is broken off once war is declared on 3 September 1939. The reader is left without any explanation of what can happen when great powers assume commitments that they cannot honour. Subsequent volumes begin with the real fighting, i.e. battles, the very essence of military history. The generally accepted consensus is based on the assumption that the conflict begun in September 1939 was a good war. Even A.J.P. Taylor, a gadfly among historians, believes it was.[7] Of course it could be argued that there is no such thing as a good war; but for Britain, the Second World War was certainly an

---

[6] Richard Overy, *1939: Countdown to War* (London: Allen Lane, 2009), 111.

[7] A.J.P. Taylor, *The Second World War: An Illustrated History* (London: Hamish Hamilton, 1975), 234.

improvement over the First. Not only were there fewer British casualties, including civilians caught in the bombing; the "real" war, the one that began in June 1940, has come to symbolize the heroism of an entire nation.

Fine, but the Phoney War was not a good war. Books on the subject, whether scholarly monographs or popular histories, cover a severely restricted time frame: 3 September 1930 to 10 May 1940. Little, if anything, is told about its consequences for the peoples of continental Europe. The war of waiting merits at best a passing reference in more general works, where, in the words of two British historians, it "is avoided as a barren landscape."[8] Another writes: "The British national memory of the Second World War treats its first nine months as . . . an uneventful and slightly tiresome preamble that must be got through before the truly important parts of the story can begin – and by 'important' is meant the parts in which the British themselves play the role as sole saviours of the world."[9] The most comprehensive single-volume treatment of the war in English ignores the "preamble" altogether.[10]

The present study raises a question that is often overlooked by historians: why go to war at all? To this, there can be only one answer: self-defence. Yet in 1939, neither Britain nor France was directly threatened by Nazi Germany. Of course Hitler was a truly bad guy; and except for a few Nazi sympathizers, nearly all chroniclers of the Second World War can hardly wait to see him defeated. But we must avoid wishful thinking. An American historian claims that in 1939 "Hitler wanted a fight [yes he did, but where?], and this time Britain and France were ready to oblige."[11] If only it were so! Neither Chamberlain

---

[8] Nick Smart and Jeremy Black, *British Strategy and Politics during the Phony War: Before the Balloon Went Up* (Westport, CT: Praeger, 2003), 165.

[9] Alan Allport, *Britain at Bay: The Epic Story of the Second World War, 1938-1941* (New York: Knopf, 2020), 160.

[10] Peter Calvocoressi and Guy Wint, *Total War: Causes and Courses of the Second World War* (London: Penguin, 1972).

[11] Philip Nord, *France 1940: Defending the Republic* (New Haven, CT: Yale

nor Daladier, the French premier, wanted a "fight" with Hitler, who, in any case, had made no plans for war in the west. A British historian is closer to the mark when he writes that the British and French governments, bound by their pledge to Poland, "wriggled desperately in an effort to escape from the trap they had set for themselves."[12] Once officially involved, the two allies could not agree on war aims. Britain was nominally at war with Hitler, France with Germany. Neither had the military strength to seek a decision, and Chamberlain assumed that the war could be won with little or no fighting. Allied strategy on the Rhine was to wait for Hitler to attack, which he did, at a time and in a manner of his own choosing.

Now that total war is no longer a viable option, Neville Chamberlain's war presents us with an object lesson in humility and patience: namely that war is not a matter to be entered into lightly. Too many books on the Second World War present it as an epic, a glorious adventure in which right prevailed over might – Churchill over Hitler. The Phoney War is largely ignored in surveys of World War II because it involved little or no fighting. But Chamberlain's ill-considered declaration of war and his subsequent do-nothing policy set the stage for Hitler's greatest triumph: the conquest of Western Europe. There was nothing glorious about the Phoney War, and that is precisely why it merits our attention. In the context of international relations, it was worse than a crime – a tragic blunder.

War is a disease for which there is no cure, only prevention. The Phoney War reminds us that any state, especially a democracy, must first understand what it will be fighting for and then carefully weigh its chances of victory before committing itself to violent action. The great powers of our own day may well take note.

University Press, 2015), 18.

[12] Leonard Mosley, *On Borrowed Time: How World War II Began* (London: Pan Books, 1971), 425.

1 Unfinished Business

The First World War is remembered chiefly for the fighting on the Western front, as massed armies flung themselves onto well-prepared defences, suffering appalling casualties for very little gain. The slaughter, which lasted more than four years, has obscured a simple fact: it was not supposed to have happened that way. No one, least of all the German general staff, expected a protracted struggle in France and Belgium. German strategy in 1914 was designed to eliminate France first by taking Paris, where all major railway lines converged. The country would then be paralyzed, leaving the German army free to deal with what was perceived to be the main enemy: Russia.

Traditional German military doctrine, dating from the Holy Roman Empire, was defensive in the west and expansionist in the east. It was embodied in the original German mobilization plan, devised shortly after the Franco-Prussian War by Helmuth von Moltke the Elder, who had led the Prussian army to successive victories over Denmark, Austria and France. He determined that in a future conflict, Germany should hold the newly-acquired blue line of the Vosges against a French assault and then deploy the bulk of its forces on the Russian front. Moltke's successor, Schlieffen, reversed the order of priority. He reasoned that Russian mobilization would take at least six weeks, during which time it would be possible to knock France out of the war.

In the event, France survived to fight another day. The Schlieffen plan, as modified by the younger Moltke, maintained the basic strategy of attacking France first. Though brilliant on paper, it encountered difficulties that neither Schlieffen nor his successors had fully anticipated. The first was simple fatigue. German troops, marching up to forty miles a day, were exhausted by the time they had to engage in real combat. The Belgians, through whose territory the German army pursued its invasion, were expected to let the aggressor pass unopposed. Churchill, like Lord Kitchener, assumed "that Belgium would make a formal protest and submit."[1] Instead, the Belgian army of six infantry divisions fought back, slowing the German advance by a couple of days. The Belgians sabotaged their own rail network; all bridges across the Meuse were destroyed, as were most telegraph lines throughout the country. Russia, though not yet fully mobilized, then staged a surprise offensive, obliging the German general staff to shift some of its forces to the east. The timely arrival of the British Expeditionary Force, a trained professional army of five divisions (four infantry and one cavalry), ninety thousand men, in northern France, also helped throw the invaders off their schedule. The French then ceased their fruitless attacks in the Vosges and moved northward to meet the advancing enemy. With British support, they repulsed the Germans at the Marne and saved Paris.

The battle of the Marne was the last important instance of mobile warfare in the west until 1918. A double line of trenches, protected by mines, machine guns, artillery and barbed wire, stretching from the Belgian coast to the Swiss border, ensured the supremacy of defence for the next four years. Yet the allied commanders continued to place their hopes in the offensive. One more "big push" by the infantry, they believed, would lead to victory. In retrospect, the waste of so many young lives seems absurd, and it was. But what could the allies do? They seemingly had no choice but to liberate the territory in France and Belgium that had been conquered by Germany.

In the years following the war, it was perhaps only natural to read history backwards and attribute the conflict, which the German general staff had originally envisaged as being directed primarily against Russia, to some deep-seated rivalry between France and Germany. "The story of Franco-German relations since 1871," wrote

---

[1] Winston S. Churchill, *The World Crisis, 1911-1914* (London: Thornton Butterworth, 1931), 117.

British historian G.P. Gooch in 1923, "is the record of France's endeavour to regain her lost territories and of Germany's attempt to retain them." In time, he concluded, all of European diplomacy became entwined about the question. "Each of the protagonists sought and found allies, until almost the whole of Europe was involved in their implacable vendetta."[2] After the war, France did in fact recover Alsace-Lorraine, pursuant to Woodrow Wilson's Fourteen Points, which Germany accepted as a basis for an armistice. Professor Gooch implies that Britain had been lured into war in order to satisfy French irredentism. Has this notion any basis in fact?

To set the record straight, there is no better starting point than the British diplomatic documents, which Professor Gooch himself helped edit. An entry dated 16 December 1910 records a meeting between Sir Edward Grey, the British foreign secretary, and Count Metternich, the German ambassador. In an obvious attempt to draw Britain away from her partner in the *Entente Cordiale*, Metternich raised the spectre of a war for Alsace-Lorraine. The French, he claimed, had never renounced their claims to the territory; they were dissuaded only by the superior might of Germany. Grey then writes:

I said France could hardly be expected formally to renounce the lost provinces, but as a matter of fact I was not conscious that an attack upon Germany to recover them played any part in her relations with other powers. I did not know the terms of the Franco-Russian alliance, but I did not suppose it embraced this point. Count Metternich said it certainly did not,[3]

In order to break out of its diplomatic isolation, to find and retain allies, beginning with Russia, France had to renounce any hint of irredentism. French statesmen, notes an American historian, "could not help but see that Russia had no interest in securing Alsace-Lorraine for

---

[2] George Peabody Gooch, *Franco-German Relations, 1871-1914* (London: Longmans, Green, 1923), 5.

[3] George Peabody Gooch and Harold Temperly, eds., *British Documents on the Origins of the War, 1898-1914*, (London: H. M. Stationary Office, 1930), VI, 575-576.

France. ..."[4] The tsar went out of his way to explain to the French ambassador that, so far as the lost provinces were concerned, "You can wait with dignity."[5]

In August of 1914, it was not Alsace-Lorraine but the Schlieffen-Moltke plan that committed Germany to a full-scale offensive against France, regardless of what French sentiments or ambitions might have been. Yet even without Alsace-Lorraine as a factor, most Britons emerged from the ordeal resentful at having to squander blood and treasure on the continent of Europe. The German declaration of war on 3 August left France with no alternative but to defend itself. Britain, which was not directly threatened, declared war against Germany the following day – ostensibly to protect Belgian neutrality, in reality to preserve (or, more accurately, to restore) the European balance of power.[6] But what did that mean to the individual British soldier, who had been called upon to fight in a foreign land against an enemy with whom he had no personal quarrel? Those who managed to survive in one piece had to endure up to four years of mud, rats, trench foot and shell shock. "No more wars for me at any price!" exclaimed one veteran. "Except against the French. If there's ever a war with them, I'll go like a shot."[7]

Britain's losses in the First World War were substantially less than those of its ally: total war dead amounted to 715,000 for the United Kingdom and 198,000 for the Empire. Metropolitan France, whose population was six million fewer than that of Britain, registered 1,327,000 killed plus 71,000 from its colonies. Moreover, France's demographic decline in the nineteenth century left it with a smaller proportion of young men available for service and a higher proportion

---

[4] William L. Langer, *The Franco-Russian Alliance* (Cambridge, MA: Harvard University Press, 1929), 89.

[5] Pierre Renouvin, *Histoire des relations internationales* (Paris: Hachette, 1955), VI, 128.

[6] Nicholas Mansergh, *The Coming of the First World War: A Study in the European Balance, 1878-1914* (London: Longmans, Green, 1949), 232-3.

[7] Robert Graves, *Goodbye to All That* (London: Penguin, 1960), 305.

of dead and wounded than all other major combatants. But at least France was defending its own soil, whereas Britain gained precious little from the conflict, save a few mandated territories taken from the Ottoman Empire and some German colonies of doubtful value in Africa. During the first two years of war, as Britain relied on voluntary enlistments to raise a mass army, a disproportionate number of casualties came from the upper classes. Public (i.e. private) school graduates filled the ranks of junior officers, who went over the top, leading their men in fruitless assaults against withering fire.

In all their history, the British people had never been called upon to make such sacrifices. Britain's traditional policy on the continent was to maintain a rough balance of power so that, in any conflict, it could intervene in favour of the weaker side and win. The Royal Navy was Britain's chief contribution to victory; on land it would customarily engage only a small force, relying on its continental allies, often aided by British subsidies, to do most of the fighting. In 1914, however, the European balance of power, on which Britain had long relied in order to limit its continental commitment, no longer existed. German industrial and military predominance was such that, as the casualty figures mounted, the British government took the unprecedented step of enacting conscription in January 1916. Even then, the allies did not achieve victory until the arrival in 1918 of two million fresh troops from the United States.

The lesson was not lost on British military strategists or the British political class. It was widely believed in Britain that Anglo-French staff talks held before 1914 had provided the French with an opportunity to draw the British into a commitment far beyond their original intentions.[8] In 1932, Captain (later Sir) Basil H. Liddell Hart published a study entitled *The British Way in Warfare*, in which he proposed a return to tradition. "For the first time in our history," he

---

[8] Philip Bell, "'Thank God for the French Army': Churchill, France and an Alternative to Appeasement in the 1930s," Christopher Baxter, Michael L. Dockrill and Keith Hamilton eds., *Britain in Global Politics*, I: *From Gladstone to Churchill* (London: Palgrave Macmillan, 2013), 179.

recalled, "we poured the nation into the army."[9] This must not be allowed to happen again. He drove the point home in *The Defence of Britain*, a best-seller of 1939. "The first responsibility of the [British] army is to protect this country." Defending the Empire came second, and "our foreign interests" ran a poor third.[10] Like his French counterpart, Charles de Gaulle, he favoured a small professional force. But in 1939 Britain had not even that. Only two divisions of conscript troops were available for active duty in France when Chamberlain declared war. Churchill fully subscribed to Liddell Hart's philosophy; he remained convinced as late as 1939 that Britain did not need a large army.[11] He counted on France to supply the bulk of the necessary land forces.

Adding to the general disillusionment was the treaty of Versailles. The German Empire had been proclaimed there in January 1871, and in France it seemed the most appropriate venue for the peace settlement of 1919. For the British, however, the very word, "Versailles," with its ornate Hall of Mirrors, conjured up the image of French predominance under Louis XIV. Had the final settlement with Germany been signed in London, Washington or even Brussels, it would hardly have incurred such opprobrium. Not until 1942 did a book appear in England defending the treaty, and then only in measured terms. The British public, like that of the Dominions and the United States, readily accepted the claim of the German government that Versailles was a *Diktat*, a dictated peace; and it retains that reputation to this very day. Actually, the treaty of Versailles followed Wilson's Fourteen Points in their broad outline and was far less oppressive than the treaty signed at Brest-Litovsk on 3 March 1918. There, Germany annexed one quarter of Russia's territory, one-third of its population,

---

[9] Basil H. Liddell Hart, *The British Way in Warfare* (London: Faber & Faber, 1932), 14.

[10] Basil H. Liddell Hart, *The Defence of Britain* (London: Faber & Faber, 1939), 279.

[11] A.J.P. Taylor, "The Statesman," A.J.P. Taylor. ed., *Churchill Revised: A Critical Assessment* ((New York: The Dial Press, 1969), 36.

one-third of its arable land, three-quarters of its coal and iron and 54 percent of its railroads. It further imposed on the hapless Russians an indemnity of six billion gold marks – a real *Diktat*. The treaty of Brest-Litovsk was annulled by the armistice in the west and has since been conveniently forgotten.

But not the treaty of Versailles. It was thoroughly discredited by British economist John Maynard Keynes in a masterful polemic which quickly became a best-seller in 1920. He described Paris during the peace conference as "a nightmare," where "every one . . . was morbid," except perhaps U. S. President Woodrow Wilson, whom he dismissed as a "blind and deaf Don Quixote." Keynes had no use for newly-restored Poland, calling it "an economic impossibility with no industry but Jew-baiting."[12] His main objection concerned reparations, which he claimed would cripple Germany financially and drag all of Europe into a permanent economic morass. In the event, Germany was not ruined and actually paid less in reparations than the net amount, after partial reimbursement, that it received in foreign loans, especially American.[13] After the Second World War, Germany – both the Western zones and the Soviet zone – paid more in reparations than the Weimar Republic ever did without having to face economic ruin.[14] Contrary to the Weimar Republic, the German successor regimes of the post-World War II era accepted defeat and a foreign military presence. Another dire prediction came from the head of the German delegation to the Paris peace conference: "Those who sign this treaty will sign the death sentence of many millions of German men, women and children." Keynes approved wholeheartedly. "I know of no adequate answer to

---

[12] John Maynard Keynes, *The Economic Consequences of the Peace* (New York: Harcourt, Brace and Howe, 1920), 5-6, 41, 291.

[13] Stephen A. Schuker, *American "Reparations" to Germany, 1919-33: Implications for the Third-World Debt Crisis* (Princeton, NJ: International Finance Section, Department of Economics, 1988), 10-11 *et passim*.

[14] Adam Tooze, *The Wages of Destruction: The Making and Breaking of the Nazi Economy* (London: Penguin, 2006), 673-4.

these words," he wrote.[15] In point of fact, not a single German died as a result of the Versailles treaty.

The German government had planned to pay for the war (assuming victory, of course) by imposing a crushing indemnity on France, so that the defeated enemy would not be able to rearm for another eighteen or twenty years. "The enemy must be vanquished completely," Kaiser Wilhelm II announced on 7 February 1915, "and I will dictate the peace terms at the point of my soldiers' bayonets."[16] In that case, the rich iron ore deposits of eastern France were to be annexed permanently to Germany, as was Luxembourg. Belgium was to become a vassal state.[17] Such measures, along with the subjugation of Russia, were intended to ensure total German domination over Europe; but with an allied victory, they were never realized and are of interest only to academic historians.

So it was the reparations question that preoccupied European statesmen for much of the postwar period. The legal basis for reparations was established in article 231 of the treaty, which had been drafted by lawyers Norman Davis and John Foster Dulles of the American delegation. It has since become known as the infamous "war guilt" clause. Actually, the article makes no mention of guilt, but refers to the *responsibility* of Germany and her allies for the damage caused by their aggression. Even Keynes admitted obliquely that Germany was primarily responsible for the war. He feared that French and British leaders ran the risk of "completing the ruin, which Germany began."[18] The allied terms can hardly have come as a surprise to the German delegation, since article XIX of the armistice convention, which Germany accepted, states plainly that Germany must pay "reparation for damage done." The damage, often caused deliberately and with no

---

[15] Keynes, *Economic Consequences*, 230.

[16] T.E. Jessop, *The Treaty of Versailles: Was It Just?* (London: Thomas Nelson, 1942), 51.

[17] Fritz Fischer, *Germany's Aims in the First World War* (New York: Norton, 1967), 110-111, 117-118, 257-271.

[18] Keynes, *Economic Consequences*, 3.

military purpose, was in fact considerable. Faced with unexpected resistance by the Belgian army, German troops laid waste to the university town of Louvain on 25-30 August 1914. Its library of 250,000 mediaeval and early modern manuscripts was burned, university buildings were destroyed and the cathedral of Saint Pierre badly damaged. German soldiers forced their way into peoples' homes and engaged in extensive looting. Three hundred men and boys were shot, as were the mayor, two magistrates, the rector of the university and all police officials. Nor was this the only example: German troops had killed 674 Belgian civilians in Dinant two days earlier.

The occupation of northern France, though not as dramatic, was no less oppressive. There were severe food and fuel shortages. Factories were dismantled and shipped to Germany. In 1915, an indemnity of one million gold marks was levied on the citizens of Sedan, while those of Lille had to pay three million. The German occupiers confiscated the gold reserves of French banks. Young Frenchmen of military age were conscripted into labour battalions. At the war's end, the retreating Germans flooded French coal mines, destroyed bridges and railways, slaughtered cattle and poisoned wells, leaving behind booby traps in those public buildings still standing.[19] A British historian paints a grim picture of the immediate postwar scene in France: "Altogether 66,000 miles of roads and 31,000 miles of railway line had been destroyed or damaged; 320,000 houses, 20,000 factories, 2,000 bridges and 600 railway stations had to be rebuilt. The national debt had soared to 150 billion francs, compared to 35 billion in 1914. The country was exhausted, and so was the economy."[20] Keynes, the arch-germanophile, recognized that France and Belgium deserved compensation. "France, in my judgment . . . has the greatest claims on our generosity."[21] He simply disputed the amount owing (which was

---

[19] Brendan Hodge, "World War I Reparations Weren't as Unfair as You Think", *The Federalist*, 29 July 2014; James T. Shotwell, *What Germany Forgot* (New York: Macmillan, 1940), 30.
[20] Gordon Corrigan, *Blood, Sweat and Arrogance, and the Myths of Churchill's War* (London: Phoenix, 2007), 109.

not fixed until May 1921, more than a year after his book was published) and insisted that it be tied to inter-allied war debts. The United States refused any such connection, leaving France with the bill for both the damages caused by Germany and the money owed to its allies.

Above all, Keynes condemned the spirit of the treaty, which he characterized as vengeful. He summarized it as follows: "For at least a generation to come, Germany cannot be trusted with even a modicum of prosperity . . . year by year Germany must be kept impoverished and her children starved and crippled, and. . . she must be ringed round by enemies. . . ."[22] What enemies? Was newly-created Czechoslovakia an enemy? Did its mere existence threaten Germany? During the brief span of the Weimar republic, relations between the two countries were in fact quite cordial.[23] Keynes did not focus on Czechoslovakia. His prime target was French Premier Georges Clemenceau, whose "aim was to weaken and destroy Germany in every possible way."[24] There is no basis for such blanket condemnation, but Keynes was not given to nuances. "In so far as the economic lines of the treaty represent an intellectual idea, it is the idea of France and of Clemenceau." Keynes accused the French of making "in the first instance the most definite and the most extreme proposals" on the question of reparations.[25] Actually, it was the British representatives at the peace conference, Lords Cunliffe and Sumner, who presented the highest figure,[26] which included indirect war expenses, such as pensions and separation allowances. These terms violated the armistice agreement, which

---

[21] Keynes, *Economic Consequences*, 150.

[21]*Ibid.*, 125-6.

[22]*Ibid.*, 267.

[23] P.E. Caquet, *The Bell of Treason: The 1938 Munich Agreement in Czechoslovakia* (London: Profile Books, 2018), 6.

[24] Keynes, *Economic Consequences* 52.

[25]*Ibid.*, 28-9.

[26] Alan Sharp, "The Big Four: Peacemaking in Paris in 1919," *History Review*, December 2009, 16; cf. Marc Trachtenberg, "Reparation at the Paris Peace Conference," *The Journal of Modern History*, March 1979, 24-55..

limited reparations to payment for direct damages. Unlike France and Belgium, Britain had suffered little direct damage from Germany on its home soil.

The very idea that Germany was to be permanently enfeebled is absurd. As Thorstein Veblen noted in his review of Keynes's petulant masterpiece, the peace negotiations of 1919 were overshadowed by the spectre of Bolshevism, which might take hold throughout much of Europe if Germany were reduced to misery.[27] The Bolshevik seizure of power in November 1917 had sown something akin to panic among the allies. The following spring, troops from various allied countries were sent to Russia – ostensibly to keep that country in the war against Germany; but they stayed after the armistice and continued to lend support to the Czechoslovak Legion and the White Russian forces. No one was more committed to this venture than Churchill, who told American journalists in 1954: "If I had been properly supported in 1919, I think we might have strangled Bolshevism in its cradle. . . ."[28] War weariness and the fierce resistance of Trotsky's Red Army led to the withdrawal of all allied contingents, except the Japanese, in 1920; but no one at the peace conference – certainly not Clemenceau – wanted Bolshevism to sweep across Europe. The Spartacist uprising in Berlin, brutally crushed in January 1919 by the paramilitary *Freikorps* at the instigation of a nominally social-democratic government, frightened the victorious powers and encouraged them to lift the blockade on foodstuffs to the vanquished foe. In March, shortly before the Versailles treaty was signed, Lloyd George warned: "If Germany goes over to the Spartacists it is inevitable that she should throw her lot with the Russian Bolshevists."[29] At the same time, Churchill expressed the hope that Germany, "by combating Bolshevism, by being a bulwark against it . . . may take the first step toward ultimate reunion with the civilised world."[30]

---

[27] *Political Science Quarterly*, September 1920, 467-72.

[28] *New York Times*, 29 June 1954.

[29] elizabethmaddaluno.wordpress.com/2017/04/15/fpnainebleau-memorandum/

Basking in the public acclaim that he had received for his initial denunciation of the Versailles treaty, Keynes proposed an extensive revision in 1922. He advised France not to worry about the Germany's military potential. "That she has anything to fear from Germany in the future which we can foresee, except what she may herself provoke, is a delusion. . . . Germany's future now lies to the east, and in that direction her hopes and ambitions, when they revive, will certainly turn."[31] In other words, France should allow Germany to dominate Central and Eastern Europe, which it eventually did – following the Munich accords. In 1924, however, France concluded a defensive military pact with Czechoslovakia, thereby blocking Germany's eastward thrust. Keynes foresaw that Germany was not particularly eager to wage another war in Western Europe, and on this point he was substantially correct. In 1914, the German general staff regarded Russia as the prime danger, as would Hitler in 1939.[32] Keynes might well condemn Clemenceau for being beastly to the poor Germans; but Hitler, once he came to power, did not seek a war with France. He didn't have to. In less than six years he managed to nullify, without a war, nearly all the restrictions imposed on Germany at Versailles.

Hitler merely continued the sabotage of the treaty begun by the Weimar Republic. On 9 January 1923, the Reparation Commission declared Germany to be in default on coal deliveries. The vote was three to one, with the British delegate in opposition. Two days later, French, Belgian and Italian engineers, protected by a small contingent of French and Belgian troops, entered the Ruhr to procure the coal. German coal miners and steel workers went on strike and were paid in fiat currency by the government in Berlin. Within a year the Reichsmark, which stood at 7,000 to the dollar in December 1922,

---

[30] See Arno J. Mayer, *Politics and Diplomacy of Peacemaking: Containment and Counterrevolution at Versailles, 1918-1919* (New York: Knopf, 1967), 754-64.

[31] John Maynard Keynes, *A Revision of the Treaty* (London: Macmillan, 1922), 189.

[32] Cf. *infra*, 246.

plummeted to 4.2 billion. The hyperinflation did not ruin the German middle classes, as is commonly alleged; they had already been ruined by the previous wave of inflation. But it did benefit large corporations, which liquidated their debt for pennies. The public loans which had financed the war were paid off by the state in similar fashion. Keynes had encouraged the German government to hyper-inflate its currency. He well understood the economic consequences of such a measure, but believed that it would help Germany politically, which it did.[33]

In itself, the Ruhr occupation was neither remarkable nor unprecedented. British and French troops had occupied Düsseldorf, Duisburg and Ruhrort – three cities that controlled all Ruhr communications – in March 1921 to enforce reparations payments. In 1923, however, Britain denounced the occupation as illegal and immoral. As passive resistance led to a vast increase in the occupying force, Germany was seen in both Britain and the United States as a martyr to the French Shylock intent on claiming his pound of flesh. More than reparations was at issue here. French Premier Raymond Poincaré sought to convince the German government and the German public that they had lost the war and should accept the Versailles settlement.[34] They were not convinced. When returning German troops had paraded in Berlin on 11 December 1918, President Friedrich Ebert, a social-democrat, greeted them as victors, saying: "I salute you, who return unvanquished from the field of battle."[35] So if Germany did not lose the war, it did not have to comply with the Versailles treaty or pay reparations.

This time, however, Germany did comply. In October 1923, the government of Wilhelm Cuno was replaced by that of Gustav Stresemann, who ended passive resistance, reformed the currency and

---

[33] Stephen A. Schuker, "J.M. Keynes and the Personal Politics of Reparations, part 2" *Diplomacy and Statecraft*, Vol. 25 No. 4 (2014), 591.
[34] Sally Marks, "The Myths of Reparations," *Central European History*, September 1978, 244-5.
[35] John W. Wheeler-Bennett, *The Nemesis of Power: The German Army in Politics, 1918-1945* (New York: St. Martin's Press, 1954), 31.

offered to pay reparations as part of a general settlement. American banker (and future Vice-President) Charles G. Dawes devised a plan whereby reparations would be staggered over a five-year period and financed largely by loans from the United States. This is essentially what Poincaré had proposed in 1922.[36] In terms of direct American investment in Europe during the interwar period, Germany received more than twice as much as Great Britain and three times that of France.[37] French and Belgian troops withdrew from the Ruhr in August 1925.

Stresemann's policy of compliance served his country well. Years before Hitler formally cancelled reparations payments on 17 May 1933, the Weimar Republic had already obtained global satisfaction on this issue. When the first tranche of bonds came due in 1928, Germany defaulted. In June 1929, a new plan was enacted, floating more U. S. backed bonds and reducing reparations payments still further. On 30 June 1931, President Hoover proposed a one-year moratorium on reparations and war debts. At the Lausanne conference of July 1932, it was decided to release Germany from all reparations claims, with a final payment to be made when conditions improve. It was never made, and Germany defaulted on the new bonds in 1935. So when the Nazis assumed power, the reparations question, which Keynes had denounced as the most iniquitous aspect of the Versailles treaty, was already a dead letter.

Nonetheless, the British establishment never forgave France for the Ruhr occupation. At the very outset, the *Times* of London wrote: "We, for our part – and in this British public opinion is almost unanimous – are satisfied that the present action of France is a sheer disaster not only to the peace and reconstruction of Europe, but even to

---

[36] Denise Artaud, "Reparations and War Debts: The Restoration of French Financial Power, 1919-1929," Robert Boyce ed., *French Foreign and Defense Policy: The Decline and Fall of a Great Power* (London: Routledge, 1998), 96-7.

[37] William O. Scroggs, "The American Investment in Germany," *Foreign Affairs*, January 1932, 324.

the prospect of obtaining reparations at all from Germany."[38] In the House of Commons, Lloyd George urged his country's government to pull France back from the brink. "I believe the French government are committing France day by day and week by week to a policy of irretrievable disaster."[39] Sir Warren Fisher, permanent secretary to the Treasury, claimed in July 1923 that the French traditionally "played the part of bullies . . . and they are doing so now."[40] No blame accrued to Belgium or Italy.

Such condemnation is rooted in the British tradition of maintaining a rough balance of power in Europe. France was seen as aspiring to continental hegemony, taking advantage of Germany's weakness, which in any case proved to be temporary. In 1932, Lloyd George begrudged France for having what seemed to be a powerful army. "France has to-day an army, with reserves, of over five millions, and thousands of heavy guns. . . . Germany has an army of only 100,000 men, and very few guns or munitions."[41] Lloyd George could hardly have been unaware that Germany had been rearming in secret since 1922[42] or that France had reduced the term of military service from three years to eighteen months in 1922 and then again to twelve months in 1928. The mere fact that France was allowed to maintain a continental army larger than that of Germany was, in his view, a threat to peace. By 1932, the British army had reverted to its traditional role as an imperial police force.

The advent of Hitler did little initially to change British perceptions. On 7 November 1933, Sir Archibald Sinclair, the Liberal

---

[38] *The Times*, 15 January 1923.

[39] 160 H. C. Deb., series 5, 19 February, 1923.

[40] Michael Dockrill, "Anglo-French Relations. 1989-1998: From Fashoda to Jospin," Philippe Chassaigne and Michael Dockrill, eds., *British Official Perceptions of France and the French, 1936*-1940 (New York: Palgrave, 2002), 94.

[41] David Lloyd George, *The Truth About Reparations and War Debts* (London: Heinemann, 1932), 139.

[42] See Hans W. Gatzke, *Stresemann and the Rearmament of Germany* (Baltimore, MD: Johns Hopkins Press, 1954), 10, 36 *et passim*.

leader, expressed his deep sympathy for the vanquished foe of 1918. "Germany must be treated fairly and justly. . . . We have promised Germany equality of status in armaments. . . . We must give it. We Liberals detest Hitlerism . . . but it battens on the refusal to meet Germany's just grievances and can only be exorcised by fairness in the treatment of German claims."[43] (In the event, Hitlerism was not exorcised even after all German grievances were met.) A week later, George Lambert of the National Liberals asked: "Why is France building an enormous [sic] number of submarines, seeing that Germany is not building any?"[44] To achieve equality in armaments, it was not enough to allow Germany to rearm; France must disarm. As Churchill noted in March 1934, "The awful danger, nothing less, of our present foreign policy is that we go on perpetually asking the French to weaken themselves. And what do we say is the inducement? We say, 'Weaken yourselves,' and we always hold out the hope that if they do it and get into trouble, we will then in some way or other go to their aid, although we have nothing with which to go to their aid."[45]

Churchill was ill-suited to excoriate British foreign policy in 1934. He had helped create it. In 1925 he wrote to Foreign Secretary Austen Chamberlain that "when France has made a real peace with Germany, Britain will seal the bond with all her strength. . . . But apart from a triple accord (Great Britain, France and Germany) we could not enter into specific obligations toward her."[46] Like Lord Curzon and Ramsey MacDonald, Churchill sought to resurrect the "Concert of Europe," a loose understanding reached among the great powers at the Congress of Vienna in 1815 to prevent a renewed outbreak of revolutionary turmoil. France, once again a monarchy and shorn of its conquests, was allowed to join the "Concert" on the condition that it no longer challenge the established order. From 1815 to 1914, no major

---

[43] 281 H C Deb, 7 November 1933, col. 86.
[44] *Ibid.*, 15 November 1933. col. 903.
[45] 287 H C Deb., 14 March 1934, col. 397.
[46] Sibyl Eyre Crowe, "Sir Eyre Crowe and the Locarno Pact," *English Historical Review*, January 1972, 64.

conflict involving all the great European powers took place. This arrangement allowed Britain to free itself from any continental commitment, save for the brief episode of the Crimean War, and to pursue its imperial ambitions. After the First World War, British statesmen hoped to revive the *Pax Britannica* of the nineteenth century by admitting a presumably reformed, peaceful Germany into the community of civilised nations. Churchill, like Keynes, was convinced that Germany's territorial ambitions would be directed eastward – i.e. against Soviet Russia.[47] This would not disrupt the established order.

Britain managed to satisfy, at least partially, German claims on the sea. Without consulting or even informing the French government, it signed a naval agreement with Germany on 18 June 1935, which abolished the constraints imposed by the treaty of Versailles on the *Kriegsmarine*. Germany was authorised to build submarines up to 100 percent of British tonnage. Total tonnage of German surface ships could now attain 35 percent of the British – not quite equality, but certainly adequate, given that Germany had no overseas empire to defend.[48] Hitler denounced the agreement in 1939.

On land, Hitler, who had introduced conscription in defiance of the Versailles treaty, took the initiative by ordering 30,000 German troops to reoccupy the Rhineland on 7 March 1936. Here was one more violation of the treaty, which in any case was thoroughly discredited in Britain. The Locarno pact of 1925, by which Britain guaranteed the territorial status quo between German and its western neighbours, was also violated. The guarantee, however, was not absolute. In November 1933, Foreign Secretary Sir John Simon assured the House of Commons that "no British government is blindly fettered by the treaty of Locarno."[49] Simon was merely stating the obvious. The

---

[47] Correlli Barnett, *The Collapse of British Power* (London: Eyre Methuen, 1972), 329-30.

[48] Sally Marks, *The Ebbing of European Ascendancy* (London: Hodder Arnold, 2002), 328.

[49] 281 H C Deb., 7 November 1933, col. 61.

pact contained no military provisions; and without an army to intervene on the continent, Britain was in no position to honour its guarantee.

So it was left for France to stop Hitler. A tenacious myth holds that the French army could easily have defeated the German force and put an end to Nazi Germany's expansionist policy. The myth seems to have originated with Churchill, who wrote: "If the French government had mobilized the French army, with nearly a hundred divisions . . . there is no doubt that Hitler would have been compelled by his own general staff to withdraw, and a check would have been given to his pretensions which might have proved fatal to his rule."[50] Even the francophile Churchill could not avoid blaming the French for missed opportunities. Where he got the figure of a hundred divisions is a mystery. Like Lloyd George, he grossly overestimated the strength of the French army. Excluding its troops in the colonies, France in 1936 had 320,000 men under arms – at most twenty under-strength divisions.[51]

The notion that French military intervention might have led to Hitler's downfall is equally fanciful. Ever since 1933, the German general staff had planned to remilitarize the Rhineland. German troops entering the territory were under orders to fight if they encountered any opposition.[52] "France," writes an American historian, "stood absolutely alone. A unilateral resort to force would have brought a storm of reprobation both from the country's putative allies and from the self-appointed guardians of the world conscience at Geneva. It would almost surely have exposed the virtual bankruptcy of the French treasury and toppled the franc off the gold standard a scant six weeks before parliamentary elections."[53] Nor could Britain be counted upon.

---

[50] Winston S. Churchill, *The Second World War*, I: *The Gathering Storm* (London: Penguin, 1985), 175.

[51] General René Tournès, "The French Army, 1936," *Foreign Affairs*, April 1936, 487.

[52] Donald Cameron Watt, "German Plans for the Reoccupation of the Rhineland: A Note," *Journal of Contemporary History*, October 1966, 193-9.

[53] Stephen A Schuker, "France and the Remilitarization of the Rhineland, 1936," *French Historical Studies*, spring 1986, 304.

In February 1936, the Foreign Office had informed the French that the demilitarized zone "did not constitute a vital British interest."[54] In a diary entry of 9 March, Colonel (later Lieutenant-General) Henry Pownall expressed the view of nearly all his compatriots: "I cannot see this country going to war because somebody has re-occupied his own territory."[55] Pownall was certainly right concerning the possibility of war. A mere show of strength on France's part would not have sufficed.

Pope Pius XI weighed in with his opinion on 16 March, telling the French ambassador to the Vatican that the Rhineland question would have been settled if France had sent two hundred thousand soldiers there immediately.[56] This is clearly wishful thinking. The French army, once mobilized, could conceivably have expelled the German contingent from the Rhineland, but there would have been casualties on both sides. And then what? France, acting alone, could not possibly conquer all of Germany. French troops, their flanks exposed and dependent on a tenuous supply line from home, would surely have had to face a German counter-attack. As for Hitler, he had withstood temporary setbacks previously, the most recent being his attempt to annex Austria in 1934. It was foiled by Mussolini, who massed Italian troops on the Brenner. German generals did not oppose their leader on that occasion, and it is highly unlikely that they would have done so if a French force had entered the Rhineland. Hitler recovered from his Austrian reversal and achieved *Anschluss* in 1938. Had he been repulsed in the Rhineland, his recovery would probably have been even swifter.

In Germany, Hitler's bloodless triumph raised him to a new pinnacle of popularity. The Rhinelanders were jubilant. Women threw flowers at the soldiers, and Catholic priests offered their blessing. The archbishop of Cologne, Cardinal Karl Joseph Schulte, officiated at a

---

[54] *Ibid.*, 312.

[55] Brian Bond ed., *Chief of Staff: The Diaries of Lieutenant-General Sir Henry Pownall*, I, *1933-1940* (London: Leo Cooper, 1972), 105.

[56] Gerhard L. Weinberg, *Hitler's Foreign Policy, 1933-1939: The Road to World War II* (New York: Enigma Books, 2010), 204.

mass to thank Hitler for "bringing back our army." Parliamentary elections were held throughout Germany on 29 March, with only Nazis as candidates. Voters were asked to approve or disapprove Hitler's Rhineland coup. The result was typical of a totalitarian state, with an approval score of 98.9 percent. There can be little doubt, however, that on this question the dictator enjoyed the massive support of his people.[57] For him, it was an easy victory. The Rhineland had become a power vacuum once allied occupation troops left in 1930. The vacuum was filled by a relatively small German force. Foreign Secretary Anthony Eden reassured his fellow MPs: "There is, I am thankful to say, no reason to suppose that the present German action implies a threat of hostilities."[58] This was true. The remilitarization of the Rhineland weakened the international position of France, whose ally, Belgium, reverted to neutrality on 15 October. It effectively liquidated the much-maligned settlement that followed the First World War but did not contribute to bringing on the Second.

The French government, meanwhile, tried to salvage what remained of its pride and status. Foreign Minister Pierre-Étienne Flandin flew to London on 11 March, in the vain hope of convincing the British to impose sanctions on Germany. Neville Chamberlain, then chancellor of the exchequer, informed him that British public opinion would not tolerate such a move.[59] A similar view was expressed by Harold Nicolson, who wrote to his wife: "The French are not letting us off one jot or tittle of the bond." If Britain did honour its guarantee, Germany would not withdraw and there would be war. "Naturally we shall win and enter Berlin [Nicolson *dixit*]. And what is the good of that? It would only mean Communism in Germany and in France, and that is why the Russians are so keen on it. Moreover the people of this country absolutely refuse to have a war."[60]

---

[57] Ian Kershaw, *Hitler*, I: *1889-1936, Hubris* (London: Penguin, 1999). 588-99.

[58] 309 H C Deb., 9 March 1936, col. 1812.

[59] Keith Feiling, *The Life of Neville Chamberlain* (London: Macmillan, 1946), 279.

British Prime Minister Baldwin told the cabinet that it was "very unfriendly" of France to press the issue while Britain had no army to speak of. His predecessor, former Labour Party leader J. Ramsay MacDonald, confided to his diary that he was satisfied with the outcome. "That blot on the peace of the world, the treaty of Versailles, is vanishing, and for that I am thankful. . . . France has again had a severe lesson, and I hope it will take it this time."[61] In fact, French statesmen had already learned their lesson during the Ruhr crisis: they understood that France could not undertake any military action in Europe without the prior consent of Great Britain.

The Rhineland episode illustrates the fatal flaw of the Versailles settlement: it was not self-executing but had to be enforced continually. Not so the treaty of Frankfurt of 1871, which ended the Franco-Prussian War. This was a dictated peace in every sense of the word. The newly established French republic, acknowledging defeat, had no choice but to accept the victor's terms. It yielded nearly all of Alsace (minus Belfort, which had held out against the enemy) and two-fifths of Lorraine. Germany imposed an indemnity – not reparations, since the war was fought entirely on French soil – of five billion gold francs. A gold franc was worth one hundredth of an ounce of gold. At today's value – say 1,800 dollars an ounce – the indemnity translates into 90 billion dollars. France paid the sum demanded in just over two years, thanks to a twenty-year bond issue bearing tax-free interest at five percent annually. It did not disturb the peace of Europe but instead worked through diplomatic channels to restore its status as a great power. Germany, meanwhile, continued to expand economically and came to dominate the European continent as never before.

Even in defeat, Germany, which had not experienced invasion or destruction by foreign armies during the war, still enjoyed economic prominence. The treaty of Versailles had not hindered its steel production, which in 1921 was three times that of France.[62] By 1925,

---

[60] Harold Nicolson, *Diaries and Letters* I, *1930-1939*, ed. Nigel Nicolson (New York: Atheneum, 1966), 249-50.

[61] Schuker, "France and the Remilitarization of the Rhineland," 314.

Germany was producing twice as much steel as Britain, whose total industrial production was still only 92 percent of the 1914 level. That of Germany had already reached 117 percent.[63] John Maynard Keynes reminded his readers that Anglo-German commerce prior to the war had been extremely beneficial to both parties. Except for imperial preference, the British Treasury, the Board of Trade and the Bank of England pressed for the liberalization of international commerce. With the return of peace and the destruction of the German navy, the revival of Germany's economy was welcomed in British financial circles.[64] In a very real sense, British appeasement of Germany began in 1919.

Though temporarily disarmed, Germany emerged from the war, relative to the rest of Europe, more powerful than it had been previously. In 1914, it was confronted by the three great powers of the Entente and had only one continental ally, Austria-Hungary, which proved to be more of a burden than an asset. Under the Versailles settlement, Germany lost thirteen percent of its former territory, including Alsace-Lorraine and the Polish Corridor, but retained its unity and industrial base. After the Second World War, Sir Lewis Namier wrote that on Armistice Day 1918, "it could have been foretold with mathematical certainty that should a united Germany in control of her resources be allowed to achieve rearmament, her conquerors would be in mortal danger."[65] Yes, but only if they refused to accept German predominance on the continent of Europe. In fact, they recognized it, at least tacitly. Throughout the inter-war period, France, the only major power willing to enforce the Versailles settlement, continued to sell iron ore to Germany, its best customer. Chamberlain, like J.M. Keynes, expected Hitler to pursue Germany's traditional policy of expansion in

---

[62] Paul Kennedy, *The Realities Behind Diplomacy: Background Influences to British External Policy, 1865-1980* (London: Fontana, 1981), 265.

[63] L.C.B. Seaman, *From Vienna to Versailles* (London: Methuen, 1955), p. 198.

[64] Kennedy, *The Realities Behind Diplomacy,* 235.

[65] Sir Lewis Namier, *Diplomatic Prelude, 1938-1939* (London: Macmillan, 1948), ix.

the east but assumed that he would behave like a proper English gentleman. The great power that had the most to fear from Germany was neither France nor Britain, and certainly not the United States, but Russia, which had been defeated in 1918.

Two of the conquerors on whose support France had relied not only allowed Germany to rearm; they persuaded themselves that their former enemy had been poorly treated. Britain in the inter-war period voluntarily reduced the size of its land army to virtually nothing and resumed its traditional policy of "splendid isolation," while the United States Senate refused even to ratify the treaty of Versailles. A revisionist school of American historians, of whom Sidney B. Fay was the most distinguished, convinced the reading public that the allies of 1914 bore at least as much responsibility for the war as the central powers.[66] Soviet Russia was excluded from European affairs until 1939. The French still maintained a sizeable land force; but without the support of Britain, Russia and the United States, an enfeebled France, burdened by reconstruction costs and human losses, could hardly be expected to oppose German expansionism on its own.

By introducing conscription in 1935, Hitler provided Germany with an army that would eventually be commensurate with his country's military potential. And he had good material to work with. Under the brilliant guidance of General Hans von Seekt, the 100,000-man *Reichswehr* of the Weimar Republic served as a vast and well-organized military academy. Enlisted men, who had signed up for a minimum of eight years' service, took turns as squad leaders. Young lieutenants played the role of division commanders.[67] The new recruits, most of whom had participated in the Hitler Youth movement, were dedicated to the Nazi regime and eager to fight for it.

In Central Europe, the destruction of the Habsburg and Romanov dynasties created a power vacuum that could be filled either

---

[66] Sidney B. Fay, *The Origins of the World War* (2 vol., New York: Macmillan, 1928).

[67] Robert M. Citino, *The Path to Blitzkrieg: Doctrine and Training in the German Army, 1920-1939* (Boulder, CO: Lynne Rienner, 1999), 90.

by the Soviet Union or by a resurgent Germany. The successor states were all weak, except one: Czechoslovakia. In 1938, it alone possessed an industrial base and a modern, well-equipped army comparable to those of Hitler's Reich.

2 Appeasement and its Discontents

Prior to 1936, Britain sought to appease Germany because it was perceived to be weak. Subsequently, Britain appeased Germany because it was seen to be strong. Even before being confirmed as prime minister on 26 May 1937, Neville Chamberlain instructed the newly-appointed British ambassador to Germany, Sir Nevile Henderson, on how to address his audience in Berlin. "Guarantee us peace and peaceful evolution in Europe, and Germany will find that she has no more sincere and, I believe, more useful friend in the world than Great Britain."[1] Chamberlain then invited Neurath, the German foreign minister, to London for talks in June. The German government cancelled the visit at the last minute, claiming that neither Britain nor France had condemned the Spanish republican navy for an alleged submarine attack on a German cruiser in the Mediterranean.[2] But Chamberlain was not deterred. Late in October he informed his sisters that he had "far reaching plans . . . for the appeasement of Europe & Asia and for the ultimate check to the mad armament race, which if allowed to continue must involve us all in ruin."[3] His policy would seem to be perfectly suited to an island nation that had disbanded its army, save for an imperial police force. It was not suited to those continental democracies, such as France and Czechoslovakia, which had a common border with Germany.

Anglo-German relations were back on track in November, when Göring invited Viscount Halifax, who was a master of foxhounds,

---

[1] L.C.B. Seaman, *Post-Victorian Britain, 1902-1951* (London: Routledge, 1991), 284.

[2] *New York Times*, 22 June 1937.

[3] Chamberlain to Ida, 30 October 1937, *The Neville Chamberlain Dairy Letters*, 280.

to a sporting exhibition in Berlin and then to a hunting party in Pomerania. Halifax, who was not yet foreign secretary, went as lord president of the (Privy) Council, having been fully briefed by Chamberlain. The foreign secretary, Anthony Eden, was not informed of the proposed visit. After the hunt, Halifax was taken to Berchtesgaden to confer with Hitler. The meeting did not begin well. On arrival, this well-bred English gentleman mistook Hitler, who wasn't wearing his uniform that day, for a footman and was about to hand him his coat and hat when Neurath hissed in his ear, "*Der Führer! Der Führer!*" Halifax made more than ample amends, however, assuring his host that Britain expected changes in the status of Austria and Czechoslovakia and merely wanted them to occur peacefully. Hitler hadn't even raised the question.[4]

What would soon become known as appeasement was actually something more: a collusion, if not actually an alliance. Britain anticipated Germany's every move and sought to facilitate it. Prime Minister Chamberlain was not just a man of peace, as often claimed; he was, consciously and intentionally "Hitler's enabler."[5] At the root of British policy toward Nazi Germany was a visceral fear of Communism. Halifax congratulated Hitler on having banished Communism from Germany, which "could rightly be regarded as a bulwark of the West against Bolshevism." Britons, he explained, were "convinced that mistakes had been made in the treaty of Versailles that had to be put right."[6] Inasmuch as the treaty of Versailles was seen as having weakened Germany, it had to be revised and perhaps dismantled altogether so that Hitler's Reich could fulfill its proper role as a bulwark against the Communist menace.

---

[4] Lois G. Schwoerer, "Lord Halifax's Visit to Germany: November 1937," *The Historian*, May 1970), 362; cf. Andrew Roberts, *"The Holy Fox," a Biography of Lord Halifax* (London: Weidenfeld and Nicolson, 1991), 70.
[5] John Ruggiero, *Hitler's Enabler: Neville Chamberlain and the Origins of the Second World War* (Santa Barbara, CA: Praeger, 2015), 68-9 *et passim*.
[6] Lionel Kochan, *The Struggle for Germany, 1914-1945* (Edinburgh: University Press, 1963), 64.

Chamberlain pronounced the visit "a great success" in laying the basis for a general settlement in Europe. He was nothing if not persistent. In a letter to his sister later that month, he wrote: "Of course they [Hitler and Göring] want to dominate Eastern Europe." Why not, after all? In Chamberlain's view and that of nearly all British Conservatives, it was better to let Germany dominate Eastern Europe than Russia. "I don't see why we shouldn't say to Germany: Give us satisfactory assurances that you won't use force to deal with the Austrians and Czecho-Slovakians [*sic*], and we will give you similar assurances that we won't use force to prevent the changes you want if you can get them by peaceful means."[7] Here it should be remembered that Britain had, at the time, no army for direct intervention on the continent of Europe. France did have a continental army, but Chamberlain obviously preferred not to see it deployed. So when he wrote that "*we* won't use force," he was referring in reality to France. Had he consulted the French government on this point? He was not in the habit of consulting the French on anything. To his other sister he claimed to be "earning much approval for the new impetus I have given to our foreign policy."[8]

British foreign policy may have been given a new impetus, but it was essentially the same foreign policy, with the same economic and ideological underpinnings. In 1934 Montagu Norman, governor of the Bank of England, told top-ranking executives of J.P. Morgan and Company that "Hitler and Schacht [president of the *Reichsbank*] are the bulwarks of civilization in Germany and the only friends we have. . . . If they fail, Communism will follow in Germany, and anything may follow in Europe."[9] Earlier, Norman had encouraged British investment in Germany as a means of keeping Bolshevism within the borders of the Soviet Union. Financial ties between Britain and Germany had

---

[7] Chamberlain to Ida, 26 November 1937, Robert Self, ed., *The Neville Chamberlain Diary Letters,* IV: *The Downing Street Years, 1934-1940* (Aldershot: Ashgate, 2005), 286-7.

[8] Chamberlain to Hilda, 5 December 1937, *Ibid.*, 288.

[9] Schuker, *American "Reparations" to Germany*, 121.

grown considerably since 1919, but were severely strained during the depression. Once the Nazis attained power, Britain tried to steer the new regime away from autarky. To this end, the Chamberlain government offered Hitler colonial concessions in Africa, which would have given Germany free access to important raw materials. But the latter was not primarily interested in Africa, preferring instead to colonize Eastern Europe.[10]

On 10 March 1938, two days before Germany annexed Austria, Horace Wilson, a senior civil servant who was Chamberlain's chief confidant and adviser, met with Theodor Kordt, counsellor at the German embassy in London. Wilson told Kordt that the prime minister was pleased to learn from Lord Lothian, a firm partisan of Anglo-German friendship who held no diplomatic post at the time but who had recently visited Germany as a private citizen, that Hitler had pronounced Britain and Germany to be the two pillars supporting the European order.[11] This was taken to mean that both powers had a mutual interest in saving Europe from Bolshevism.[12] Soviet Ambassador Ivan Maisky had spoken with Halifax on 1 March and came away convinced that "the new leaders of British foreign policy will not move a finger in regard to either Central Europe or Spain." He dismissed Chamberlain as "a consummate reactionary, with a sharply defined anti-Soviet position."[13]

The main obstacle to German expansion in the east was Czechoslovakia. The Czechoslovak Republic had proclaimed its independence on 18 October 1918, following a memorandum of

---

[10] Scott Newman, *Profits of Peace: The Political Economy of Anglo-German Appeasement* (Oxford: Clarendon Press, 1996), 58-62.

[11] G.C. Peden, "Sir Horace Wilson and Appeasement," *The Historical Journal*, December 2010, 995.

[12] Adrian Phillips, *Fighting Churchill, Appeasing Hitler: Neville Chamberlain, Sir Horace Wilson, & Britain's Plight of Appeasement, 1937-1939* (New York: Pegasus Books, 2019), 162.

[13] Gabriel Gorodetsky ed., *The Maisky Diaries*, trad. Tatiana Sorokina and Oliver Ready (New Haven, CT: Yale University Press, 2015), 102-3.

understanding signed in Pittsburgh, Pennsylvania the previous May by leading members of the Czech and Slovak expatriate communities (actually more Slovaks than Czechs) in the United States. The new state enjoyed the enthusiastic support of President Woodrow Wilson. Hitler, an Austrian German, detested the Czechs and resolved to wipe Czechoslovakia off the face of the map at the earliest possible occasion, not least because it was a democracy, in fact the only democracy in Central Europe at the time. British and French firms had major investments in the country's industries, especially its arms industry. The London Rothschilds had a majority interest in the Vitkovice steel plant, with its ties to the British weapons manufacturer, Vickers. The French engineering firm of Schneider-Creusot was heavily invested in the Skoda works, whose output alone in 1938 was slightly greater than the entire munitions production of Great Britain.[14] Czechoslovakia was by then the largest exporter of small arms in the world. The Bren gun, which was adopted by the British army in 1938 as its standard light machine gun, was a Czech design.

British military intelligence, such as it was, had already written off Czechoslovakia in November 1933 as a "ramshackle republic," incapable of resisting a German offensive.[15] The British premier shared this view. No sooner was Austria annexed to Nazi Germany than Chamberlain wrote to his sister: "You have only to look at the map to see that nothing that France or we could do could possibly save Czecho-Slovakia [sic] from being over-run by the Germans if they wanted to do it. The Austrian frontier is practically open; the great Skoda munitions works are within easy bombing distance of the German aerodromes. . . . " The Czechoslovak question, he thought, would be merely a pretext for going to war with Germany, a war which Britain was in no condition to wage. This helps explain why the British government claimed to view Czechoslovakia as a lost cause. At a

---

[14] Caquet, *The Bell of Treason*, 5-6; William McElwee, *Britain's Locust Years, 1918-1940* (London: Faber and Faber, 1962), 265.
[15] Wesley K. Wark, *The Ultimate Enemy: British Intelligence and Nazi Germany, 1933-1939* (London: Tauris, 1985), 102.

cabinet meeting on 18 March 1938, Sir Thomas Inskip, the minister for coordination of defence, predicted that "Germany could overrun Czechoslovakia in less than a week."[16]

Czechoslovakia had an alliance with France since 1924, but Chamberlain claimed to have absolutely no confidence in the French government.[17] In a letter dated 16 January 1938 to a Mrs. Marion Prince of Boston, he wrote: "Unhappily France keeps pulling her own house down about her ears." But he had steadfast respect for the British people, who "realize that we are in no position to enter light-heartedly upon war with such a formidable power as Germany, much less if Germany were aided by Italian attacks on our Mediterranean possessions and communications."[18] So it was basically British, rather than Czech, military weakness that dictated Britain's official pacifism.

Chamberlain looked at the map and saw Czechoslovakia as vulnerable. He was, of course, influenced by the British chiefs of staff, whose reports, based on outdated information, failed to take into account the real strength of the Czechoslovak army or the fortifications along the country's mountainous border with Germany.[19] Above all, he wanted good relations with the Nazi regime at almost any price, even if others had to pay it. Military historians have looked at the map and drawn quite different conclusions. True, the Skoda works, as well as Prague itself, could have been bombed by German aircraft, but Vienna – now a part of Hitler's Reich – was within range of Czech heavy artillery. A bombing plane can be brought down by anti-aircraft fire or by fighter interceptors. The Czechs had both. A British historian has established that the air defences over Czechoslovakia in 1938 were superior to those of France in 1940.[20] To this day, no one has found a way to intercept an artillery projectile.

---

[16] Roberts, *"The Holy Fox,"* 93.

[17] Chamberlain to Ida, 20 March 1938, *The Neville Chamberlain Diary Letters,* 306-7.

[18] Feiling, *The Life of Neville Chamberlain*, 323-4.

[19] Milan Hauner, "Czechoslovakia as a Military Factor in British Considerations of 1938," *Journal of Strategic Studies*, I, (1978), 195.

Man for man, the Czechoslovak army was the strongest in Central Europe, indeed in all of Europe. In a note to London dated 6 October 1937, the British military attaché in Prague, Lieutenant-Colonel H.C.T. Stronge, wrote that it was well equipped and fully capable of resisting an initial German assault.[21] The following May, Czechoslovakia ordered the partial mobilization of its forces in response to reports (which were of British origin and later proved to be erroneous[22]) that Germany was about to attack. The U. S. military attaché in Prague, Major Lowell M. Riley, noted that "the assembly and movement of Czech troops was [sic] smoothly and well conducted." The mobilized reservists seemed eager to fight. Once in position, they performed their duties with zeal and discipline.[23] At that time, the Czechs were busily fortifying their frontier with Austria. Their progress was noted by Stronge, who reported in September that even the weakest sections had defensive value.[24] Had the Germans attacked at that point, they would have encountered hundreds of Czech light and medium tanks, which had more powerful cannon, thicker armour plating, increased speed and better traction than comparable German models.[25] After Munich, these were impressed into the German army. Of all the German tanks which overran France in 1940, nearly one third was of Czech manufacture. The Czechoslovak army would have had the further advantage of fighting in familiar terrain and enjoying internal lines of communication and supply.

---

[20] Greg Baughen, *The Rise and Fall of the French Air Force: French Air Operations and Strategy, 1919-1940* (London: Fonthill, 2018), 136.

[21] Hauner, "Czechoslovakia as a Military Factor," 204.

[22] J. W. Bruegel, *Czechoslovakia Before Munich: The German Minority Problem and British Appeasement Policy* (Cambridge: Cambridge University Press, 1973), 187.

[23] Igor Lukes, "The Czechoslovak Partial Mobilization in May 1938: A Mystery (almost) Solved," *Journal of Contemporary History*, October 1996, 702.

[24] Williamson Murray, *The Change in the European Balance of Power, 1938-1939* (Princeton: Princeton University Press, 1984), 122.

[25] Ivan Pfaff, "Wir wären hängengeblieben," *Die Zeit*, 16 September 1988.

The Czechoslovak resistance infuriated Hitler, who was now more determined than ever to crush Czechoslovakia by force of arms.[26] It greatly worried Chamberlain, who suddenly realized that this small country might not be so easily swept away after all. France, by virtue of its defensive alliance with Czechoslovakia, was pledged to go to war if its ally was attacked by Germany, possibly implicating Britain. Would Britain guarantee its support? No, said Chamberlain flatly. In an address to the House of Commons on 24 March 1938, he explained that "His Majesty's Government feel themselves unable to give the prior guarantee suggested."[27] Czechoslovakia, on the other hand, counted on its alliance with France, as its ambassador to France, Osusky, confidently told the American chargé d'affaires, Wilson, just two days after Germany had annexed Austria. He was encouraged by the recent debate on foreign affairs in the French parliament during which the premier, Camille Chautemps, the foreign minister, Yvon Delbos, and several other members vowed to uphold the alliance.[28] "Should the occasion arise," assured Delbos, "our commitments to Czechoslovakia will be faithfully executed." Paul Reynaud, an arch-enemy of appeasement, referred to "the fine Czechoslovak army and its powerful armament." Premier Chautemps reminded his colleagues that it was a point of honour for France to maintain the independence of its ally.[29]

Delbos had made an official visit to Prague on 15 December 1937, during which he met with President Benes for six hours. Benes did not fail to remind his French guest of Czechoslovakia's military strength. In a speech at the six-hundred year old Prague City Hall, Delbos emphasized the ties, both diplomatic and cultural, that united the two countries. The French statesman clearly wanted to maintain the alliance.[30] Shortly after a visit to the Soviet Union in 1932, he had

---

[26] Keith Robbins, *Munich 1938* (London: Cassell, 1968), 227.

[27] 333 H C Deb., March 24, 1938, col. 1405.

[28] Wilson to Hull, 14 March 1938, FRUS, (1938) I, 483-4.

[29] J O C, 26 February 1938, pp. 631-2. 647, 655.

[30] Igor Lukes, *Czechoslovakia Between Stalin and Hitler: The Diplomacy of*

proposed readmitting Russia into the European comity of nations as a counterweight to a vengeful Germany.[31] The subsequent wave of purges in Stalin's empire discouraged him, as it did Benes. Czechoslovakia, democratic and well-armed, was a more reliable partner. In 1933 and again in 1936, it had refused Nazi Germany's offer of a non-aggression pact. But with Chamberlain and Halifax determined to give Hitler free rein in Central Europe, French support of Czechoslovakia was compromised from the start.

It was a cardinal principle of French foreign policy throughout the inter-war period that the unwritten entente with Britain had priority over all other considerations. France would not have survived the First World War without British support. From 8 August to 11 November 1918, British and Imperial forces captured nearly as many prisoners of war as the French, American and Belgian armies combined.[32] Faced with a resurgent Germany, French statesmen assumed that a strong military contribution from Britain would be decisive in the event of a future war. A French parliamentarian, Ernest Pezet, defined the problem succinctly in February 1938: "It would be agonizing for France to be faced with the tragic alternative of having to choose between the states of Central Europe and our relationship with England."[33] In reality, there was no alternative: the entente with Britain came first. As Home Secretary Sir Samuel Hoare reminded the Committee of Imperial Defence in December, "Whatever the French may think, their interests are so bound up with ours that they could not afford to stand aloof from us."[34] Britain was very much in the driver's seat, as it had been almost continuously since 1919. France, as a direct

---

Eduard Benes in the 1930s (New York: Oxford University Press, 1996), 84.

[31] Yvon Delbos, *L'expérience rouge* (Paris: Au Sans Pareil, 1933), 228, 247.

[32] John Terraine, *The First World War, 1914-1918* (London: Macmillan, 1965), 183.

[33] J O C Débats, 25 February 1938, 573.

[34] Michael Dockrill, *British Establishment Perspectives on France, 1936-1940* (London: Macmillan, 1999), 156-7.

result of the First World War, was relegated to the front passenger seat, which is known in French as *la place du mort*.

The main bone of contention between Nazi Germany and the Czechoslovak Republic was, officially at least, the Sudetenland, the frontier region facing Germany and Austria. Here resided most of the 3.5 million ethnic Germans of Czechoslovakia. In Britain, there was no shortage of well-meaning busybodies who, from the first, thought it unjust that the Sudeten Germans should not be citizens of Germany or Austria. Such was the opinion of left-wing polemicist H.N. Brailsford, who bemoaned the fact that the principle of national self-determination was not fully respected on the continent of Europe. "The worst of these cases," he wrote in 1920, "is the subjection of over three million Germans to Czech rule,"[35] National self-determination was never an absolute, however. At the Paris peace conference, it had been decided that Bohemia-Moravia formed a "natural region" that should not be broken up. The Sudetenland was an integral part of the Bohemian economy, and to join it to Germany or Austria would leave the new Czechoslovak state without the chain of mountains that constituted its geographical line of defence.[36]

Lloyd George took a very different stand. In a memorandum dated 25 March 1919, he wrote: "I cannot conceive of any greater cause of future war than that the German people, who have certainly proved themselves one of the most vigorous and powerful races in the world, should be surrounded by a number of small states, many of them consisting of people who have never previously set up a stable government for themselves, but each containing large masses of Germans clamouring for reunion with their native land."[37] Here, the prime minister held the formerly subject peoples of Central Europe –

---

[35] Henry Noel Brailsford, *After the Peace* (London: Leonard Parsons, 1920), 47.

[36] Lord (William) Strang, *Home and Abroad* (London: André Deutsch, 1956), p. 131.

[37] elizabethmaddaluno.wordpress.com/2017/04/15/Fontainebleau-memorandum/

most of them Slavs – to be incapable of self-government. Until 1918, the native land of the Sudeten Germans was not Germany, but Austria-Hungary. Once Austria was annexed to Nazi Germany, however, the Sudeten Germans could convincingly claim German citizenship.

By the summer of 1938, the Sudetenland was constantly in the news. Even Winston Churchill wrote in a newspaper article dated 18 August that he looked forward to "a fair and friendly settlement of the Sudeten-German problem."[38] The problem was largely of Hitler's making. In 1935, Nazi Germany began secretly to finance and direct the Sudeten German Party (*Sudetendeutsche Partei* or SdP), which won two-thirds of the ethnic German vote in the elections of that year. Its leader, a former gymnastics instructor named Konrad Henlein, visited London three times, twice in 1937 and once in 1938, at the invitation of the Foreign Office. He met with Arnold Toynbee, Sir Robert Vansittart, Anthony Eden and Churchill, to whom he presented himself as a loyal citizen of Czechoslovakia, whose only aim was to get a better deal for his people.[39]

In fact, the Sudeten Germans already had a very good deal. A memorandum submitted to the British Foreign Office by the Czechoslovak government in April 1938 showed in great detail that its treatment of minorities was scrupulously fair. Their legislative representation in percentage terms corresponded exactly to their numerical importance. Not only did the German speakers have a complete school system in their own language, including two technical colleges and one university; Poles and Magyars were similarly provided for.[40] Daladier confirmed these assertions. At the Anglo-French conversations held in London in April 1938, he held that "Czechoslovakia had done more for the minorities than any other European state." He had himself visited that country several times, and

---

[38] Winston S. Churchill, *Step By Step, 1936-1939* (London: Thornton Butterworth, 1939), 274.
[39] John W. Wheeler-Bennett, *Munich, Prelude to Tragedy* (New York: Duell, Sloan and Pearce, 1965), 53-4.
[40] DBFP, 3rd series, I, 188-95.

in the Sudeten districts "everywhere he had seen German schools and German officials." Therefore "it was not really at [*sic*, on] Prague that it was necessary to bring pressure to bear."

Chamberlain, who had never been to Czechoslovakia, admitted that "he did not know enough about the details to express any opinion. . . . He had, however, been told by friends who had recently visited Czechoslovakia that the Czechoslovak government had promised rather more than they had, in fact, carried out."[41] He was inclined to believe his unnamed friends, who, like him, had no other policy than to give way to Germany. Notwithstanding the objections of his French interlocutor, he was determined to put pressure on Prague, and on Prague alone. For Hitler and his surrogate Henlein, the Sudeten question was a mere pretext for destroying Czechoslovakia.[42] The slogan of the SdP, "We want a home in the Reich" (*Wir wollen Heim ins Reich*) indicates clearly that its aim was not autonomy, but annexation to Nazi Germany. Many inhabitants of the Sudetenland were opposed to such a move. They included the Czech minority, German-speaking Jews and the anti-Nazi *Sudetendeutsche*.

The Henlein faction won an important diplomatic victory when Chamberlain announced, on 25 July 1938, that he was sending Viscount Runciman, former president of the Board of Trade, to Prague as a "mediator." The *New York Times* correspondent in London noted dryly that no comparable emissary was being sent to Berlin. Chamberlain could call himself a man of peace, but this was no attempt at mediation. Runciman, who had little knowledge of Central Europe, was given the mission to browbeat the Czechoslovak government into submission. As the *New York Times* correspondent explained, "Mr. Chamberlain is exerting strenuous pressure in Prague to make Czechoslovakia satisfy the Sudeten Germans and their real leaders in Berlin."[43] When Lord Runciman arrived at the railway station in

---

[41] "Record of Anglo-French Conversations held at No. 10 Downing Street on April 28 and 29, 1938," *Ibid.*, 216-19.
[42] R.A.C. Parker, *Chamberlain and Appeasement: British Policy and the Coming of the Second World War* (New York: St. Martin's Press, 1993), 146.

Prague, he was greeted not only by representatives of the government, but by two leaders of the SdP, who were presented to him by the British minister to Czechoslovakia, Basil Newton.[44] Runciman did his best to make the Czechs yield to Nazi pressure, but the most they would do was to offer increased autonomy to all ethnic minorities. The Sudetenland was to not be detached from Czechoslovak territory.

As tension mounted, Daladier proposed to Chamberlain on 13 September 1938 that they should both confer with Hitler.[45] Chamberlain brushed the French premier aside. Without previously informing Daladier, he invited himself to see Hitler at Berchtesgaden on 15 September. Had Daladier been present, he would certainly have reminded Hitler that France had an alliance with Czechoslovakia; and this is precisely what Chamberlain wanted to avoid. At no time was the French government told in advance of Chamberlain's moves. At Berchtesgaden he expressed willingness to let Germany annex the Sudetenland outright as long as he did not use force.[46] Hitler actually expected a warning,[47] but Chamberlain was more than helpful. In a note to Runciman, he expressed the hope that that an agreement with Hitler would make "Germany and England the twin pillars of European peace and barriers against Communism."[48]

So what Chamberlain called appeasement was in essence a tacit alliance with Germany against the Soviet Union. The collusion was not limited to the British government or the Bank of England. It permeated all of British life. Not until Britain was actively at war did its film industry produce a documentary denouncing the menace to civilisation represented by Nazism. Throughout the inter-war period, many Britons,

---

[43] *New York Times*, 26 July 1938.

[44] G.E.R. Gedye, *Fallen Bastions: The Central European Tragedy* (London: Victor Gollancz, 1939), 434.

[45] Hugh Ragsdale, *The Soviets, the Munich Crisis, and the Coming of World War II* (Cambridge: Cambridge University Press, 2004), 94.

[46] Keith Robbins, *Appeasement* (Oxford: Blackwell, 1980), 71.

[47] Bruegel, *Czechoslovakia before Munich*, 238.

[48] Maurice Cowling, *The Impact of Hitler: British Politics and British Policy, 1933-1939* (Cambridge: Cambridge University Press, 1975), 186.

and certainly those in government, saw the menace as coming from Moscow, not Berlin.[49] A fifteen-minute current events analysis, made in the United States as part of the *March of Time* series and entitled *Inside Nazi Germany*, was banned outright in 1938 by the British Board of Film Censors.[50] The theatre too was subject to censorship. In December 1938, Sir Alexander Cadogan, permanent under-secretary for Foreign Affairs, wrote to the lord chamberlain on behalf of the Foreign Office, stipulating that "all direct references to Germany, to Herr Hitler, or to other prominent personages must be avoided" in plays presented on the British stage.

Even the nominally independent BBC felt the heavy hand of the government. When a usually light-textured broadcast by Harold Nicolson, *The Past Week*, first dealt with the Czechoslovakian crisis in the summer of 1938, it received favourable comment from the public. On 5 September, the Foreign Office issued a strong recommendation that he avoid the subject altogether. Nicolson was incensed, but agreed to prepare another talk. The new script mentioned the recent beating-up at the altar of the Bishop of Rothenburg by Nazi thugs. It was censured by the BBC as being too contentious.[51] The newspaper press was not muzzled directly, but Chamberlain controlled the flow of news so that no alternative to his appeasement policy was seen to exist. Most mass-circulation dailies were owned by press lords who were close to the Conservative Party.[52] In Washington, Jay Pierrepont Moffat, who headed the State Department's European division, expressed surprise "that through all this crisis . . . the governments of the democracies have not taken their people or their parliaments into their confidence

---

[49] Roberts, *"The Holy Fox,"* 107.

[50] George Perry, *The Great British Picture Show* (London: Hart-Davis, MacGibbon, 1974), 85. The short documentary can be viewed on YouTube.

[51] Anthony Adamthwaite, "The British Government and the Media, 1937-1938," *Journal of Contemporary History*, April 1983, 287.

[52] Richard Cockett, *Twilight of Truth: Chamberlain, Appeasement and the Manipulation of the Press* (London: Weidenfeld and Nicolson, 1989), 111 *et passim*.

and that there has been more accurate news in the Berlin papers than in the British."[53]

Despite these thinly disguised attempts at censorship, not all Britons allowed themselves to be misled by their government. A Mr. H.G. Wood of Birmingham wrote to a local newspaper: "May I suggest in all seriousness that a solution to the present crisis in Central Europe be found along the lines of an interchange of populations? Let those Sudeten Germans who are unwilling to accept the terms now offered to them [by the Prague government] migrate into Germany and let their place in Czechoslovakia be taken by non-Aryans of whom Herr Hitler wishes to be rid." Whatever the practical difficulties inherent in his proposal, the author clearly understood that the Sudeten Germans were not the only disadvantaged minority in Central Europe. "Such a shifting of population," he added, "would be more just than any shifting of frontiers."[54]

Having ignored Daladier, Chamberlain then went through the motions of consulting him. The French premier, his foreign minister and the French ambassador to Great Britain were invited to 10 Downing Street on 18 September to be informed of the recent tête-à-tête in Berchtesgaden. Daladier attempted to invoke reasoned argument. He reminded Chamberlain of France's treaty obligations to its ally. Ceding the Sudetenland to Germany, he explained, would "lead to the complete destruction of the Czechoslovak state" - and eventually to a general war in Europe. Halifax replied with an argument that had become a staple of British policy, "that whatever action were taken by ourselves, by the French government, or by the Soviet government, at any given moment, it would be impossible to give effective protection to the Czechoslovak state."[55]

Hitler soon raised the ante. At Berchtesgaden Chamberlain had proposed, and Hitler had accepted, the gradual transfer to Germany of

---

[53] Nancy Havison Hooker ed., *The Moffat Papers, 1919-1943* (Cambridge, MA: Harvard University Press, 1956), 214.

[54] *The Birmingham Post*, 15 September 1938.

[55] DBFP, 3rd Series, II, 381-5.

areas in the Sudetenland where ethnic Germans were a majority. Naturally, Chamberlain had not consulted with the Czechoslovak government on this point. During his second meeting with Hitler at Bad Godesberg on the morning of 24 September he was presented with a list of demands that were unacceptable not only to the French, but to a majority in the British cabinet. Even Halifax dissented discreetly. Hitler's conditions included the cession of Czechoslovak territory to Poland and Hungary, the stationing of German troops in the Sudetenland on 1 October, and a plebiscite following the transfer to confirm the *fait accompli*. Czechoslovakia was given until 28 September to comply or face an invasion from Germany. At this the French, in the words of a British historian, "had finally reached their sticking point."[56] Both France and Czechoslovakia rejected the terms of the Godesberg memorandum outright. Chamberlain wanted to accept Hitler's demands but explained to the cabinet that "if we now possessed a superior force to Germany, we should probably be considering these proposals in a very different spirit."[57]

In anticipation of Hitler's *Diktat* and with the prior approval of Britain and France, Czechoslovakia ordered full mobilization on 23 September. Half the Sudeten Germans of military age defected to Germany (which was just as well, since they would have been issued uniforms but not weapons), and many ethnic Poles failed to report. Still, more than a million men, including many reservists, answered the call.[58] A British reporter in Prague found them to be enthusiastic and eager for battle.[59] Three weeks previously, Lieutenant-Colonel Stronge had sent an aide-mémoire to the ambassador, in which he disputed Hitler's recent claim that Germany could crush Czechoslovakia in three

---

[56] Robert Self, *Neville Chamberlain, a Biography* (Aldershot: Ashgate, 2006), 318-20.

[57] Roy Douglas, *In the Year of Munich* (London: Macmillan, 1977), 61.

[58] Stephen Kotkin, *Stalin: Waiting for Hitler, 1929-1941* (New York: Penguin, 2017), 567.

[59] David Faber, *Munich 1938: Appeasement and World War II* (New York: Simon and Schuster, 2008), 343.

weeks. The Czechoslovak army, he maintained, was well-led and well-armed. The troops' morale was good. Stronge saw no reason why Czechoslovakia could not hold out, on its own, for several months.[60] His assessment was shared by the German generals who inspected Czech border fortifications shortly after the Munich agreement. They estimated that it would have taken the German army four months to breach this formidable line of defence.[61] And even then, not all of Czechoslovakia would have been conquered.

Stronge's report was not well received in London, since it ran counter to government policy. If Czechoslovakia held out for more than three weeks, France would inevitably be drawn into the conflict, possibly implicating Britain. Once the terms of the Godesberg memorandum, which both Chamberlain and Halifax called an ultimatum,[62] appeared in the press, Sir Eric Phipps, the British ambassador in Paris, reported to London that French public and parliamentary opinion "has undergone a complete change," favouring resistance.[63] Reports from British consular offices throughout France confirmed the view that the French were "resolute and resigned to the necessity of making a stand now."[64] General Gamelin, the French army chief of staff, visited London on 26 September to inform Chamberlain that France would fight and draw off German troops from Czechoslovakia.[65]

The French change of heart made war a distinct possibility. So Chamberlain took to the airwaves on the evening of 27 September in order to prepare his compatriots for the worst. A consummate showman who viewed his first meeting with Hitler as a "coup" full of "dramatic

---

[60]Stronge to Newton, 3 September1938, DBPF, 3rd series, II, 258-9.

[61] McElwee, *Britain's Locust Years,* 265.

[62] 339 H C Deb, 3 October 1938, col. 43; 110 H L Deb., 3 October 1938, col. 1300.

[63] Phipps to Halifax, 26 September 1938, DBFP 3rd series, II, 546-7.

[64] John Harvey, ed., *The Diplomatic Diaries of Oliver Harvey* (London: Collins, 1970), 200.

[65] Barnett, *The Collapse of British Power,* 544.

force,"[66] he initiated measures of civil defence and had gas masks issued to civilians. Such precautions were hardly necessary, since Germany had no serious plans to bomb London.[67] German bombers of the day, operating from bases inside Germany, lacked the range to stay over England for more than a few minutes and could not carry a sufficient payload to do much damage. Fighter squadrons and anti-aircraft batteries around London were not immediately activated, as Sir Thomas Inskip did not deem it necessary.[68] No operational plans existed for the evacuation of civilians from London and other major cities.[69] The prospect of aerial bombardment served to glorify Chamberlain's role as a peacemaker. "How horrible, fantastic, incredible it is," he intoned, "that we should be digging trenches and trying on gas-masks here because of a quarrel in a far-away country between people of whom we know nothing."

In reaction to the Godesberg memorandum, Britain mobilized the Home Fleet, there being little else to mobilize. This gesture was largely symbolic since the navy could play no direct role in Central Europe. The French call-up of 600,000 reservists was somewhat more credible. The Soviet Union also had a defensive pact with Czechoslovakia; its application depended on that of France. So Stalin ordered units of the Red Army to man the country's western frontier. But Russia had no common border with Czechoslovakia. Romania might let Soviet troops cross its territory, but Poland definitely would not. Of the five Soviet army groups mobilized, four were stationed on the border with Poland.[70] Perhaps Stalin too was engaged in a ruse;

---

[66] Chamberlain to Ida, 19 September 1938, *The Neville Chamberlain Diary Letters*, 346.

[67] Brian Bond, *British Military Policy between the Two World Wars* (Oxford, Clarendon Press, 1980), 283.

[68] General Hastings Ismay, *The Memoirs of General the Lord Ismay* (London: Heinemann, 1960), 91.

[69] David Reynolds, *Summits: Six Meetings that Shaped the Twentieth Century* (New York: Basic Books, 2007), 83.

[70] Ragsdale, *The Soviets, the Munich Crisis*, 167.

having purged his army of some of its ablest commanders, he certainly had no taste for war. Nonetheless, the mere possibility of a Soviet presence in Central Europe frightened the British ruling classes out of their wits. Nevile Henderson, the British ambassador in Berlin, and Basil Newton, the British minister in Prague, shared a deep-seated animosity towards the USSR, one that was common in the Foreign Office.[71]

Even without Soviet participation, armed resistance to Nazi Germany was not doomed to failure. General Gamelin told a journalist in 1938 that half the German divisions had insufficient training and were led by inexperienced officers.[72] This assessment is confirmed by a British historian, who writes that "the German army in 1938 was clearly not in a position to inflict a battlefield defeat on the French." For Germany, a war with both Czechoslovakia and France "would surely have been a disaster."[73] The *Westwall*, otherwise known as the Siegfried Line, was still a construction site; the concrete had not yet hardened. By September, only 517 bunkers were completed.[74] Under the terms of its alliance with Czechoslovakia, France was not expected to intervene directly in Central Europe. Its support would consist of limited forays across the Rhine. Merely by declaring war on Germany, France would immobilize substantial elements of the German army.[75] As the Second World War was to show, the Nazis needed a quick victory. A war of attrition in 1938, before Germany annexed Czechoslovakia and most of Western Europe, could probably drain the

---

[71] Peter Neville, "Nevile Henderson and Basil Newton: Two British Envoys in the Czech Crisis, 1938," Igor Lukes and Erik Goldstein eds., *The Munich Crisis, 1938: Prelude to World War II* (London: Frank Cass, 1999), 265.

[72] Milos Hajek and Josef Novotny, "Munich: Politique et armée tchécoslovaques," *Revue d'histoire de la Deuxième Guerre mondiale*, October 1963, 15.

[73] Tooze, *The Wages of Destruction*, 270.

[74] Williamson Murray, "The Strategy of the 'Phoney War': A Re-evaluation," *Military Affairs*, February 1981, 15.

[75] David Vital, "Czechoslovakia and the Powers, September 1938," *Journal of Contemporary History*, October 1966, 38.

German economy;[76] and here a British naval blockade, undertaken with the benevolent neutrality of the Soviet Union, might have been effective. Czechoslovakia's military commanders had not envisaged the possibility that their country would have to fight alone. Its armed forces were to be engaged in coordination with those of France.[77] Britain was still unable to exert any direct military pressure on Germany; but France, allied with Czechoslovakia, was in a far better position that it would be a year later with Poland on its side. In his memoirs Churchill recognized that France and Czechoslovakia in tandem had a military advantage over Germany.[78] If there was ever an opportunity to stop Hitler, or at least to contain him, this was it. But in 1938, Chamberlain was not interested in stopping Hitler.

The House of Commons met in extraordinary session on the afternoon of 28 September to hear the prime minister explain that negotiations with Germany over Czechoslovakia were at an impasse. Toward the end of his speech, he was handed a note that Hitler, at the suggestion of Mussolini, had just proposed a four-power conference at Munich to settle the question amicably. When Chamberlain, who had sought just such an invitation, announced that he would accept it (thereby committing Daladier), cheers rang out from nearly all quarters. The leaders of the principal opposition parties – Attlee and Lansbury for Labour and Sinclair for the Liberals – all wished him God-speed. The lone dissenting voice was that of the Communist MP William Gallacher, who protested against the dismemberment of Czechoslovakia.[79] Churchill wisely kept silent. It would hardly serve to attack the prime minister at the height of his popularity.

Basking in his glory, Chamberlain smiled to the newsreel cameras as he made a short statement just before taking off for Munich on 29 September. "When I was a little boy," he recalled, "I used to

---

[76] Zara Steiner, *The Triumph of the Dark: European International History, 1933-1939* (Oxford: Oxford University Press, 2011), 652-3.

[77] Vital, "Czechoslovakia and the Powers," 49.

[78] Churchill, *The Gathering Storm*, 311.

[79] 339 H C Deb., September 28, 1938, cols. 5-28.

repeat: If at first you don't succeed, try, try and try again. That's what I am doing." His decision to go by air captured the public imagination. Among political leaders, only Hitler and Roosevelt had made regular use of the airplane. Shortly after his return, Lord Lloyd of Dolobran, president of the British Council and a close friend of Halifax, quipped: "If at first you don't concede, fly, fly again."[80] In his radio address, Chamberlain had promised, "I would not hesitate to pay even a third visit to Germany if I thought it would do any good;" and the British electorate was, at this point, solidly behind him, as was the King, who had written to Chamberlain on 16 September, telling him "how much I admire your courage & wisdom in going to see Hitler in person."[81]

The Munich conference was a sinister farce. There was no written agenda and no one presiding. Maisky had asked Halifax about the program and was told that the agenda would depend largely on Hitler's mood.[82] Since no minutes were taken, we can only assume that such negotiations as there were took place directly between Hitler and Chamberlain. The two major figures were not on an equal footing. While Hitler was supported by his foreign minister, Chamberlain had left Halifax at home. He preferred to be accompanied by Sir Horace Wilson. The participants did not sit around a table but on chairs arranged in a circle, with the British and French leaders too far from one another for consultation – not that Chamberlain was particularly interested in what Daladier might have to offer.[83] Mussolini had little to contribute, and Daladier was by then too ashamed to say very much. He had tried to reach Chamberlain by telephone for consultations before the latter took off for Bavaria but received no answer. Again, on arrival in Munich, he found Chamberlain to be unobtainable.[84] Once the

---

[80] Erik Goldstein, "Neville Chamberlain, the British Official Mind and the Munich Crisis," *Diplomacy and Statecraft*, vol.10, issues 2-3 (1999), 289.
[81] Chamberlain Papers, NC7/3/29.
[82] *The Maisky Diaries*, 142.
[83] Reynolds, *Summits*, 92.
[84] Robert and Isabelle Tombs, *That Sweet Enemy: The French and the British from the Sun King to the Present* (New York: Knopf, 2007), 535.

conference ended, the Czechoslovak representatives, who had been excluded from the entire proceedings and kept in their hotel under German police guard, were summoned to Chamberlain's hotel suite at 1:30 in the morning to learn of the outcome. After nine hours with Hitler, the British prime minister was understandably tired. He claimed to have done his best; but Daladier, who was also present, was visibly dejected and did not look directly at the Czechs. He knew that they felt betrayed by France.[85]

The Czechoslovak government, under extreme pressure from Britain and France, had allowed on 26 September that it would be willing to participate in an international conference "to find a different method of settling the Sudeten German question from that expounded in Herr Hitler's proposals."[86] Chamberlain rejected the very idea that Czechoslovakia might have some say in the matter. Its representatives at Munich were given no alternative but to accept the agreement, which required Czechoslovakia to cede all border fortifications to Germany intact and annulled the treaties it had concluded with France and the Soviet Union. As they read the terms, Chamberlain yawned - discreetly at first, then openly.[87]

Hitler did not obtain everything he had demanded at Bad Godesberg, but he did get the Sudetenland. He would help himself to the remaining spoils of Czechoslovakia later. Now that war had been averted, Chamberlain was immensely proud of himself. Before leaving Munich, he conferred personally with Hitler and presented him with a typewritten note containing an agreement that Britain and Germany would never go to war with each other again – an agreement which Chamberlain himself was to violate in less than a year's time. Hitler, who had no designs on Britain, signed immediately without asking for an official written translation. Chamberlain had not consulted Daladier before taking this initiative, or his own diplomatic corps. On arriving in London, he waved the sheet of paper before the newsreel cameras and

---

[85] DBFP, 25 September 1938, 3rd series, II, 530.
[86] Jan Masaryk to Halifax, DBFP, 26 Setember1938, 3rd series, II, 551.
[87] Lukes, *Czechoslovakia Between Stalin and Hitler,* 252-3.

announced that he had achieved "peace with honour." General Franz Halder, the German army chief of staff in 1938, took a different view. "Never in history," he recalled later, "has there been such a betrayal. A country, with an army at least equal to ours, forced to give up the strongest defence line in Europe."[88] The Czech border fortifications had been built largely with French capital.[89]

On learning the results of the Munich conference, six top-ranking Czech generals called on President Benes and argued that their country must go to war then and there. The army was already mobilized, and the population was united (at least among the Czechs and Slovaks). The Western powers, they said, would eventually follow; and even if they did not, the army had a duty to defend the national soil. They begged, they entreated; some wept. But Benes, as commander-in-chief, refused to give the order. Czechoslovakia, he warned, would probably have to face Poland as well as Germany; and even though the Czechoslovak army was far stronger than the Polish, a war against two enemies was inadvisable, especially without French support.[90]

No honour accrued to France. On 1 October, General Jan Syrovy, who had replaced President Benes as head of the Czechoslovak government, made a radio broadcast to his compatriots, which ended: "We were abandoned. We stood alone."[91] Czechoslovakia was indeed abandoned, and General Syrovy did not have to specify by whom. In the days that followed, the French embassy in Prague was deluged with French decorations, medals and citations which Czechoslovak citizens no longer wanted. For lack of visitors, the *Alliance française* was about to close. French diplomas were returned to the *Institut*, and Czech parents withdrew their children from the *Lycée*, which was rumoured to be transformed into a Czech secondary school.[92] The French

---

[88] Robert Boothby, *I Fight To Live* (London: Victor Gollancz, 1947), 174.

[89] Alexandre Zévaès, *Histoire de six ans, 1938-1944* (Paris: Éditions de la Nouvelle Revue Critique, 1944), 40.

[90] Vital, "Czechoslovakia and the Powers," 62.

[91] Caquet, *The Bell of Treason*, 194-5.

[92] Faucher to Daladier, October 6, 1938, DDF, 2nd series, XII, 93-6.

ambassador in Berlin, André François-Poncet, was overheard to comment: "See how France treats the only allies who remained faithful to her."[93]

More ominous forebodings came from Moscow. In mid-September 1938, the French ambassador, Robert Coulondre, warned that if Britain and France abandoned Czechoslovakia, the Soviet Union, in order to avoid total isolation, might come to some sort of agreement with Nazi Germany, regardless of ideological differences.[94] Coulondre, who was widely regarded as the ablest member of a highly professional diplomatic corps, met with Vladimir Potemkin, the Soviet vice-commissar for foreign affairs, on 4 October. The Russian was sympathetic, but coldly realistic. "My poor friend," he said, referring to Munich, "what have you done? For us, I see no outcome other than a fourth partition of Poland."[95]

Looking back on these events, Coulondre recalled that the French people, confusedly at first, then clearly, perceived that Munich was "one of the most tragic turning-points in our history." It signified a retreat from France's traditional role as a major European power, its "downfall – the word is not too strong. Yes, Munich sounded the death-knell of a certain France, the France of yesteryear, the France that still existed in 1914, the France which, in the secret of our hearts, we shall always long for."[96] In the opening paragraph of his war memoirs, Charles de Gaulle wrote: "In short, as I see it, France cannot be France without greatness."[97] At Munich, France was shown to be totally bereft of greatness, since a great power does not forsake its ally. The French military defeat of 1940 merely confirmed its reduced status.

---

[93] Telford Taylor, *Munich, the Price of Peace* (New York: Doubleday, 1979), 48.

[94] Coulondre to Bonnet, 17 September 1938, DDF 2nd series, XI, 278-9.

[95] Robert Coulondre, *De Staline à Hitler. Souvenirs de deux ambassades* (Paris: Hachette, 1950), 165.

[96]*Ibid.*, 181.

[97] Charles de Gaulle, *Mémoires de guerre,* I: *L'Appel, 1940-1942* (Paris: Plon, 1954), 5. The French word *grandeur* should not be translated as "grandeur," but as "greatness."

De Gaulle's anglophobia, his open contempt for the "Anglo-Saxons," as he liked to call them, remains a conundrum for most English-speaking observers. Yet an explanation may be found in the strained relations between the two former allies during the inter-war years. From 1919 on, successive British governments sought to strengthen Germany at the expense of France. Neville Chamberlain was merely the heir to this lamentable tradition, although he did expand on it considerably. Regarding Czechoslovakia, he put interminable pressure on France not to honour its prior commitment to that country. At a meeting of the foreign policy committee of the cabinet on 21 March 1938, Halifax explained that it was essential "to dissuade France from going to the aid of Czechoslovakia."[98] It is often assumed that France had a largely independent foreign policy – that it gave up its great-power status willingly.[99] In fact it was pushed into the abyss by Britain. In 1938, as throughout most of the inter-war period, the French were in turn "ignored and then browbeaten"[100] by their erstwhile allies.

During and after the Czech crisis, the British government and the British public displayed little understanding of the French position, and their indifference is largely reflected in British historiography. The remarkably detailed account by Keith Robbins of the entire tragedy hardly mentions France at all.[101] Only Sir Lewis Namier, writing shortly after the war, quotes Coulondre's appraisal of Munich sympathetically.[102] For France, Munich represented not only a serious blow to its prestige and the loss of a stalwart ally. It may also have affected French soldiers' morale during the Phoney War. Those who had been mobilized during the confrontation over Czechoslovakia were

---

[98] Telford Taylor, *Munich, the Price of Peace,* 637.

[99] A.J.P. Taylor, *The Origins of the Second World War* (London: Hamish Hamilton, 1961), 168, 187-8.

[100] Anthony Adamthwaite, "Reactions to the Munich Crisis," Neville Waites ed., *Troubled Neighbours: Franco-British Relations in the Twentieth Century* (London: Weidenfeld and Nicolson, 1971), 191.

[101] Keith Robbins, *Munich 1938* (London: Cassell, 1968).

[102] Sir Lewis Namier, *In the Nazi Era* (London: Macmillan, 1952), 142.

soon sent home. Many conscripts expected to be similarly released from duty in the winter of 1939-1940.[103]

The Chamberlain government's utter disregard for French interests can be seen in the pressure it exerted on France to choose a foreign minister acceptable to Britain. When Édouard Daladier assumed the premiership in April 1938, he wanted to retain in that post Joseph Paul-Boncour, who had served as foreign minister in the outgoing cabinet of Léon Blum. Paul-Boncour was a determined adversary of the dictators; he had once referred to Mussolini as a "carnival Caesar" (*un César de carnaval*) and believed that France should provide military assistance to the Spanish republic. In a dispatch to the French embassy in London, he argued that in the interest of peace, the two democratic powers should oppose Hitler's designs on Czechoslovakia.[104] He reiterated his position in a meeting with the British ambassador, Sir Eric Phipps. That was enough to make him persona non grata in Whitehall. Phipps intervened directly in French foreign affairs by persuading Daladier to appoint a noted appeaser, Georges Bonnet, to succeed Paul-Boncour, whom he considered "a disaster." Here, he was clearly acting on behalf of Chamberlain, whose influence in foreign affairs was decisive. British tutelage of its fellow democracy was now complete.[105] "France," in the words of a Canadian historian, "had to be guided and manipulated like some unruly offspring."[106]

With Bonnet, Britain's appointee, at the Quai d'Orsay, the so-called "appeasement" policy could proceed without hindrance. Throughout 1938 and much of 1939, the French foreign minister was effectively an instrument of British policy. In July, Phipps reminded Bonnet that his government objected to the stance taken by General

---

[103] Adamthwaite, "Reaction to the Munich Crisis," 192.

[104] Paul-Boncour to Corbin, 21 March 1938, DDF, 2nd series, IX, 4-5.

[105] John Herman, *The Paris Embassy of Sir Eric Phipps: Anglo-French Relations and the Foreign Office, 1937-1939* (Brighton: Sussex Academic Press, 1998), 5, 79-80, 86-7. 179.

[106] Robert J. Young, *In Command of France: French Foreign Policy and Military Planning, 1933-1940* (Cambridge, MA: Harvard University Press, 1978), 213.

Faucher, head of the French military mission to Czechoslovakia, who "was inclined to encourage the Czechs to be unduly obdurate in their negotiations with the Sudeten Germans." Would he get Faucher "to change his attitude in this respect"?[107] Bonnet was only too eager to comply, effectively negating any attempt at firmness by his own government. Faucher resigned his post on 23 September and put himself at the disposal of the Czechoslovak armed forces.[108]

Daladier's repeated attempts at reasoned argument with Chamberlain proved to be fruitless. The latter had made up his mind before taking office, and he viewed the Munich accord as his greatest triumph. To him, it mattered little that Czechoslovakia had been rendered defenceless and France shorn of its status as a great power. Czechoslovakia, allied with France, was the linchpin of the Versailles system, which sought not to crush Germany but to contain it and thus ensure collective security. The British government had strongly advised the French in 1924 against making alliances with the successor states of Central Europe.[109] Now its policy seemed fully vindicated.

Addressing the House of Lords early in October, Halifax hailed the Munich accords as a necessary revision of the Versailles treaty.[110] In the Commons, Inskip was even more explicit. "I should think that everybody admits that the treaty of Versailles has been unsuccessful in effecting the suppression and encirclement of Germany." The term "encirclement" apparently refers to Germany's position between France and Czechoslovakia. With Czechoslovakia amputated of the Sudetenland, Germany could – or at least should – no longer feel encircled. Inskip doubted "that any sane government would restore and recreate Czechoslovakia with its former boundaries." (Britain presumably had the right to redraw the boundaries of any state.) He reassured his fellow MPs that "His Majesty's Government feel under a

---

[107] Phipps to Halifax, 16 July 1938, DBFP, 3rd series, I, 577-8.

[108] *New York Times*, 24 September 1938.

[109] Roy Douglas, *The Advent of War, 1939-1940* (New York: St. Martin's Press, 1978), 147.

[110] 110 H L Deb., 3 October 1938, col. 1306.

moral obligation to Czechoslovakia to see that the integrity of Czechoslovakia is preserved." What was left of it, that is. The rump, he announced proudly, was protected by a British "guarantee."[111] Not all MPs were convinced. On 1 November, Attlee declared: "I do not know what has become of the moral guarantee. . . . The question we have to ask is whether, dismembered and fragmented, there is hope for an independent Czechoslovakia. I hope there is, but it looks extremely doubtful." Chamberlain's reply, "that we are not now contemplating the equipment of an army on a continental scale," cast further doubt on the efficacy of a moral guarantee and on the sincerity of his government in proposing it.[112]

In any event, it was not Czechoslovakia that mattered, but Germany. Now that the vanquished foe of 1918 was freed of its humiliations, it could not possibly harbour any more grievances – or so Chamberlain believed. He reminded the press on 11 September that "Herr Hitler has repeatedly expressed his own desire for peace, and it would be a mistake to assume that these declarations were insincere."[113] With the dreaded treaty of Versailles out of the way, he was confident that Europe could look forward to a sustained period of tranquility.

---

[111] 330 H C Deb., 4 October 1938, cols. 300-304.
[112] 340 H C Deb., 1 November 1938, cols. 65, 86.
[113] DBFP, 3rd series, I, 692.

3 A Change of Tactics

The euphoria that had accompanied Chamberlain's return from Munich proved to be of short duration. When Parliament reconvened on 3 October, Chamberlain defended the Munich accords as being an improvement on Hitler's demands at Bad Godesberg. The improvement, if any, was largely cosmetic. Instead of seizing the Sudetenland overnight, Germany occupied it progressively in ten days.[1] Chamberlain claimed that the Czechs had accepted the amputation of their territory prior to the Munich conference – a doubtful proposition at best. He further argued that the "new Czechoslovakia," now shorn of its frontier defences, was more secure that it had ever been.[2] Not all MPs were convinced.

Immediately prior to Chamberlain's speech, Alfred Duff Cooper, first lord of the Admiralty, announced his resignation, the only cabinet minister to do so. He stated flatly that Britain (and presumably France) should have gone to war instead of yielding to Hitler – and not specifically for Czechoslovakia. "It was not for Serbia that we fought in 1914. It was not even for Belgium, although it suited some people to say so. We were fighting then, as we should have been fighting last week, in order that one great power should not be allowed, in disregard of treaty obligations, of the laws of nations and the decrees of morality to dominate by brutal force the continent of Europe."[3]

These were brave words, to be sure, but totally at variance with the mood of the times. Britain, as nearly everyone knew, was in no position to make war; and no one wanted a repeat of 1914. The treaty obligations to which Duff Cooper referred were those of Versailles,

---

[1] Phillips, *Fighting Churchill, Appeasing Hitler*, 188.

[2] 339 H C Deb, 3 October 1938, series 5, cols. 42-46.

[3] *Ibid.*, cols. 29-32.

which by then was thoroughly discredited in Britain, if not in France. The objections to the Munich accord voiced by other parliamentarians were of a different nature. Clement Attlee, who had initially welcomed Chamberlain's decision to fly to Munich, now had second thoughts. "We have felt humiliation. This has not been a victory for reason and humanity. It has been a victory for brute force. . . . We have seen the cause of democracy, which is, in our view, the cause of civilisation and humanity, receive a terrible defeat." But unlike Duff Cooper, Attlee did not propose going to war. His position was that of other anti-appeasers, such as Churchill and Paul-Boncour: he believed that "the best chance of preventing war was a firm declaration by Britain, France, the Union of Socialist Soviet Republics [*sic*] and all other states open to be brought in, to stand against aggression. I still think that we would have stopped this tragedy."[4] In other words: show Hitler that you mean business, and he'll back down.

This was clearly wishful thinking. Chamberlain was correct in assuming that Hitler's threat to make war on Czechoslovakia, if the Sudetenland was not ceded to Germany, was genuine. Duff Cooper, who thought that Britain and France ought to have taken up the challenge, accepted this premise. But not Churchill. In his speech to the House of Commons on 5 October, he first admitted "that we have sustained a total and unmitigated defeat, and that France has suffered even more than we have." With the passage of time, his assessment has been fully validated. Less convincing, however, was his supposition that France and Britain, had they maintained close contact with Russia, could have rallied other European states, including Poland (!), to oppose Hitler's designs on Czechoslovakia. "Such a combination . . . would, I believe, have given strength to all those forces in Germany which resisted this departure. . . ." Britain should have declared "straight out and a long time beforehand that she would, with others, join to defend Czechoslovakia against unprovoked aggression."[5] At this stage, Churchill continued to believe in the good Germany which could

---

[4] *Ibid.*, cols. 51-58.
[5] 339 H C Deb., 5 October 1938, series 5, cols. 363-364.

effectively oppose Nazi expansionism. To encourage the good Germans and deter Hitler, he was, in essence, proposing the creation of a "peace front." A loose grouping of European states under that name, sponsored by Britain and France, did, in fact, come into existence in the spring of 1939, but it failed to bring peace.

Chamberlain held fast to his policy, which, he informed the cabinet on 31 October "is one of appeasement. We must aim at establishing relations with the dictator powers, which will lead to a settlement in Europe and a sense of stability."[6] The dictatorships included Germany and Italy, but not Stalin's Russia, which played no role in his diplomatic initiatives. Shortly before his death in November 1940, he wrote to Stanley Baldwin: "Never for one single instant have I doubted the rightness of what I did at Munich. . . ."[7] At Chamberlain's initiative, he and Halifax made an official visit to Paris on 23 November 1938. He intended, *inter allia*, "to give [the] French people an opportunity for pouring out their pent-up feelings of gratitude and affection" for his having preserved the peace.[8] Instead, when they arrived at the Gare du Nord, they were greeted with cries of "*A bas Munich!*" and "*Vive Eden!*"[9] In some French circles, Chamberlain was now called "*Monsieur j'aime-Berlin.*"

The meeting between British and French leaders at the Quai d'Orsay was devoted mainly to preparations for war. France and Germany had just signed an agreement to renounce any territorial claims between them, but the French were taking no chances. Daladier had agreed to the dismemberment of Czechoslovakia in order to draw Britain closer to France. If Britain were attacked directly, he promised that France would come immediately to its aid. In return, he argued in favour of an increase in British offensive capability, in the air and on

[6] Ian Colvin, *The Chamberlain Cabinet* (New York: Taplinger, 1971), 173.
[7] Feiling, *The Life of Neville Chamberlain*, 456.
[8] Chamberlain to Hilda, 6 November 1938, *The Neville Chamberlain Diary Letters*, 361.
[9] Richard Overy, *The Origins of the Second World War* (Abingdon: Routledge, 2008), 262.

the ground. "Munich then," writes an American historian, "at last got the French what they wanted: a serious continental commitment from the British."[10] Alas no. The British continental commitment was largely symbolic. Chamberlain explained that Britain was concentrating on the production of anti-aircraft guns and fighters to defend its home territory. He admitted that the medium and heavy artillery of a future expeditionary force, which could comprise at first only two divisions, was "obsolescent, if not obsolete." Britain "was also deficient in tanks." On the question of Czechoslovakia, Halifax was deliberately vague. "There was no precise definition of the guarantee," he explained. Bonnet insisted on more definite terms, as in the Locarno treaty (hardly a convincing precedent), but the British visitors refused to commit themselves further.[11] To his sister, Chamberlain wrote that the meeting had gone well. He had never been to the French foreign ministry (or the Élysée Palace or the Hôtel de Ville) before and was suitably impressed. "We only ran into one snag, when we discussed the guarantee of Czecho [sic]."[12]

The Jewish question had already intruded on Chamberlain's plans for an entente with Hitler. On the night of 8-9 November, the Nazis unleashed a monstrous pogrom, known as *Reichskristallnacht*, or the Night of Broken Glass, throughout Germany. Jewish-owned shops were vandalized and synagogues set on fire. More than a 90 Jews were murdered, and some 30,000 sent to concentration camps. "I am horrified by the German behaviour to the Jews," he confided to his sister. "There seems to be some fatality about Anglo-German relations which invariably blocks every effort to improve them."[13] He persisted nonetheless.

---

[10] Nord, *France 1940*, 17.

[11] "Record of Anglo-French Conversations held at the Quai d'Orsay on 24 November 1938," DBFP, 3rd series, III, 286-304.

[12] Chamberlain to Hilda, 27 November 1938, *The Neville Chamberlain Diary Letters*, 364.

[13] Chamberlain to Ida, 13 November 1938, *Ibid*, 363.

While seeking better relations with Hitler, Chamberlain did initiate several rearmament measures, in particular to improve Britain's air defences. Radar installations and a modern fighter force incurred unprecedented expenses, especially since a Spitfire cost nearly three times as much to produce as a Messerschmitt 109. Yet he effectively refuted any notion that his appeasement policy was merely a device to gain time. On returning from Munich, he sought the support of Lord Swinton, whom he had recently dismissed as secretary of state for air. Swinton, who was still a powerful force in the Conservative Party, told him: "I will support you, Prime Minister, provided that you are clear that you have been buying time for rearmament." Chamberlain once again produced the piece of paper he had signed with Hitler and exclaimed, "But don't you see, I have brought back peace!"[14] So he thought. But his far-reaching plans of 1937 for general appeasement did not halt the arms race, as he had hoped.[15] Throughout Europe, militarisation was given a new impetus by the Munich accords. Even peace-loving Britain had to rearm.

Daladier, meanwhile, was faced with the consequences of Munich in a way that eluded his British counterpart. Mussolini, who was emboldened by France's betrayal of its Central European ally, imagined himself to be a world-class statesman, the leader of a world-class power. He had proposed the Munich conference and was now determined to reap the benefits thereof. Inasmuch as Germany had gained the Sudetenland, he believed that Italy could and should recover lost territory. In late November, he informed the Fascist council that for security reasons, "we need Tunisia and Corsica."[16] During a session of the Italian Chamber of Deputies on 30 November, Ciano, the foreign minister, promised to uphold what he called "the interests and national aspirations of the Italian people." At these words, the secretary-general of the Fascist party, Lieutenant-General Achille Starace, jumped to his

---

[14] Colvin, *The Chamberlain Cabinet*, 168.

[15] Cf. *supra*, 38.

[16] Reynolds M. Salerno, *Vital Crossroads: Mediterranean Origins of the Second World War* (Ithaca, NY: Cornell University Press, 2002), 83.

feet and led the black-shirted deputies in cries of "Tunisia! Tunisia!" From the public gallery other Fascists chimed in with "Djibouti! Corsica!" [17] Nice was added to the list later.

Other than Mussolini himself, who was seated in the front row, anyone with the slightest measure of discernment could see that these claims were specious and had no chance of acceptance. Unlike the Sudetenland, which was populated largely by ethnic Germans, Nice and Corsica were, by 1938, thoroughly French; their inhabitants had no desire to be annexed by Fascist Italy. In Tunisia the Arab majority was overwhelmingly pro-French; even the small independence movement known as the *Néo-Destour* preferred France to Italy. The Italian colony in Tunis, which had long been dominated socially and economically by Jews from Livorno (Leghorn), was now effectively decapitated by Mussolini's recent anti-Jewish decrees.[18]

And there was France to contend with. Although it was assumed, in France as in Britain, that Germany was stronger than Czechoslovakia, no Frenchman believed that Italy had to be appeased on military grounds. The Italian claims were viewed as derisory and unworthy of even the slightest consideration. Knowing that he had the full support of his fellow citizens, Daladier arrived on board a French warship in the Corsican capital, Ajaccio, on New Year's Day 1939. In reply to the words of welcome by the town's mayor, he reminded his audience (not that anyone needed reminding) that Corsica had given Napoleon Bonaparte to France. He also recalled that some 40,000 Corsicans died for France during the Great War. His speech made for excellent newsreel footage, as did the exuberant reception he received in Tunisia. As he drove through the streets of Bizerte, people shouted *"Vive la France! Vive Daladier!"* while women threw flower petals at his car. Later, the Bey of Tunis made a stirring speech, saying: "You may be certain that Tunisians will, if necessary, rally to France. I give you this assurance here. France has the right to the infinite thanks of the

---

[17] Richard G. Massock, *Italy From Within* (New York: Macmillan, 1943), 107.
[18] Denis W. Brogan, *The Development of Modern France* (London: Hamish Hamilton, 1940), 728.

people of Tunis for the work it has done here, and Tunis will show her gratitude."[19]

The Fascist outburst did not escape notice in the British House of Commons, where Chamberlain was questioned early in December 1938 about his plans to confer with Mussolini in Rome. Brigadier-General Spears asked whether, in view of the recent scene in the Italian parliament and France's refusal to yield, the prime minister's visit could serve any useful purpose. Chamberlain explained that he had received assurances from the Italian government that it was in no way implicated in the incident; and therefore, "I see no reason to alter the arrangements for my visit to Rome next month." Attlee then asked: "Does the right honourable gentleman believe that spontaneous demonstrations take place in Italy under present conditions?" Chamberlain replied weakly that he accepted the official Italian explanation.[20]

Appeasing Italy was, at the time, the centrepiece of British policy in Europe. A month before being questioned in Parliament, Chamberlain had written to his sister, "An hour or two *tête-à-tête* with Musso[lini] might be extraordinarily valuable in making plans for talks with Germany. . . ."[21] To his other sister he wrote that the "ridiculous demonstration" in Rome could only unite all French citizens against the dictators and encourage British opponents of Fascism. But just as he sought good relations with Hitler in spite of anti-Jewish persecutions in Germany, so he cultivated Mussolini regardless of Italian irredentism.[22] Halifax, while recognizing British and French primacy in Western Europe, had told the cabinet on 3 October 1938 that Italy should be given a free hand in the Mediterranean. "Although we do not expect to detach Italy from the Axis, we believe the agreement [between London

---

[19] Alexander Werth and Denis W. Brogan, *The Twilight of France, 1933-1940* (New York: Harper, 1942), 315.

[20] 342 H C Deb., 5 December 1938, series 5, col. 852.

[21] Chamberlin to Hilda, 6 November 1938, *The Neville Chamberlain Diary Letters*, 361.

[22] Chamberlain to Ida, 4 December 1938, *Ibid.*, 366.

and Rome] will increase Mussolini's freedom of manoeuvre and so make him less dependent on Hitler. . . ."[23] The foreign secretary seems to have forgotten that much of the Mediterranean lay in Western Europe and that France had important interests there.

When Chamberlain and Halifax left for Rome on 10 January 1939, they made a courtesy stop in Paris, where they were informed that the French government would not accept any British mediation in its dispute with Italy. Daladier was well aware of Lord Runciman's recent mission to Prague, where he did not mediate at all, but instead sought to intimidate the Czechs. A similar British mission, this time directed at France, was just what Mussolini wanted; and when Chamberlain refused to authorise one, the Rome conference was limited to polite exchanges, leading nowhere.[24] The British premier, whose self-confidence never faltered, pronounced it a remarkable success, inasmuch as Mussolini "wanted peace and was ready to use his influence to get it."[25] Chamberlain informed the cabinet on 1 February that if the current Franco-Italian tension led to war, Britain might well remain neutral, lest its support for France lead Germany to enter the conflict on Italy's side.[26] Daladier, who privately referred to Chamberlain as a "desiccated stick," told the U. S. ambassador that "he fully expected to be betrayed by the British."[27] Actually, there was no danger that Mussolini would press his claims to the point of war; but having failed to obtain what he wanted most, namely British pressure on France to cede territory, he drew even closer to Hitler. Thus ended the British government's grand design for a general European settlement based on appeasing the dictator powers.

---

[23] Salerno, *Vital Crossroads*, 77.

[24] Werth and Brogan, *The Twilight of France*, 319.

[25] Chamberlain to Hilda, 15 January 1939, *The Neville Chamberlain Diary Letters*, 373.

[26] John Charmley, *Chamberlain and the Lost Peace* (London: Hodder & Stoughton, 1989), 189.

[27] Orvill H. Bullitt ed., *For the President, Personal and Secret: Correspondence Between Franklin D. Roosevelt and William C. Bullitt*, 6 February 1939 (London: André Deutsch, 1972), 310.

The appeasement of Nazi Germany continued because there was really no other possibility. Without Czechoslovakia as an ally, the two Western democracies were in a far weaker position than they had been before Munich. Many well-informed people in Britain continued to defend Chamberlain's policy on the grounds that, even in 1938, Germany would have been victorious. Such was the opinion of George M. Trevelyan, the eminent British historian, who was asked by an American colleague, Roger Merriman, what he thought of the current situation. In his reply, dated 28 January 1939, Trevelyan wrote: "In the last war England plus France plus Italy plus Russia plus Japan plus (half way through) the United States only just beat Germany and Austria. How do you expect England plus France alone to 'crush the dictators' with Germany, Austria, Italy and Japan against us?"[28] Trevelyan conveniently excluded Czechoslovakia from the equation; by January 1939, in any case, it was no longer a factor.

Merriman passed on Trevelyan's letter to President Roosevelt, who had been his student at Harvard. Roosevelt had initially approved Chamberlain's initiative in seeking an understanding with Hitler, although privately he had misgivings regarding British policy toward Czechoslovakia.[29] By early 1939, he was obliged to revise his public stance by none other than the British ambassador in Washington. "I wish the British would stop this 'We, who are about to die, salute thee' attitude," he wrote in his reply of 15 February. "Lord Lothian was here the other day, started the conversation by saying he had completely abandoned his former belief that Hitler could be dealt with as a semi-reasonable human being, and went on to say that the British for a thousand years had been the guardians of Anglo-Saxon civilization - that the scepter or the sword or something like that had dropped from their palsied fingers - that F.D.R. alone could save the world - etc., etc."

Roosevelt continued: "I got mad clear through and told him that just so long as he or Britishers like him took that attitude of complete

---

[28] http://docs.fdrlibrary.marist.edu/psf/box32/t304g03.html
[29] Harold L. Ickes, *The Secret Diary of Harold L. Ickes*, II *The Inside Struggle, 1936-1939* (New York: Da Capo Press, 1974), 468.

despair, the British would not be worth saving anyway." His conclusion foretells the future power relationship between the two English-speaking democracies: "What the British need today is a good stiff grog, inducing not only the desire to save civilization but the continued belief that they can do it. In such an event, they will have a lot more support from their American cousins – don't you think so?"[30]

Chamberlain had little use for Roosevelt, who had devalued the dollar in 1934 and offered Britain no relief on the payment of war debts. The Americans, he claimed, were "a nation of cads."[31] On this question, as on most others, he never changed his mind. When Sir Ronald Lindsay retired as British ambassador to the United States in June 1939, Chamberlain was consulted about a replacement. He replied that "the Americans are so rotten, it does not matter who we send there."[32] For his part, Roosevelt had no illusions about Chamberlain, of whom he said in 1937, "We must recognize that fundamentally he thoroughly dislikes Americans."[33] The British premier's anti-American stance did not deter Roosevelt from sending him a secret message early the following year, in which he proposed an international conference to be held in Washington, one that would include the leaders of Germany and Italy. A British historian comments: "Roosevelt would have faced the dictators with the necessity to declare themselves and their demands before the world – and use the consequences to alert American opinion, even more deeply asleep than our own. He *needed* that conference [emphasis in the original]; for us it was a life-buoy thrown to a drowning man."[34] Ambassador Lindsay urged Chamberlain to accept the proposal, which he viewed as a genuine attempt to ease

---

[30]http://www.masshist.org/database/viewer.php?item_id=1842&mode=large&img_step...

[31] Robert Self, *Neville Chamberlain: a Biography* (Aldershot: Ashgate, 2006), 189-90.

[32] Taylor, *Munich, the Price of Peace*, 660.

[33] Reynolds, *The Creation of the Anglo-American Alliance*, 25.

[34] A.L. Rowse, *Appeasement: a Study in Political Decline, 1933-1939* (New York: Norton, 1961), 67.

international tension. To withhold support, he added, could negate the recent progress made in Anglo-American relations. Chamberlain rejected the plan, because it might cut across his own diplomatic initiatives.[35]

The British premier's personal diplomacy was put to the test on 15 March 1939, when German troops entered Prague, effectively annexing all of Bohemia and Moravia to the Reich. In his radio address of 27 September 1938, he had declared: "After my visits to Germany I have realized vividly how Herr Hitler feels that he must champion other Germans." In fact, Hitler did not champion *all* other Germans. He left the German-speaking population of northern Italy to the tender care of Mussolini; and he made no claims for the Germans of North Slesvig, which had been returned to Denmark, or for Eupen-Malmédy, which was annexed outright by Belgium, both under the Versailles treaty. The last two groups, as loyal subjects of Kaiser Wilhelm II, actually had German nationality in 1918. At the time, Hitler was still an Austrian and did not become a German citizen by naturalization until 1930. The prime minister then added, "He told me privately, and last night he repeated publicly, that after this Sudeten German question is settled, that is the end of Germany's territorial claims in Europe."[36] Daladier had warned Chamberlain on 18 September that Hitler was using the Sudeten issue as a pretext to destroy Czechoslovakia.[37] Hitler told his military commanders on 23 November: "It was clear to me from the first moment that I could not be satisfied with the Sudeten-German territory. That was only a partial solution. The decision to march into Bohemia was made."[38]

Was Chamberlain naive, credulous? On presenting the Munich accords to the House of Commons on 3 October 1938, he claimed that "under the new system of guarantees, the new Czechoslovakia will find

---

[35] Churchill, *The Gathering Storm,* 226-7.
[36] Neville Chamberlain, *In Search of Peace* (New York: Putnam's, 1939), 275.
[37] Richard Lamb, *The Drift to War, 1922-1939* (London: Bloomsbury, 1991), 246.
[38] Namier, *Diplomatic Prelude,* 405.

a greater security than she has ever enjoyed in the past.[39] He certainly hoped it would, having written to the Archbishop of Canterbury the previous day: "I am sure that some day the Czechs will see that what we did was to save them for a happier future."[40] His optimistic declaration came back to haunt him after the Prague coup. In the upper house of Parliament, Lord Snell, a Labour Party stalwart who had been elevated to the peerage in 1931, took issue with the prime minister for being "too simple" to understand that Hitler could not be trusted. Halifax emphatically denied that Chamberlain was the least bit simple. "I can assure your Lordships that neither the prime minister nor I, myself, nor any member of His Majesty's Government has failed at any moment to be acutely conscious of the difference between belief and hope."[41] In plain English, this meant that the government somehow hoped that Hitler would keep his word, but did not believe it possible. The total collapse of Czechoslovakia could hardly have come as a surprise. In a dispatch of May 1938, Newton, the British minister in Prague, had endorsed the conclusions of the Paris peace conference that Bohemia-Moravia formed a natural region. "I am doubtful whether any attempt to divide it up would provide a permanent solution."[42]

Indeed, some evidence exists that Britain had been ready from the very start to throw Czechoslovakia to the wolves. A dispatch from the German embassy in London dated 8 June 1938 records the advice given by "an influential Englishman" (unnamed) to a German acquaintance of the ambassador: "Don't shoot Czechoslovakia, strangle her." The ambassador understood this to mean that anything that Germany could gain without recourse to arms would be accepted by the British government.[43] Shortly after Munich, Chamberlain met privately with Jan Masaryk, the Czechoslovak minister to Britain, who reported

---

[39] 339 H C Deb, 3 October 1938, col. 46.

[40] John W. Wheeler-Bennett, *King George VI, His Life and Reign* (London: Macmillan, 1958), 355.

[41] 112 H L Deb., 20 March 1939, cols. 300, 314.

[42] Newton to Halifax, 16 May 1938, DBFP 3rd Series, I, 300-3.

[43] Dirksen to Ribbentrop, 8 June 1938, DGFP, series D, II, 393.

being told: "I am sorry, but Czechoslovakia has to go."[44] And so it went.

Now Chamberlain had to answer for his policy of sacrificing the only democracy in Central Europe in order to appease Nazi Germany. When he promised Daladier to guarantee what remained of Czechoslovakia, he admitted that Britain "had no army which could march to Czechoslovakia, and it was a long way to send an air force."[45] It made no sense to guarantee a rump state shorn of its border fortifications, especially when the guarantor lacked an army. The time to support Czechoslovakia was while it still had the means of defending itself.[46] In the House of Commons on 15 March, he justified the British government's inaction with the lame excuse that since Czechoslovakia had ceased to exist because of "internal disruption," (the secession of Slovakia, encouraged by Vienna radio), the guarantee was no longer operative. In fact, it had never been issued formally. Early in December 1938, Halifax explained to the British minister in Prague that "His Majesty's Government are not prepared to consider a guarantee which might oblige them, alone or with France, to come to the assistance of Czechoslovakia in circumstances in which effective help could not be rendered."[47] Given that no effective help could be rendered in any case, the British government had already extricated itself from Inskip's promise.[48] On learning of Hitler's Prague coup, Halifax was somewhat relieved. He told the French ambassador that "it had brought to a natural end the somewhat embarrassing commitment of a guarantee."[49] Chamberlain did admit, however, that the Germans had just occupied militarily a "territory inhabited by people with whom they have no

---

[44] Bartley C. Crum, *Behind the Silken Curtain* (New York: Simon and Schuster, 1947), 62.

[45] David Dilks ed., *The Diaries of Sir Alexander Cadogan, O. M., 1938-1945* (London: Cassell, 1971), 101.

[46] Zévaès, *Histoire de six ans*, 43.

[47] Halifax to Newton, 8 December 1938, DBFP, 3rd series III, 304-5.

[48] Cf. *supra*, 65.

[49] Halifax to Phipps, 15 March 1939, DBFP 3rd series IV, 273.

racial connection. These events cannot fail to be a cause of disturbance to the international situation."[50]

Two days later the prime minister gave a speech in his home constituency of Birmingham. It was originally supposed to be about domestic affairs, but the *fait accompli* in Prague so incensed British public opinion that he had to deal with it. He defended the Munich accords (as he would to his dying day) by claiming that the question at issue was not new. "This was something that had existed ever since the treaty of Versailles – a problem that ought to have been solved long ago if only the statesmen of the last twenty years had taken broader and more enlightened views of their duty." So the treaty of Versailles was to blame – once again! Besides, he added pathetically: "Nothing that we could have done, nothing that France could have done or Russia could have done could possibly have saved Czecho-Slovakia from invasion or destruction." Presumably, his listeners had already forgotten his earlier claim that, amputated of its defence frontier, Czechoslovakia was more secure than ever. Having justified his appeasement policy, he then asked rhetorically what reliance could be placed on Hitler's assurances. "Is this the end of an old adventure or is it the beginning of a new?" Chamberlain had received a slap in the face, one which could compromise his standing with the electorate. But he explained that he was "not prepared to engage this country by new unspecified commitments under conditions which cannot now be foreseen."[51] He would keep his hands free and wait on events.

Waiting on events meant doing nothing. With the benefit of hindsight, this was the best, indeed the only, option available.[52] The alternative was a European war, for which Britain was singularly unprepared. In March 1938, General Ironside wrote in his diary: "There is no [British] army and there cannot be an army. . . ."[53] He was

---

[50] 345 H C Deb., 15 March 1939, series 5, cols. 438, 440.

[51] *New York Times*, 18 March 1939.

[52] See Alan Alexandroff and Richard Rosecrance, "Deterrence in 1939," *World Politics*, April 1977, 410n.

[53] General Edmund Ironside, *Time Unguarded: The Ironside Diaries, 1937-*

commenting on the recent military appropriations debate, during which Churchill admitted that, as to the army, "we are weaker in every respect, relatively and actually, than we were in 1914, but the army is not at the present time a prime factor in our safety. . . ."[54] Throughout the inter-war period, the Royal Navy and the Royal Air Force received the lion's share of military allotments. The situation changed once war was declared, as the army budget overtook those of the other services. Doing nothing was a form of appeasement, but not the proactive appeasement so recently practised by Neville Chamberlain. Since becoming prime minister in 1937, he had made it a top priority to anticipate Hitler's territorial ambitions and to satisfy them so that Germany could annex Austria and the Sudetenland without recourse to armed force. The amputation, and later the destruction, of Czechoslovakia left Hitler free to dominate all of Eastern Europe and pursue Germany's traditional policy of expansion to the east. So it would have been best, from Britain's standpoint, simply to leave him alone.

But can a great power do nothing and still remain a great power? In London rumours flew fast and furious. On 16 March, the day before Chamberlain's Birmingham speech, the Romanian minister in London, Vergil Tilea, informed the Foreign Office that Germany was about to absorb Hungary and had issued an ultimatum to Romania. There was no substance to this claim, but it was followed by other wild notions that Hitler was planning to attack Poland, the Netherlands, Ukraine and even Britain – all within a few months.[55] At a cabinet meeting on 29 March, Halifax admitted that "there was probably no way in which France and ourselves could prevent Poland and Romania from being overrun. We were faced with the dilemma of doing nothing, or entering into a devastating war. If we did nothing, this in itself would mean a great accession to Germany's strength and a great loss to ourselves of sympathy and support in the United States, in the Balkan

---

1940 (New York: D. McKay, 1951), 22 March 1938, 51.

[54] 332 H C Deb., 7 March 1938, col. 1600.

[55] Charmley, *Chamberlain and the Lost Peace,* 169-70.

countries, and in other parts of the world." Chamberlain was more optimistic regarding Britain's chances in the event of war. "By manning the Maginot Line, we [i.e. France] should be holding up large German forces which would otherwise be available for overrunning Poland and Romania."[56] Once the Phoney War began, the Maginot Line tied up three times as many French troops as German.[57] Chamberlain could not have anticipated this paradox. He tried mightily to avoid war; but if it did break out, he assumed that the Maginot Line was the Western democracies' assurance of success.

The cabinet meeting of 29 March marked a decisive turning-point in British foreign policy. That afternoon, Halifax was told by Ian Colvin, who had been recently expelled from Berlin as correspondent of the *News Chronicle*, that Germany had "everything ready" for a "swoop on Poland," after which Hitler would turn his attention to the British Empire.[58] As recently as early February, the Polish ambassador in London, Count Edward Racynski, had reported to Warsaw that British leaders considered all of Eastern Europe to be outside their country's sphere of interest.[59] Chamberlain, who was a prey to rumour-mongers, nearly fell for the reporter's fanciful tale. We know now that Hitler had no aggressive designs on Poland or Romania in March 1939,[60] but Chamberlain had already decided that "Poland was very likely the key to the situation." The time had come, he informed the cabinet on 18 March, "for those threatened immediately or ultimately by German aggression to get together."[61]

To his sister Chamberlain explained, "I must confess that if the small states won't face up to this sort of penetration even when backed

---

[56] Sidney Aster, *1939: The Making of the Second World War* (London: André Deutsch, 1973), 94-5.

[57] Taylor, *The Second World War*, 49.

[58] Charmley, Chamberlain *and the Lost Peace*, 173.

[59] Sir Nicholas Henderson, "A Fatal Guarantee: Poland, 1939," *History Today*, October 1997, 19.

[60] Alexandroff and Rosecrance, "Deterrence in 1939," 412.

[61] Colvin, *The Chamberlain Cabinet*, 189.

up by us, I see nothing for us to do unless we are prepared ourselves to hand Germany an ultimatum. We are not strong enough ourselves & we cannot command sufficient strength elsewhere to present Germany with an overwhelming force. Our ultimatum would therefore mean war, and I would never be responsible for presenting it. We just have no go on rearming & collecting what help we could from outside in the hope that something would happen to break the spell, either Hitler's death or a realization that the defence was too strong to make attack feasible."[62] Here, then, was a candid admission that even with France as an ally, Britain could not prevail against Germany. How was Chamberlain to extricate himself from this predicament?

His solution was deterrence. By guaranteeing the independence of Poland, Britain would deter Hitler from committing further acts of aggression – or so Chamberlain hoped. He presented the guarantee to Parliament on 31 March, reminding his fellow MPs that the British government had always favoured "free negotiation between the parties concerned of any differences that may arise between them." Then he added that "in the event of any action which clearly threatened Polish independence, and which the Polish Government accordingly considered it vital to resist with their national forces, His Majesty's Government would feel themselves bound at once to lend the Polish Government all the support in their power."[63] The guarantee was poorly drafted. No mention was made of frontiers or whether Danzig was included. The putative aggressor was not named. The British government had only Germany in mind; but if Russia ever invaded Poland (which it eventually did) the guarantee would presumably oblige Britain to make war on that country as well.[64] Unfortunately, there was no credible British deterrent, other than words. Even with France as an ally, Britain had assumed a stance that it could not maintain.[65]

---

[62] Chamberlain to Ida, 26 March 1939, *The Neville Chamberlain Diary Letters*, 396.

[63] 345 H C Deb., 31 March 1939, series 5, col. 2415.

[64] John Gunther, *Inside Europe* (New York: Harper, 1940), 133.

Chamberlain added that the guarantee had been communicated to Warsaw and that the French government subscribed to it fully. In fact, the actual text of the guarantee was made public before anyone in Paris had time to comment on it.[66] On Poland, notes an American historian, "the British acted on their own, unbidden by the French."[67] Churchill adds a touch of the dramatic: "Great Britain advances, leading France by the hand, to guarantee the integrity [*sic*: the independence] of Poland – that very Poland which, with hyena appetite, had only six months before joined in the pillage and destruction of the Czechoslovak state."[68] Addressing the House of Lords, Halifax declared: "Our pledge to Poland marks a new and momentous departure in British policy."[69] The guarantee was without precedent in British history, indeed in all of history. As Sir Alexander Cadogan explained to U. S. Ambassador Joseph Kennedy, Britain was leaving the final decision of declaring war to another power.[70] No British ally, and certainly not France, had ever enjoyed such a privilege.

The guarantee had been issued against the advice of the chiefs of staff, who knew that Britain could not intervene militarily to defend Poland. To Chamberlain, this did not matter. He felt compelled to make a gesture which would show both Hitler and the British people that he was ready to oppose aggression.[71] Ambassador Maisky remarked pointedly to Halifax on 31 March that his government had not been informed of Chamberlain's intention to issue the guarantee.[72] In May,

---

[65] Richard Rosecrance and Zara Steiner, "British Grand Strategy and the Origins of World War II," Richard Rosecrance and Arthur A Stein eds., *The Domestic Bases of Grand Strategy* (Ithaca, NY: Cornell University Press, 1993), 131.

[66] P.M.H. Bell, *France and Britain, 1900-1940: Entente and Estrangement* (London: Longmans, 1996), 224.

[67] Nord, *France 1940*, 17.

[68] Churchill, *The Gathering Storm*, 311.

[69] 112 H L Deb., 2 April 1939, col. 575.

[70] Kennedy to Hull, 31 March 1939, FRUS (1939), I, 105-6.

[71] Mosley, *On Borrowed Time*, 196-7.

the chiefs of staff advised the cabinet that a mutual assistance pact with the Soviet Union would carry more weight, but Halifax demurred on the grounds that if Britain drew closer to Russia, "we should run a serious risk of breaking the common front which we are endeavouring to establish."[73] He had told his cabinet colleagues on 20 March that "if we had to make a choice between Poland and Soviet Russia, it seemed clear that Poland would be the greater value."[74]

That France should allow itself to be pushed into a possible war over Poland seems to defy all logic. Unlike Czechoslovakia, which had been France's most faithful ally, Poland had signed a non-aggression pact with Germany in 1934, the first ever concluded by Hitler. On 27 September 1938, three days before Munich, it sent an ultimatum to Prague demanding the cession of a border region inhabited largely by ethnic Poles. The Czechs yielded on 1 October. In November, Poland annexed even more territory, bringing its total gains to more than one thousand square kilometres and 228,000 inhabitants, of whom 133,000 were Czech and 20,000 German-speaking.[75] Hitler had encouraged the Polish scavenge; he was delighted that Poland, along with Hungary, participated in the dismemberment of Czechoslovakia. It reinforced his claim to promote national self-determination. Colonel Beck, the Polish foreign minister, considered Czechoslovakia to be an "artificial creation," which was condemned to disappear sooner or later. Like Hitler, he believed that, if left alone, it would become a "hotbed of Bolshevism."[76] Beck was decidedly cool to the alliance with France and had urged the French to cede Tunisia to Italy.[77] As a result, they had

---

[72] *The Maisky Diaries*, 169.

[73] Anita Prazmowska, *Britain, Poland and the Eastern Front, 1939* (Cambridge: Cambridge University Press, 1987), 138.

[74] *Ibid.*, 51.

[75] Wheeler-Bennett, *Munich, Prologue to Tragedy.* 338.

[76] Keith Eubank, *The Origins of World War II* (Wheeling, IL. Harlan Davidson, 2004), 128-9.

[77] Jean-Baptiste Duroselle, *La décadence, 1933-1939* (Paris: Imprimerie Nationale, 1979), 392.

come to distrust Poland profoundly.[78] In November, Bonnet sought unsuccessfully to strip the Franco-Polish alliance of its binding character and transform it into a simple treaty of friendship.[79]

The French decision to risk a war with Germany makes sense only if one takes Italy into account. At the first full staff conversation with their British counterparts on 29 March, French strategists explained that they would adopt a purely defensive posture toward Germany, but were prepared to launch an offensive against Germany's ally, Italy.[80] They were convinced, with ample justification, that France would be victorious, thereby humiliating both partners to the Axis. The French navy dominated the western Mediterranean. Its two battle cruisers, the *Dunkerque* and the *Strasbourg*, both of which were commissioned in 1938, surpassed in speed and armament their Italian rivals.[81] The French also had an aircraft carrier, the *Béarn*. The Italians had none. As the summer wore on, however, it became apparent that Italy would adopt a non-belligerent stance in 1939, as the British had hoped. Non-belligerence meant that Italy, while remaining an ally of Germany, would abstain from fighting. Thus was undermined the only strategic basis for going to war over Poland.

It is sometimes assumed that Daladier endorsed the guarantee simply to maintain the British connection. This was certainly a factor, but not a determining one. Like its ally, the French government feared that if it reneged on its earlier commitment, it risked pushing Poland into the arms of Hitler.[82] In the event, Poland was forced into the arms of both Hitler and Stalin; neither France nor Britain could save it. On the Polish question, France fell in line with Britain in order to salvage what remained of its dwindling status. Daladier, who distrusted the British,[83] knew that his country had been humiliated at Munich; and he

---

[78] Young, *In Command of France*, 230.

[79] Prazmowska, *Britain, Poland and the Eastern Front*, 25.

[80] Brian Bond, *France and Belgium, 1939-1940* (Newark, DE: University of Delaware Press, 1979), 31.

[81] Murray, *The Change in the European Balance of Power*, 105.

[82] Young, *In Command of France*, 233.

now believed that France was compelled to oppose further German expansionism lest it cease to be a great power. Speaking to a group of war veterans in November 1938, he warned that France ran the risk of becoming "a second-rate, subordinate nation, with no prestige other than its past greatness." It must choose "between a slow decline and its rebirth by virtue of effort."[84] A month later, Gamelin warned Daladier to expect a test a test of strength with Germany in the spring or summer of 1939. France would renounce being a great power, he wrote, if it failed to meet the challenge.[85] Italy's bombastic claims to Nice, Corsica and Tunisia served further to strengthen French resolve.

British resolve emanated from the humiliation endured by Chamberlain when Hitler annexed Bohemia and Moravia. A Foreign Office memorandum issued in May 1939 read in part: "The principal object of our guarantee to Poland was to deter Germany from any further act of aggression. . . ."[86] But would it be sufficient? Churchill didn't think so. In a speech to the House of Commons on 3 April, he first congratulated the prime minister for what he called "the surprising transformation of the last few weeks." For deterrence to be effective, however, Britain needed the participation of the Soviet Union. "Having begun this new policy there can be no turning back. . . . To stop here with a guarantee to Poland would be to halt in no-man's land under fire of both trench lines and without the shelter of either. . . . Having begun to create a grand alliance against aggression, we cannot afford to fail. . . . The worst folly, which no one proposes we should commit, would be to chill and drive away any natural co-operation which Soviet Russia in her own deep interests feels it necessary to afford."[87]

Lloyd George was even more emphatic. Prior to addressing the House, he had conferred with Chamberlain and asked what the role of the Soviet Union would be in a coalition against Nazi Germany.

---

[83] Cf. *supra*, 73.

[84] Édouard Daladier, *Défense du pays* (Paris: Flammarion, 1939), 94-95.

[85] Elisabeth du Réau, *Édouard Daladier. 1884-1970* (Paris: Fayard, 1993), 312.

[86] DBFP, 3rd series, V, 642.

[87] 345 H C Deb., 3 April 1939, series 5, cols. 2500-2502.

Chamberlain replied that neither Poland nor Romania wanted Soviet participation, but not to worry. "Our information is that the Germans will not risk a two-front war." Lloyd George then asked, "And where is the 'second front' to be?" On being told, "Poland," he ridiculed the very notion that Poland, "a country with a weak economy and torn by internal strife, a country that has neither aviation nor a properly equipped army" could hold out against Hitler's legions.[88] "Without the Soviet Union," he said in conclusion, "your policy is a reckless gamble."[89] In Parliament, he expressed doubt that Britain, even with the support of France, could fulfill a military commitment in the east. "If war occurred to-morrow, you could not send a single battalion to Poland." A consummate politician who understood the mood of the country, he struck a patriotic note: "Britain has been admired, Britain has been respected, Britain has been hated and Britain has been feared, but she has never been laughed at." The Poles were "a brave people," but valour alone could not win battles against a superior force. "If we are going in without the help of Russia, we are walking into a trap." Should the Poles refuse Russian help, "the responsibility must be theirs."[90]

As Chamberlain noted, the Poles certainly did not want Russian help. They had repulsed the Bolsheviks and gained territory at Russia's expense in the war of 1919-1921. Poland's main defences faced east, not west, and Poland had not signed a non-aggression pact with the Soviet Union. The Polish government feared, with some justification, that if Soviet troops entered Poland to protect it from Nazi Germany, they would not leave.[91] As for Russia, the Munich accord convinced

---

[88] *The Maisky Diaries*, 170; cf. Michael Jabara Carley, *1939: The Alliance that Never Was and the Coming of World War II* (London: House of Stratus, 2000), 114.

[89] Hugh Dalton, *The Fateful Years: Memoirs, 1931-1945* (London: Friedrich Muller, 1957), 242.

[90] 345 H C Deb., 3 April 1939, series 5, cols. 2507-2511.

[91] Andrew David Stedman, *Alternatives to Appeasement: Neville Chamberlain and Hitler's Germany* (London: Tauris, 2011), 151.

Stalin that France and Britain were effectively in league with Hitler and had rejected collective security. In a marathon speech to the eighteenth congress of the Soviet Communist Party on 10 March 1939, he warned that one of its prime tasks in foreign policy was "to be cautious and not to allow our country to be drawn into conflicts by warmongers who are accustomed to having others pull the chestnuts out of the fire for them."[92] Taken in context with Potemkin's earlier reference to a fourth partition of Poland,[93] Stalin's warning would seem to indicate that a Soviet *rapprochement* with Nazi Germany was already in the offing. Ambassador Coulondre, who had been transferred from Moscow to Berlin, reported to the Quai d'Orsay early in May that Germany was moving closer to Russia.[94]

Chamberlain's appeasement policy had not yet run its course. Late in March (i.e. after German troops entered Prague), the British government delivered six million pounds' worth of Czechoslovak gold to Berlin.[95] There was, however, no going back on the guarantee to Poland. On 6 April, Colonel Beck met with Halifax in London. He first sought to ingratiate himself with his host by announcing that the guarantee was reciprocal, a symbolic gesture at best. On the really important questions of collective security, he remained obdurate. A pact with the Soviet Union, he claimed, would provoke Hitler and "possibly accelerate the outbreak of a conflict." He warned that if Britain signed an agreement with Russia, his government would have to dissociate itself publicly. Nor would Poland enter into a defensive alliance with Romania. That, he said, would drive Hungary into the German camp.[96] Beck availed himself of the opportunity to seek Britain's help in relieving Poland of its "surplus" Jews, numbering at least 3.3 million,

---

[92] Quoted in Anthony P. Adamthwaite, *The Making of the Second World War* (London: George Allen & Unwin, 1977), 211.

[93] Cf. *supra*, 61.

[94] Coulondre to Bonnet, 7 May 1939, *Le Livre jaune français*, 154.

[95] Harold Macmillan, *Winds of Change, 1914-1939* (London: Macmillan, 1966), 596-7.

[96] Aster, *The Making of the Second World War*, 124-5.

who, he assumed, could surely find refuge in the vast reaches of the British Empire. The official statement from London expressed sympathy for this proposal. In reality, the various Imperial administrations were not ready to welcome more than a token contingent of the 500,000 German Jews.[97] A British government White Paper, issued in May of 1939, severely limited Jewish immigration to Palestine, at that precise moment when the Jews of Europe were most in need of a haven.

Almost from the start, it was obvious that the guarantee to Poland, far from assuring peace, increased the danger of war. On this point, Liddell Hart was unequivocal. "The Polish guarantee," he wrote, "was the surest way to produce an early explosion, and a world war" because it eliminated any possibility of a compromise between Germany and Poland.[98] Hitler had welcomed Poland's claims on Czechoslovak territory and sought an understanding with Warsaw by removing the prime source of conflict: Danzig. On 24 October 1938, Ribbentrop made the following proposals to Jozef Lipski, the Polish ambassador: (1) Danzig would revert to the Reich; (2) an extraterritorial road and rail link between Pomerania and East Prussia would be laid across the Corridor, which would remain under Polish control; (3) Danzig would be a free port, and Poland would receive a guarantee for its goods in the Danzig area; (4) Poland and Germany would recognize their common boundaries; (5) the non-aggression treaty between the two nations would be extended 25 years, and Poland would join the Anti-Comintern pact.[99] The mutual recognition of the German-Polish border was a major concession on Hitler's part, since it meant giving up certain revisions to the Versailles treaty, such as the return of East Upper Silesia to Germany, that had been demanded by the Weimar Republic under Stresemann.[100]

---

[97] *New York Times*, 7 April 1939.
[98] B. H. Liddell Hart, *The Memoirs of Captain Liddell Hart* (London: Cassell, 1965), II, 217-20.
[99] Simon Newman, *March 1939: The British Guarantee to Poland* (Oxford: Clarendon Press, 1976), 158.

Just three weeks before Britain declared war on Germany, Churchill confided to Lloyd George that Hitler's terms were "not unreasonable."[101] The Third Reich had a perfectly legitimate claim to Danzig: unlike the Sudetenland, it had been part of Imperial Germany. Of its 400,000 inhabitants, only 15,000 were Poles. Henderson wrote to Sir Horace Wilson in May, "The Prague coup has altered our whole outlook towards Hitler but it has not altered the merits of the Danzig-Corridor case in themselves. I may be wrong but I am personally convinced that there can be no permanent peace in Europe until Danzig has reverted to Germany. The Poles cannot be master of the 400,000 Germans in Danzig – ergo the Germans must be."[102] Henderson's pro-German sentiments should not detract from the force of his argument, which closely reflected Chamberlain's policy on the territorial dispute between Germany and Poland. The prime minister retained him in his ambassadorial post until war was actually declared.

A British historian notes the irony of the situation. "It would have been so much easier," he writes, "to make a *prima facie* case for appeasing Germany in the case of Poland than had been possible in the case of Czechoslovakia. . . . Having abandoned, in 1938, an industrious democracy, loyal to the principles of the League of Nations, and an untiring worker in the field of collective security, Britain and France in 1939 placed the decision as to their declaration of war in the hands of a state ruled by an incompetent and purblind oligarchy who preferred government by junta rather than by parliament, and who, in the years 1920-38, had embarked upon military or diplomatic forays against Germany, Russia, Lithuania and Czechoslovakia, which resulted in no small accretion of territory." Czechoslovakia had a far more liberal policy toward its ethnic minorities than Poland, which in 1934 openly repudiated provisions of the Minorities Treaty it had

---

[100] Rolf-Dieter Müller, *Enemy in the East: Hitler's Secret Plans to Invade the Soviet Union*, trans. Alexander Starritt (London: Tauris, 2015), 101.

[101] Cecil H. King, *With Malice Toward None: A War Diary* (London: Sedgwick & Jackson, 1970), 13.

[102] Newman, *The British Guarantee to Poland*, 213-14.

signed in 1919 and 1920. [103] Ever since Poland had opened a seaport in Gdynia, Danzig was no longer its only outlet to the Baltic.

A war for Danzig seemed remote in March 1939. Moreover, Nazi Germany had certain ideological affinities with autocratic Poland. Both were fiercely anti-Communist and fiercely anti-Semitic. Until 8 November 1938, there was actually more anti-Jewish violence in Poland than in Germany. Between 1935 and 1937, ninety-seven Polish Jews had been killed; and in 1937 alone, some 7,000 others were put on trial for "having insulted the Polish nation."[104] Hitler initially viewed Poland as a forward "bastion of civilization," protecting Germany from the Bolshevik menace.[105] At the death of Marshal Pilsudski, the Polish head of state, in May 1935, Hitler ordered a memorial mass to be held in Saint Hedwig's Church in Berlin. He was himself in attendance and greeted Ambassador Lipski at the church entrance in front of the press photographers. As early as 1936, Göring visited Warsaw to propose a joint offensive against Russia. Poland would "impose order" in the north and Germany would take the south.[106] Fearing a hardening of relations as a result of British policy, Ribbentrop met with Lipski again on 21 March 1939 to inform him that Hitler wished to make a "fresh attempt" at a settlement and would welcome a visit from Beck.[107] At that meeting, Lipski promised "a beautiful monument in Warsaw" for Hitler if he could find a solution to "the Jewish question."[108] Hitler saw Poland as a useful, if subordinate, ally in what he considered to be an

[103] Wheeler-Bennett, *Munich, Prologue to Tragedy,* 375

[104] Kotkin, *Stalin,* 687.

[105] Slawomir Debski, "Polish Perceptions of the Strategic Situation on the Eve of the Second World War," Michael H. Clemmesen and Marcus S. Faulkner eds., *Northern European Overture to War, 1939-1941* (Leiden: Brill, 2013), 192.

[106] Müller, *Enemy in the East,* 70.

[107] Aster, *The Making of the Second World War,* 90.

[108] Waclaw Jedrzejewicz ed., *Diplomat In Berlin, 1933-1939, Papers and Memoirs of Jozef Lipski, Ambassador of Poland* (New York: Columbia University Press, 1968), 411.

inevitable war with the Soviet Union. If he wanted to retain Polish support against Russia – the real enemy in his view – he would have to honour the territorial concessions made the previous October.

A leading British biographer of Hitler finds "no evidence that Hitler had committed himself to war to obtain [Danzig and passage across the Corridor] or to the dismemberment of Poland," which might have been allied to Nazi Germany much as Hungary was to be.[109] Germany's annexation on 23 March of Memel, which had been transferred to Lithuania under the Versailles treaty, made the Poles wary of any proposal from Berlin.[110] Yet Hitler still hoped to avoid war with Poland, as he had with Lithuania. On 25 March he sent a directive to the army commander in chief which read in part: "The Führer *does not* wish to solve the Danzig question by force [emphasis in the original]. He does not wish to drive Poland into the arms of Britain by this." Force would be applied only if the Polish government proved uncooperative.[111] That same day, Beck sent a dispatch to Lipski, who was about to meet with Ribbentrop: "Please stress," he wrote in conclusion, "that we consider blocking the penetration of Communism into Poland one of the supreme tasks of our state."[112] The British guarantee of 31 March left little room for an amicable solution. Three days later, Hitler issued a directive concerning preparations for war. In an annex he wrote that he still wished to maintain peaceful relations with Poland; but should the Polish government's attitude toward Germany change for the worse, "it might be necessary to settle the account for good."[113]

---

[109] Alan Bullock, "Hitler and the Origins of the Second World War," Esmonde M. Robertson ed., *The Origins of the Second World War* (London: Macmillan, 1971), 211.

[110] Henderson, "A Fatal Guarantee," 22.

[111] DGFP series D, VI, 117.

[112] *Diplomat in Berlin*, 507.

[113] H.R. Trevor-Roper ed., Hitler's War Directives, 1939-1945 (London: Sidgwick and Jackson, 1964), 3.

There seems to have been no mass support for the guarantee in Britain itself. An editorial in the *Sunday Express* of 23 July 1939 read in part: "The settlement of Polish affairs in relation to Germany should be left to Colonel Beck, who is a thoroughly popular and entirely familiar figure in Berlin. With Poland out of the way we can give some thought to our domestic concerns."[114] The newspaper was correct in assuming that Beck could have come to terms with Hitler, but he was emboldened by the British guarantee and refused to compromise.[115] Poland was not out of the way – far from it. Yet the entire political class in Britain, with the notable exception of Lloyd George, endorsed the guarantee "in the fond belief," writes Liddell Hart, "that that it would check Hitler. Never has there been a more astonishing case of collective self-delusion under the influence of righteous indignation."[116]

More guarantees to potential victims of the dictator states were forthcoming. Romania and Greece received an Anglo-French guarantee on 13 April, following Italy's invasion of Albania; Turkey came next, on 12 May. This was not collective security: Poland was under no obligation to come to the aid of Romania; Greece and Turkey were not cast as allies. Only Britain, with France in tow, undertook to defend the other participants in what was soon to be called the "Peace Front," but without making any specific military commitments. Nowadays the Peace Front barely merits a footnote in history books, but in 1939 it was taken quite seriously by Chamberlain, who had recently discovered the virtues of firmness. He explained to the House of Commons that "we are trying to build up, not an alliance between ourselves and other countries, but a peace front against aggression. . . ."[117] There were, as usual, a few sceptics. In London, someone coined the phrase, "A guarantee a day keeps Hitler away."[118] On 6 June, Alexis Léger,

---

[114] Quoted in Norman Angell, *For What Do We Fight?* (London: Hamish Hamilton, 1939), 170.

[115] Newman, *The British Guarantee to Poland*, 153.

[116] Basil Liddell Hart, "The Military Strategist," Taylor ed., *Churchill Revised*, 205.

[117] 347 H C Deb., 19 May 1939, series 5, col. 1839.

secretary-general of the French foreign ministry, had lunch at a posh restaurant in the Bois de Boulogne with Jacques Chastenet, editor of the prestigious daily, *Le Temps*. Chastenet, who had serious reservations about the entire policy of verbal deterrence, could not resist asking sarcastically: "And which country have you guaranteed this morning?"[119]

None of this grandstanding impressed Hitler, whose talent for improvisation once again manifested itself. Having failed to obtain an understanding with Poland, he quickly reversed course and ordered plans to be drawn up for the invasion of that country. He was convinced that even if Britain and France declared war pursuant to their guarantee, they would not actually launch an offensive against Germany;[120] and events proved him right. In mid-May, Henderson assured the German government that if a general war did break out, it would be conducted defensively by the Western powers.[121] The Poles, meanwhile, were confident that their army could successfully resist any aggression.[122] Besides, with the support of the two greatest empires in the world, how could they possibly lose? So they refused to yield. On 29 June, the Polish president, Ignaz Moscicki, proclaimed on the radio that the Corridor and its seacoast were "invaluable" and "the air and sun of our national life." In Gdynia, crowds chanted "We want Danzig." Throughout the country, Poles took an oath to defend their "eternal right" to the Baltic and "to maintain an invincible guard in the mouth of the Vistula."[123]

The British government assumed that the Poles understood that Britain guaranteed their country's independence, not its territorial integrity. They would have to be reasonable and make certain

---

[118] Adamthwaite, *The Making of the Second World War*, 91.

[119] Anthony Adamthwaite, *France and the Coming of the Second World War, 1936-1939* (London: Frank Cass, 1977), 329.

[120] Alexandroff and Rosecrance, "Deterrence in 1939," 414.

[121] "Memorandum by the State Secretary", 15 May 1939, D G F P, series D, VI, 503.

[122] Jean Daridan, *Le chemin de la défaite, 1938-1940* (Paris: Plon, 1980), 126.

[123] *New York Times*, 30 June 1939.

concessions to Hitler.[124] Chamberlain explained in Parliament that the guarantee "is not concerned with some minor little frontier incident." It was issued in order to preserve the peace, not to bring on war. "I am no more a man of war to-day than I was in September."[125] In mid-July, he wrote to his sister that if the dictators showed a modicum of patience, "I can imagine that a way could be found of meeting German claims while safeguarding Poland's independence and economic security."[126] But the guarantee left Britain with no leverage; Poland alone would decide how to deal with Nazi Germany.

Chamberlain was convinced that the guarantee would make Hitler reasonable. "One thing is, I think, clear," he wrote to his sister later in July, "namely that Hitler has concluded that we mean business and that the time is not ripe for a major war."[127] Showing Hitler that Britain "meant business" had been the chief argument of the anti-appeasers; Chamberlain now adopted it as his policy. And it failed completely. As Weizsäcker, the German state secretary, explained to Ambassador Henderson in May, "the British guarantee of Poland was not taken very seriously in Germany."[128] Hitler did not back down, and neither did the Poles. In a diary entry of 30 August, Sir Henry Channon wrote: "Meanwhile we are still urging Germany and Poland to negotiate."[129] Ambassador Kennedy met with Chamberlain the same day and reported to Washington that "he is more worried about getting the Poles to be reasonable than the Germans."[130] Kennedy had telephoned Sumner Welles, the permanent undersecretary of State, on 14 August to say that the British wanted the Americans to put pressure

---

[124] Dalton, *The Fateful Years*, 239.

[125] 345 H C Deb., 3 April 1939, cols. 2483-2484.

[126] Chamberlain to Hilda, 15 July 1939, *The Neville Chamberlain Diary Letters*, 428.

[127] Chamberlain to Ida, 23 July 1939, *ibid.*, 431.

[128] "Memorandum by the State Secretary," 15 May 1939, DGFP, series D, VI 503.

[129] Robert Rhodes James ed., *Chips: The Diaries of Sir Henry Channon* (London: Weidenfeld and Nicolson, 1067), 210.

[130] Kennedy to Hull, 30 August 1939, FRUS (1939), I, 392.

on the Poles to arrive at a compromise with Hitler. They were precluded from doing it themselves by the guarantee. Moffat rejected the idea, as did Roosevelt and Cordell Hull, the secretary of State. "As we saw it here," he wrote, "it merely meant that they wanted us to assume the responsibility of a new Munich and to do their dirty work for them."[131]

The hoped-for compromise could apply only to the points raised by Hitler: Danzig and the Corridor. Ten days before Chamberlain issued his fateful guarantee, Halifax told the Polish ambassador, "So far as Danzig was concerned, for example, our view might be that if Poland and Germany could settle the question by direct negotiations, so much the better; but if the question should develop is such as way as to threaten Polish independence, then I thought that His Majesty's Government would have to treat it as a question which was of the gravest concern to themselves."[132] In other words, if Danzig proved to be a mere pretext for destroying Poland, as was the Sudetenland for Czechoslovakia, Britain would have to take a stand. By encouraging compromise, the British government indicated that it did not consider Danzig to be such a pretext and that the question need not become a *casus belli*. Unlike the Sudetenland, with its frontier fortifications, Danzig was not vital to Polish defence.

The British guarantee to Poland did not signify an end to appeasement, merely a hiatus. Not until war was declared did Chamberlain reshuffle his cabinet to include Churchill and Eden. He was not ready to antagonize Hitler or the Conservative Party.[133] An article in the New York *Journal of Commerce*, which appeared in mid-May 1939, reveals a remarkable understanding of the situation. It begins: "The strong support which a policy of international political appeasement enjoys among British businessmen and bankers reflects the sound self-interest of these groups. A war would inevitably have to be paid for chiefly by the large-income classes, for one thing. In

---

[131] *The Moffat Papers,* 253.

[132] Halifax to Kennard, 21 March 1939, DBFP, 3rd series, IV, 436.

[133] See Ruggiero, *Hitler's Enabler,* 126.

addition, it is often overlooked that Germany is a leading purchaser of British goods." In 1938, greater Germany (including Austria and the Sudetenland) was Britain's fourth largest export market, passing the United States. The article continues: "Conversations looking toward an expansion of Anglo-German trade have been interrupted by recent political developments. It may be assumed, however, that as soon as the political tension abates, they will be resumed."[134] As Britain's businessman-in-chief, Neville Chamberlain certainly wanted commercial relations with Germany to expand. He fully expected the political tension to abate.

Abrogating, or even severely curtailing, trade with Germany would deprive Britain of much-needed foreign exchange and increase unemployment. Britain's chief exports to Germany were coal and textiles, which could easily be procured elsewhere. Its chief imports from the Reich were precision instruments and machine tools, for which there were few other reliable sources.[135] In June Halifax explained to the House of Lords, "We know that a truly prosperous Germany would be good for all Europe and be good for us. . . . Our one desire is to throw all our weight in the scale of peaceful settlement. . . . Any of Germany's claims are open to consideration round a table."[136]

In light of the British guarantee to Poland, all overtures to Germany had to be secret. When Robert Hudson, who directed the Department of Overseas Trade, announced to reporters on 22 July that Britain had offered Germany a loan valued at several hundred million pounds in return for international control of German armaments, a scandal erupted, obliging Chamberlain to issue an immediate denial.[137] "There is no proposal for a German loan," he announced to Parliament.[138] To his sister he wrote that "there are other and discreeter [*sic*]

---

[134] "British Trade with Germany," *Journal of Commerce and Commercial*, 19 May 1939.

[135] Newman, *The British Guarantee to Poland*, 83-4.

[136] 113 H L Deb., 8 June 1939, col. 361.

[137] Watt, *How War Came*, 400-1.

[138] 350 H C Deb., 24 July 1939, col. 1025.

channels."[139] These included a meeting in Berlin with Hitler on 27 July by Lord Kemsley, proprietor of the *Sunday Times* and the *Daily Sketch*, who reported back to Downing Street four days later. Earlier that month, the pop historian and editor of Chamberlain's speeches, Arthur Bryant, had met with Walther Hewel, a close friend of Hitler, who had participated in the failed Munich putsch of 1923 and would commit suicide at the end of the war. Bryant travelled to Germany, with Chamberlain's consent, as a private citizen and sent a report to the prime minister on his return.[140] The overall effect of these back-channel attempts at preserving the peace was to convince Hitler that Britain was not serious about going to war over Poland.[141]

Inasmuch as the Polish government refused any Russian support, the British guarantee effectively precluded an alliance with the Soviet Union, as Chamberlain explained to the cabinet in April. The most he wanted from the Soviets was benevolent neutrality.[142] He did authorize an Anglo-French mission to Moscow in July, although he had confessed privately "to the most profound distrust of Russia."[143] This was essentially a political move designed to placate the French government and many British parliamentarians, especially on the left. The allied delegation, after a five-day sea voyage and a rail journey from Leningrad, finally reached Moscow on 11 August. The following day, Marshal Voroshilov exhibited a document giving him full powers to negotiate and sign a military convention. He then asked to see those of his guests. The French representative, General Doumenc, dutifully produced the proper credentials. His British counterpart, Admiral Drax,

---

[139] Chamberlain to Hilda, 30 July 1939. *The Neville Chamberlain Diary Letters*, 435.

[140] Phillips, *Fighting Churchill, Appeasing Hitler*, 295.

[141] Watt, *How War Came*, 407.

[142] Louise Grace Shaw, "Attitudes of the British Political Elite towards the Soviet Union," *Diplomacy and Statecraft*, vol. 13, issue 1, 57. See also Graham Stewart in *The Times*, 3 September 1999.

[143] Chamberlain to Hilda, 19 March 1939, *The Neville Chamberlain Diary Letters*, 396.

had none, but sent a telegram to London requesting the necessary papers. At this, Voroshilov asked whether the French and British general staffs believed that the Soviet army would be admitted to Poland in order to meet a German invasion force. Since neither Doumenc nor Drax could give such assurance, Voroshilov concluded that "further conversations will not have any real meaning."[144] For six days, the French foreign ministry tried to persuade the Polish government to allow the passage of Soviet troops across its territory, but to no avail.[145] Chamberlain stood aside. His "one fear," wrote an early critic of the Munich settlement, was "that we should drift into a Franco-Russian combination against the dictators." He suspected that Russia "was eager to egg on the Western powers to war with Germany" without giving them effective help.[146]

The view from Moscow was radically different. A military convention with Britain and France would commit the Soviet Union to war with Germany while taking the pressure off its putative allies. Stalin had already made it clear that he was not interested in pulling their chestnuts out of the fire. He had, in fact, sought an understanding with Hitler in 1934.[147] The negotiations with the Western democracies in mid-August were possibly a feint designed to pressure Nazi Germany into concluding a satisfactory agreement.[148] The latter had much to offer the Soviets: first of all, a respite from war, which the Red Army, weakened by the recent purges, was disinclined to wage. Stalin was well aware of Russia's military weakness.[149] On 27 July, an official of the German foreign ministry put the question bluntly to the Soviet

---

[144] Aster, *The Making of the Second World W*ar, 300-3.

[145] Richard Overy and Andrew Wheatcroft, *The Road to War* (London: Macmillan, 1989), 211.

[146] Leopold S. Amery, *My Political Life*, III: *The Unforgiving Years, 1929-1940* (London: Hutchinson, 1953), 262-3.

[147] Aster, *The Making of the Second World War*, 314.

[148] Overy and Wheatcroft, *The Road to War*, 138-9.

[149] Gabriel Gorodetsky, "Les dessous du pacte germano-soviétique," *Le Monde diplomatique*, July 1997, 22-3.

chargé d'affaires: "What could England offer Russia? At best participation in a European war and the hostility of Germany. What could we offer? Neutrality . . . and, if Moscow so wished, a German-Russian understanding on mutual interests."[150] Specifically, an accord with Germany would enable Russia to recover territory lost to Poland in the war of 1919-1921 and gain access to the Baltic. A non-aggression pact, coupled with a secret agreement to divide Poland, was duly concluded between Germany and the Soviet Union on 23 August. In contrast to the low-level Anglo-French delegation, Hitler sent Ribbentrop, his foreign minister, by air to meet with Stalin.

Chamberlain had assumed that the Soviet Union, even if rebuffed by Britain and France, would remain neutral. On learning of the Nazi-Soviet pact, he realized that an invasion of Poland was imminent. In a conversation with Joseph Kennedy, he admitted that nothing could be done to save the Poles. "I have done everything that I can think of, and it seems as if all my work has come to naught."[151] Having tried back-channel conciliation, he reverted to deterrence, the policy he had proclaimed in March. In an urgent message to Hitler, he wrote: "Whatever may prove to be the nature of the German-Soviet agreement, it cannot alter Great Britain's obligation to Poland." He then harkened back to the First World War. "It is alleged that if His Majesty's government had made their position more clear in 1914, the great catastrophe [for Britain especially] would have been averted." This time, however, "there shall be no such tragic misunderstanding." A new catastrophe could be averted if the parties accepted a "truce" to allow for "peaceful discussions."[152] Hitler replied the following day that Germany, like any other state, had a right to protect its sphere of interest. In effect, he was telling Chamberlain to mind his own business and not to meddle in the affairs of Eastern Europe. Germany, he insisted, had no aggressive designs on England or France and in fact

---

[150] Sir Lewis Namier, *Europe in Decay: A Study in Disintegration, 1936-1940* (New York: Macmillan, 1950), 246.

[151] Kennedy to Hull, 23 August 1939, FRUS vol. I: General, 355-6.

[152] Henderson to Halifax, 23 August 1939, DBFP 3rd series, VII, 170-1.

sought their friendship. If they went to war for Poland, however, Germany would mobilize its forces immediately.[153]

Daladier too sent a personal (and rather pathetic) letter to Hitler, appealing to him as a fellow war veteran to seek conciliation rather than confrontation. While the French people wanted peace and friendship with their German neighbours, he warned that France would keep its word to Poland.[154] In his reply, Hitler recalled his earlier statement that the transfer of the Saar to Germany in 1935 had put an end to any territorial claims that Germany might have on France. The region's rich coal deposits had been granted to France by the League of Nations in 1920 for fifteen years as compensation for the flooding of French coal mines by the retreating Germans in 1918. In a democratically-conducted plebiscite dominated by Nazi propaganda, 90.3 percent of the Saarlanders voted for a return to Germany. All remaining German claims concerned Danzig and the Corridor, which had been torn from the Reich by the treaty of Versailles. Hitler, whose proposal for a settlement had been rejected by the Poles, was now determined to recover both. He urged France not to make war on Poland's account.[155]

Prior to corresponding with Daladier, Hitler had received the French ambassador, Robert Coulondre, to whom he repeated the assurance that, having renounced Alsace-Lorraine, he had no quarrel with France. It would be tragic, he continued, if French and German blood should be shed over Poland, with which he had sought an understanding; but the British guarantee had made the Poles intransigent. Coulondre replied that the French government was doing its utmost to maintain peace and had repeatedly urged the Poles to exercise restraint. A war between France and Germany, he added, would leave only one victor: Trotsky. Hitler interrupted him: "Then why did you give Poland a blank cheque?"[156]

---

[153] Henderson to Halifax, 24 August 1939, *Ibid*, 177-9.
[154] Bonnet to Coulondre, *Le Livre jaune français*, 26 August 1939, 319-20.
[155] Coulondre to Bonnet, *Ibid.*, 27 August 1939, 332-5.
[156] Coulondre to Bonnet, *Ibid.*, 25 August 1939, 312-14.

To his fellow Nazis in the Reichstag, Hitler declared on 1 September that Germany had no interests in Western Europe.[157] This was true at the time: he had made no plans for war in the west.[158] He did not seek war with Britain and France, but he would not shirk from it. In a speech to his generals on 22 August, he foresaw – correctly – that Britain would not help Poland and could send at most three divisions to France in the immediate future. He sensed intuitively that Chamberlain's Polish policy was, in the words of a British historian, "a piece of bluff";[159] and as Sir Eric Phipps had observed during the Czech crisis, one could not bluff Hitler.[160] The French army, the dictator added, was short of men due to a declining birth rate. Its artillery was obsolete. "France did not want to embark on this adventure." The allies had only two ways of fighting Germany: (1) blockade, which would not be effective because of Germany's autarky and its sources of supply from Russia, and (2) a direct attack from the Maginot Line. "I consider this impossible." Hitler's assessment was correct. Far more than Chamberlain, he understood the power relationship on the European continent. He greatly resented the British government's newly-found interest in Eastern Europe. "My proposals to Poland concerning Danzig and the Corridor were frustrated by England's intervention. Poland has changed her tone toward us." Therefore he claimed to have no choice but to attack.[161] The campaign against Poland, writes a German historian, was "in no sense . . . *the* war that Hitler sought" at this stage. "To his mind, the European war that came on September 3 was as incomprehensible as it was contrary to his aims."[162]

---

[157] Réau, *Édouard Daladier, 1884-1970*, 390.

[158] Karl-Heinz Frieser with John T. Greenwood, *The Blitzkrieg Legend: The 1940 Campaign in the West* (Annapolis, MD: Naval Institute Press, 2011), 18.

[159] Norman Davies, *Europe at War, 1939-1945: No Simple Victory* (London: Macmillan, 2006), 145.

[160] Douglas, *In the Year of Munich*, 128.

[161] Max Domarus ed., *Hitler: Speeches and Proclamations, 1932-1945*, trans. Chris Wilcox (Waucinda, IL: Bolvhazy-Carducci, 1997), III, 1664-1669.

[162] Andreas Hillgruber, *Germany and the Two World Wars*, trans. William C.

On 25 August, the British government made one last-ditch attempt at deterrence: a formal Anglo-Polish alliance. Liddell Hart wrote at the time that such a gesture "inevitably adds fuel to the flames,"[163] but the Foreign Office was convinced that Britain had recovered the initiative. The German government was "wobbling," read one memorandum. "The latest indications are that we have an unexpectedly strong hand."[164] Oliver Harvey, who was private secretary to Halifax, wrote in his diary on 27 August: "It looks to us here as if Hitler was wobbling."[165] On 28 August, Cadogan surmised that "Hitler has cold feet."[166] Four days later, Germany invaded Poland.

Kirby (Cambridge, MA: Harvard University Press, 1981), 77.

[163] Liddell Hart, *Memoirs* II, 255.

[164] "Minute by Mr. Kirkpatrick," 27 August 1939, DBFP, 3rd series, VII, 314-15.

[165] John Harvey, ed., *The Diplomatic Diaries of Oliver Harvey, 1937-1940* (London: Collins, 1970), 306.

[166] David Dilks, ed., *The Diaries of Sir Alexander Cadogan, 1938-1945* (London: Cassell, 1971), 203.

4 Limited Liability

It is generally assumed that the Second World War began in September 1939. One author, senior historian of the Imperial War Museum, suggests that this is when the world went to war.[1] Nothing could be further from the truth. Most countries, in particular the United States, remained neutral. Japan was bogged down in China, which it had invaded in 1937. The Soviet Union did join Nazi Germany in a fourth partition of Poland once Warsaw had fallen. Except for a war against neighbouring Finland, it remained on the sidelines until it was itself invaded by Germany in June 1941. The Finnish war lasted four months; Poland, the first victim of the Hitler's legions, was conquered in three weeks. After that, Europe settled down to a period of relative tranquility, which lasted until the German offensive against Norway, the Low Countries and France in the spring of 1940. It was a "phoney war" from the start, the kind of war that Neville Chamberlain was comfortable with – a sort of armed appeasement. The war of nerves, which had shaken the civilian populations of Britain and France for more than a year, was over; the real war had yet to begin.

As the *Wehrmacht* sliced through Poland, Chamberlain's dilemma was not whether to intervene militarily but simply, whether to declare war.[2] Only after two full days of fierce fighting, including German bombardment of civilian targets, did he announce to Parliament and the British people that Britain was at war with Germany, and even that step was taken with the greatest reluctance. On 1 September, some fifteen hours after the German offensive had begun, he reminded the House of Commons that his government had done

---

[1] Terry Charman, *Outbreak 1939: The World Goes to War* (London: Virgin Books, 2009).
[2] Prazmowska, *Britain, Poland and the Eastern Front*, 181.

everything possible "to keep open the way for an honourable and equitable settlement of the dispute between Germany and Poland." Unless Germany withdrew its forces from Poland, Britain would break off relations and declare war. This, as Arthur Greenwood, who was sitting in for Labour Party leader Clement Attlee, noted in his rejoinder, was a loophole offered to Hitler.[3] It was yet another desperate attempt on Chamberlain's part at avoiding a conflict.

The following day, the prime minister informed Parliament of a proposal made by Mussolini for a five-power conference, which would include Poland, to achieve a peaceful settlement. "If the German government should agree to withdraw their forces, then His Majesty's Government would be willing to regard the position as being the same as it was before the German forces crossed the Polish frontier." Since this was hardly likely, he had to admit that the British government was "in a somewhat difficult position," one made even more difficult by France's wish for an additional delay before declaring war. He expected a reply from Paris within a few hours.[4] This did not satisfy most British MPs, who felt that their country's honour required going to war then and there. American journalist John Gunther understood that after the fiasco over Czechoslovakia, they did not want Britain to appear weak.[5] Later that evening, Chamberlain telephoned Daladier, saying that "there had been an angry scene in the House of Commons" and that "if the French government were to insist on a time-limit of forty-eight hours to run from midday tomorrow, it would be impossible for the government to hold the situation here."[6]

In plain terms, this meant that the government risked being overthrown unless war was declared promptly. Halifax, to whom Chamberlain had expressed fear for his political survival earlier that

---

[3] 351 H C Deb., 1 September 1939, series 5, 351, 127-32.

[4] *Ibid.*, 2 September 1939, cols. 281-4.

[5] Gunther, *Inside Europe*, xiv.

[6] Minute by Sir A. Cadogan, DBFP, 3rd series, VII, 2 September 1939; cf. Anthony P. Adamthwaite, *France and the Coming of the Second World War, 1936-1939* (London, Frank Cass, 1977), 349.

evening, said that he "had never seen the prime minister so disturbed."[7] Under pressure from an inflamed legislature, the arch-appeaser had to act, and he could not act alone. He had to put France at risk in order to save his own political skin. As he admitted candidly to Daladier, "he quite realized that it was France who must bear the burden of the German attack," it being assumed that Germany would wage war simultaneously on two fronts, as it had done in 1914. This is why the French sought a delay; they needed time to mobilize their army and evacuate civilians from areas near the German border.[8] But Chamberlain insisted that "some step" be taken immediately. That step could only be a joint declaration of war by the two allies.

At this point, the corridors of Parliament were abuzz with rumours that the French were "ratting."[9] French ambassador Charles Corbin was assailed with aggressive questions from British journalists and parliamentarians, who could not understand France's delay. He tried to explain that mobilizing an army of some five million men took several days at best. France had to be ready for an imminent German offensive against its territory. No one was more impatient with the French than Churchill, who telephoned Corbin to threaten France that if it did not go to war immediately, the British would retreat into their island and take no further interest in continental affairs. In a dispatch to the Quai d'Orsay, Corbin recalled that Churchill's voice raised in anger "caused the telephone to vibrate." (*Ses éclats de voix font vibrer le téléphone.*)[10] Brendan Bracken, Churchill's chief confidant who was soon to become his parliamentary secretary, was present during the conversation. He told Hugh Dalton of the Labour Party that Churchill treated the French ambassador "like an old washerwoman." (Worse, in fact: even an old washerwoman deserves respect.) If the French "ratted" on the Poles as they had "ratted" on the Czechs, said Churchill, he would leave France to her fate. When Corbin referred to technical

---

[7] Parker, *Chamberlain and Appeasement*, 341.

[8] Bell, *France and Britain*, 225.

[9] Channon, *Diaries*, 213-14.

[10] Corbin to Bonnet, 7 September 1939, DDF, 2nd series, XIII, 471.

difficulties in going to war, Churchill replied, "Technical difficulties be damned! I suppose that you would call it a technical difficulty for a Pole if a German bomb dropped on his head."[11]

In his war memoirs, Churchill was somewhat less abrasive. He did reproach France for having abandoned "her faithful ally, Czechoslovakia," but added that the Britain had encouraged the French to renege on their commitments. Of course in his view Albion was not the least bit perfidious and "would certainly have fought if bound by treaty obligations."[12] Churchill seems to have forgotten that Britain was, in fact, bound by its verbal guarantee to defend what remained of Czechoslovakia after Munich. So Britain too had "ratted" on the Czechs. Duff Cooper, who embarked on a lecture tour of the United States in the fall of 1939, recalled that Americans were not, at the time, especially pro-British. They generally hoped that Britain would win; but only a minority wanted the United States to intervene militarily in Europe. "The policy of appeasement had gone far to discredit Great Britain," he noted.[13]

Appeasement had not been totally abandoned on the afternoon of 2 September, as the government sought some way to avoid a real war. That day, Sir Samuel Hoare confided to a German journalist: "Although we cannot in the circumstances avoid declaring war, we can always fulfil the letter of a declaration of war without immediately going all out."[14] That France had to mobilize its entire army apparently did not concern him. While MPs in the Commons smoking room, having fortified themselves with liquid courage, insisted that the Polish guarantee become operative immediately, the cabinet withdrew to deliberate. It decided to wait another day and see whether the Italian proposal for a five-power conference might yet materialize.[15] In the event of war, the time gained would facilitate the preparation of air

---

[11] Dalton, *The Fateful Years*, 271.
[12] Churchill, *The Gathering Storm*, 288.
[13] Alfred Duff Cooper, *Old Men Forget* (New York: Dutton, 1954), 271.
[14] Newton, *Profits of Peace*, 133-4.
[15] Channon, *Diaries*, 212.

defences and the enactment of emergency regulations for civilians. So the French delaying action was not entirely unwelcome.[16]

Once war was declared, Churchill, as first lord of the Admiralty, planned to send British warships into the Baltic, but was overruled by his admirals. They warned that surface vessels without fighter protection would be vulnerable to attack from the air.[17] After the war, he recognized that Britain lacked the military strength to honour its guarantee.[18] Nor did it help that the Polish high command, yielding to British and French pressure, cancelled an order of general mobilization on 29 August, only to re-issue it the following day. As a result, only a third of the Polish army was fully deployed to face the German offensive.[19] The Western allies wanted to keep the door open for a possible last-minute conciliation.[20] The Polish economy was still not on a war footing – much to dismay of the country's military leaders.[21] Poland expected direct and immediate support from Britain and France, but that was not forthcoming.

The allies' predicament was assessed accurately by Count Ciano, the Italian foreign minister, who wrote in his diary on 3 September: "In what way can France and England bring help to Poland? And when Poland is liquidated, will they want to continue a conflict for which there is no longer any reason?"[22] Other neutral observers – and some British – were equally sceptical. With Poland reeling from repeated German assaults, Dalton asked Churchill on 13 September why Britain had not initiated any air strikes to relieve that

---

[16] Graham Stewart, *Burying Caesar: Churchill, Chamberlain and the Battle for the Tory Party* (London: Weidenfeld and Nicolson, 1999), 381.

[17] Graham T. Clews, Ch*urchill's Phoney War: A Study in Folly and Frustration* (Annapolis, MD: Naval Institute Press, 2019), 40-5.

[18] Churchill, *The Gathering Storm*, 311.

[19] Tim Bouverie, *Appeasement: Chamberlain, Hitler, Churchill, and the Road to War* (New York: Tim Duggan Books, 2019), 380n.

[20] Prazmowska, *Britain, Poland and the Eastern Front*, 173.

[21] Debski, "Polish Perceptions of the Strategic Situation," 200.

[22] Galeazzo Ciano, *The Ciano Diaries, 1939-1943*, ed. Hugh Gibson (New York: Howard Fertig, 1973), 137.

country. He was told that American opinion would be more sympathetic toward Britain if the first victims of aerial warfare were British and not German.[23] From the outset, Churchill always had one eye cocked on the United States; but in this case, he miscalculated. As Leopold Amery noted in his memoirs, "American public opinion, far from applauding our self-restraint, was shocked by our callous refusal to do anything to help the Poles,"[24]

Churchill's earlier assertion that the French might be "ratting" on Poland now rang a bit hollow. Putting pressure on France to join Britain as a co-belligerent was simply a frank recognition that without France as an ally, a British declaration of war would be totally meaningless. Only France, among Western democracies, had an army of any importance; Britain had virtually none. Churchill had warned earlier that without the participation of the Soviet Union, any coalition against Germany was doomed to fail.[25] Yet there he was, pushing for war even after the Nazi-Soviet pact had been signed. The simple fact is that with or without Russia, Churchill needed a war in order to regain power and influence. It is universally acknowledged that Churchill would never have become prime minister were it not for the Second World War. But first, he had to enter the government. On 1 September, Chamberlain asked him if he was willing to participate in a war cabinet. He was more than willing. For many years, Churchill had been in political exile, ostracised by the establishment, including the King, as a warmonger. When the royal couple visited Canada in June 1939, King George VI met with Mackenzie King, the Canadian prime minister, who recorded in his diary: "The King indicated he would never wish to appoint Churchill to any office unless it was absolutely necessary in time of war. I confess I was glad to hear him say that because I think Churchill is one of the most dangerous men I have ever known."[26] Labour MP Herbert Morrison, who was later to serve as home secretary

---

[23] Dalton, *The Fateful Years*, 277-8.
[24] Amery, *The Unforgiving Years,*), 332.
[25] Cf. *supra*, 86.
[26] Mackenzie King Diaries, No. 20426, 10 June 1939.

in a coalition government under Churchill, had described him in 1935 as "a fire-eater and a militarist."[27]

On 2 September, there being as yet no declaration of war, Churchill was still not formally offered a ministerial post. That evening, he sent a plaintive message to Chamberlain: "I have not heard anything from you since our talks on Friday, when I understood that I was to serve as your colleague, and when you told me that this would be announced speedily."[28] Churchill's uneasiness helps explain his temper tantrum with the French ambassador. A war cabinet including Churchill was announced the following day. Chamberlain hoped that naval affairs would keep him fully occupied and leave him little opportunity to influence policy.[29]

As it happened, the French were not "ratting." They too did not want to appear weak. On 2 September, Daladier made a solemn pledge to the Chamber of Deputies that France would honour its commitments to Poland. Failure to do so, he warned, would leave his country "isolated, discredited, scorned, without allies and – have no doubt – subject to a frightful assault." Daladier had obviously learned the lesson of Munich: France would forfeit all claims to be a great power if it reneged once again on its commitments. Bonnet had pressed Mussolini late in August to sponsor a four-power conference on the Danzig question,[30] but was overruled by Daladier, who informed the British government that he "was definitely determined to reject any proposal for a general conference of the Munich kind."[31] On Czechoslovakia, writes an American historian, "Britain was the imperious 'governess' and France her sometimes restive but on the whole compliant charge."[32]

---

[27] Robert Rhodes James, "The Politician," Taylor ed., *Churchill Revised*, 120.

[28] Churchill, *The Gathering Storm*, 362.

[29] John Charmley, *Churchill: The End of Glory* (London: Hodder & Stoughton, 1993), 372.

[30] Fabrice Grenard. *La Drôle de Guerre. L'entrée en guerre des Français, septembre 1939 – mai 1940* (Paris: Belin, 2015), 83.

[31] Phipps to Halifax, 29 August 1939, DBFP, 3rd series, VII, 379.

[32] Nord, *France 1940*, 6

By September 1939, Daladier had quite enough of the governess. The concluding sentence of his speech, which had been interrupted by frequent applause from all sides, reveals his innermost feelings. "Gentlemen, today France is in command."[33]

Except that it wasn't. Britain continued to determine allied war policy.[34] France was still under British tutelage.[35] Nowhere was this more apparent than in the French premier's abrupt dismissal of Bonnet as foreign minister on 13 September. Bonnet's presence in the cabinet helped shore up Daladier's parliamentary majority; but the British government, which had effectively chosen Bonnet as foreign minister the previous year, now decided that he had to go.[36] Cadogan wrote to Phipps on 6 September that "it will be difficult to establish confident and sincere collaboration with the French so long as M. Bonnet is active at the Quai d'Orsay."[37] On 2 September, however, Daladier's policy was not dissimilar to that of Bonnet. Like Bonnet – and like Chamberlain – he was still looking for some way to avoid war. To sustained applause, he promised that France would welcome an attempt at conciliation if it had any chance of success. He knew that his country had little to gain and possibly everything to lose from a conflict with its more powerful neighbour; but France could not shirk responsibility without losing what remained of its dwindling prestige. The French premier mentioned peace far more often than war in his speech, but he did recognize that a war was in progress and that it could threaten France's security. He did not ask his fellow parliamentarians to help eradicate the scourge of Nazism or the horrors of dictatorship. The present crisis, as he saw it, was simply the result of Hitler's bad faith.

---

[33] J O C Débats. 2 September 1939, 1952.

[34] Alfred Fabre-Luce, *Journal de la France, 1940-1944* (Geneva: Éditions du Cheval Ailé, 1946), 168.

[35] Jean-Pierre Azéma, *1940. L'année noire* (Paris: Fayard, 2010), 51.

[36] François Bédarida, "La 'gouvernante anglaise'," René Rémond and Janine Bourdin eds., *Édouard Daladier, chef de gouvernement* (Paris: Presses de la Fondation Nationale des Sciences Politiques, 1977), 239.

[37] Dockrill, *British Establishment Perspectives on France*, 143.

"I put the question to the French people and to all peoples: what value can we place on the recently renewed guaranty given for our eastern frontier, for our Alsace (loud applause), for our Lorraine (loud applause), now that the guaranties for Austria, Czechoslovakia and Poland have been violated and Poland invaded?" The war credits of 90 billion francs were approved unanimously by a show of hands in both the Chamber and the Senate, but there was no formal declaration of war by parliament, as prescribed in the constitution of the Third Republic. For this, he was reprimanded by Flandin and other pro-appeasement parliamentarians.[38] France simply went to war the following day, following Britain's hesitant lead.

Chamberlain announced Britain's declaration of war in a spirit of extreme gravitas. "This is a sad day for all of us, and to none is it sadder than to me. Everything that I have worked for, everything that I have hoped for, everything that I have believed in during my public life, has crashed into ruins." By contrast, Greenwood, who had berated Chamberlain the previous day over his hesitancy, was positively buoyant. "Resentment, apprehension, anger reigned over our proceedings last night, aroused by a fear that delays might end in national dishonour and the sacrifice of the Polish people to German tyranny. . . . This morning we meet in an entirely different atmosphere – one of relief, one of composure, and one of resolution. The intolerable agony of suspense from which all of us have suffered is over; we now know the worst. The hated word 'war' has been spoken by Britain, in fulfilment of her pledged word and unbreakable intention to defend Poland and so to defend the liberties of Europe." He concluded: "May the war be swift and sure."[39]

It was swift and sure – for Germany. Given that Britain, in spite of her pledged word, did absolutely nothing in 1939 to defend Poland, and precious little in 1940 to defend the liberties of Europe, it might have been better if France had "ratted." French national pride, which had been degraded at Munich, now reasserted itself. A public opinion

---

[38] Réau, *Édouard Daladier*, 472; Zévaès, *Histoire de six ans*, 52-4.
[39] 351 H C Deb, 3 September 1939, cols. 291-4.

poll showed that 76 percent of French citizens favoured going to war if Germany attacked Poland.[40] General mobilization, which was decreed on 1 September, proceeded smoothly; the proportion of draft-dodgers (*insoumis*) was low, 1.5 percent, and no greater than in 1914.[41] Yet nowhere was to be seen the enthusiasm displayed at that time by many of those who had been called to the colours. An American journalist in Paris reported: "Except for the Communists, very few Frenchmen thought that the government was wrong to declare war. Yet the vast majority answered the call to arms like somnambulists."[42] (Once Britain and France declared war on Germany, there was no enthusiasm in Berlin either.[43]) For the French, the situation in 1939 was markedly different from that of 1914, when Germany initiated the war on France and, in a rapid offensive, conquered much of its territory in the north and north-east. France had no choice but to defend itself in the hope of liberating the region under German occupation. Recovering Alsace-Lorraine came second. In 1939, France had no territorial grievances when it declared war on Germany.[44] French morale, both civilian and military, generally held throughout the bloodbath of 1914-1918. Would it hold this time? And would the conscripts of the First World War have responded so cheerfully if they had known what awaited them?

Twenty-five years later, France found itself engaged in a war whose outcome was at best doubtful. The French high command was well aware of the brutal arithmetic that gave Germany a clear advantage in manpower and war production. France in 1939 had 2.6 million men

---

[40] Tombs, *That Sweet Enemy,* 539.

[41] William D. Irvine, "Domestic Politics and the Fall of France in 1940," Joel Blatt, ed., *The French Defeat of 1940. Reassessments* (Providence, RI: Berghahn Books, 1998), 94.

[42] Edmund Taylor, *The Strategy of Terror: Europe's Inner Front* (Boston: Houghton Mifflin, 1940), 152.

[43] William L. Shirer, *Berlin Diary: The Journal of a Foreign Correspondent, 1934-1941* (New York: Knopf, 1941), 201.

[44] Pierre-Frédéric Charpentier, *La Drôle de Guerre des intellectuels français, 1939-1940* (Paris: Lavauzelle, 2008), 273.

of military age, as opposed to 6.5 million in Germany. French steel production was 7.9 million tons annually, or about a third of the German output, 22.5 million tons.[45] At a meeting of the *Conseil supérieur de la guerre* on 2 September, two generals favoured going to war, two strongly opposed, and the other fifteen had serious reservations.[46] Of all French cabinet ministers, Bonnet seems to have understood the existing power relationship most clearly. He had been a leading proponent of an alliance with the Soviet Union as a means of keeping Germany at bay.[47] With the signing of the Nazi-Soviet pact, however, he argued that France should "reconsider her attitude and profit by the respite thus gained to increase her military strength."[48] Bonnet's appeasement policy was wrong in September 1938 when France, allied with Czechoslovakia, had a fighting chance to contain Germany; but he was right a year later. "The only reason to declare war," he wrote in his memoirs, "is to win it."[49]

Chamberlain did not believe that the allies could win on the battlefield. "What I hope for," he wrote to his sister early in September, "is not a military victory – I very much doubt the possibility of that – but a collapse of the German home front. For that it is necessary to convince the Germans that they cannot win."[50] Liddell Hart, the leading

---

[45] Grenard, *La Drôle de Guerre*, 113-14.

[46] Robert O. Paxton, *Parades and Politics at Vichy: The French Officer Corps under Marshal Pétain* (Princeton, NJ: Princeton University Press), 65-6.

[47] Talbot C. Imlay, *Facing the Second World War: Strategy, Politics and Economics in Britain and France, 1938-1940* (New York: Oxford University Press, 2003), 45. The title is somewhat misleading since Chamberlain never anticipated a Second World War. The prospect of a prolonged conflict involving the Soviet Union and the United States, with Britain also engaged in a war against Japan, was totally abhorrent to him.

[48] Christopher Thorne, *The Approach of War, 1938-1939* (London: Macmillan, 1967), 180.

[49] Georges Bonnet, *Défense de la paix. De Munich à la guerre* (Paris: Plon, 1967), 593.

[50] Chamberlain to Ida, 10 September 1939, *The Neville Chamberlain Diary Letters*, 445.

British proponent of defensive warfare whose concepts greatly influenced Chamberlain, had explained earlier that year: "Our object is fulfilled if we can convince the enemy that he cannot conquer."[51] Five weeks prior to Britain's declaration of war, Chamberlain had written to his sister: "Let us convince [Germany] that the chances of winning a war without getting thoroughly exhausted in the process are too remote to make it worth-while."[52] This remained his policy once war officially began: he still hoped to avoid fighting. In a note of 4 October to Roosevelt, Chamberlain reiterated his grand strategy, adding that "I believe that they [the Germans] are already half way to this conviction [that they cannot win]." If the U. S. embargo on the sale of war matériel to belligerents is repealed, he wrote further, "I am convinced that the effect on German morale will be devastating."[53] Relying on conventional wisdom that the defence was intrinsically superior to the offence, he explained to his sister: "An attack must surely mean colossal losses for the attacker, and surely H. must feel a certain doubt as to how long the German people will stand such losses."[54] He might have recalled that Germany's recent victory over Poland had not resulted in colossal losses for the attacker. But France was different: like his cabinet colleagues, the prime minister was convinced that the Maginot Line was impregnable and that the French army would surely hold.

More wishful thinking came from Halifax, who eagerly anticipated a revolution in Germany which would overthrow Hitler.[55]

---

[51] Liddell Hart, *The Defence of Britain*, 43.

[52] Chamberlain to Hilda, 30 July 1939, *The Neville Chamberlain Diary Letters*, 435.

[53] Kennedy to Roosevelt, enclosure, 5 October 1939, FRUS (1939), I, 674-5.

[54] Chamberlain to Hilda, 15 October 1939, *The Neville Chamberlain Diary Letters*, 458.

[55] Peter Ludlow, "Le débat sur les buts de paix en Grande-Bretagne durant l'hiver 1939-1940," Comité d'histoire de la 2ième Guerre mondiale, *Français et Britanniques dans la Drôle de Guerre* (Paris: Éditions du Centre National de la Recherche Scientifique, 1979), 119.

A dispatch from Ambassador Henderson in the final days of peace helped lay the basis of the government's optimistic war policy. It cited a retired German army officer working in the war censorship department who told the British military attaché in Berlin that 70 percent of the German people opposed Hitler. The Nazi party, he claimed, was divided: only Himmler actively favoured war "as a possible chance of saving the regime." The army, though bound by its oath of allegiance to Hitler, was uneasy at the prospect of having to fight Britain and France.[56] The officer's assessment may have been correct at that particular time, but Hitler was not about to abdicate. During the Phoney War, Halifax was further encouraged by reports from the political intelligence department of the Foreign Office predicting the impending collapse of the German home front. In November it held that "the pressure of the allied blockade is beginning to make itself felt" as there were indications of "apprehension about the future." By January 1940, "signs of strain" were evident, but a "malaise" and a "downward trend" in public morale had not yet produced "signs of a break."[57]

Henderson's influence seems to have outlasted his diplomatic posting in Berlin. Whenever the Chamberlain cabinet needed to be apprised of the situation in Germany, the most authoritative source remained the former ambassador. Less than 48 hours before the outbreak of war in the east, he had written: "If we are ever to get the German army and nation to revolt against the intolerable government of Herr Hitler," Germany's "grievances . . . which are not of Herr Hitler's making . . . must be eliminated." Among these grievances, "the city of Danzig as distinct from the port must revert to Germany; there must be direct and extraterritorial communication between the Reich and East Prussia; and the German minority in Poland must be got rid of by means of some exchange of population. . . . The whole of the nation

---

[56] Henderson to Halifax, 30 August 1939, DBFP 3rd series, VII, 419.
[57] Guy Nicholas Esnouf, "British Government War Aims and Attitudes Towards a Negotiated Peace, September 1939 to July 1940," unpublished Ph.D. thesis, King's College, London, 1988, 167.

and even the most moderate sections of it would not regard any other basis as fair to Germany."[58] Fairness to the German nation was seen as essential to establishing good relations with a successor regime.

It was in this spirit that RAF bombers flew over Germany on 7 September, dropping ten million leaflets, which read in part: "This war is utterly unnecessary. Germany was in no way deprived of justice. Was she not allowed to re-enter the Rhineland, to achieve the *Anschluss*, and to take back the Sudeten Germans in peace? . . . You, the German people, can, if you will, insist on peace at any time. We also desire peace and are prepared to conclude it with any peace-loving government in Germany."[59] The message was clear enough: all the Germans had to do at this point was to get rid of Hitler and his regime. Surely that was not beyond their capabilities? At the very least, it would save Britain a lot of bother. But what about France? Would it demobilize once the Nazis were overthrown? A French translation of the leaflet appeared a few days later in a Paris newspaper.[60] Its readers cannot have been very happy to learn that virtually every able-bodied Frenchman between the ages of 20 and 50 had been called up to wage a war that was utterly unnecessary.

The mobilization of five million men, or roughly one-quarter the entire male population of France, made sense only in the event of an immediate German invasion. No such invasion could begin until the German army had defeated Poland, and none actually occurred until May 1940. As the days and weeks went by without any serious fighting in the west, it became obvious that this *levée en masse* deprived the French economy of much-needed manpower. In the Renault works alone, the main centre of tank production, the number of employees fell from 32,000 to 17,000.[61] So a partial demobilization was decreed. In all, some 550,000 conscripts returned to their jobs in key war

---

[58] Henderson to Halifax, 30 August 1939, DBFP 3rd series, VII, 409.

[59] *Manchester Guardian*, 8 September 1939.

[60] *Excelsior*, 11 September 1939.

[61] Pierre Rocolle, *La guerre de 1940*, I: *Les illusions, novembre 1918 - mai 1940* (Paris: Armand Colin, 1990), 192.

industries. Another million, including farmers needed for the autumn harvest, received occupational deferments.[62] The morale of civilians was severely dampened by widespread censorship of the press and the lack of any relevant news on the radio. Some French citizens with short-wave receivers kept abreast of the situation by listening to broadcasts in French from American networks. "Certainly," wrote Janet Flanner, *The New Yorker* correspondent in Paris, "this must be the first war that millions of people on both sides continued to think could be avoided even after it had officially been declared."[63]

In Britain, civilian morale suffered as a result of the prevailing inactivity. As Harold Nicolson confided to his diary on 24 September, "The whole stage was set for an intensive and early attack by Germany [presumably by air], which would have aroused our stubbornness. The government had not foreseen a situation in which boredom and bewilderment would be the main elements. . . . The result is general disillusion and grumbling, from which soil defeatism may grow."[64] Among ordinary Britons, there seems to have been little defeatism, but rather a general lassitude and profound scepticism about the war. One man remarked sarcastically that "if we go on like this, we're sure to win the war. That is, when Hitler dies of old age and the German people take pity on us." A working-class woman concluded, "There's something wrong with the organisation at the top." On 17 October, a man in a North London pub was heard to say: "This is a funny business. Why don't they begin fighting? Is it a war or isn't it? They're holding something back or don't want to fight. They just let the Germans get all nice and ready without trying to stop them. The boys are fed up. . . . Everyone's losing heart, that's it."[65] Major-General Sir Ernest Swinton,

[62] George O. Flynn, *Conscription and Democracy: The Draft in France, Great Britain, and the United States* (Westport, CT: Greenwood Press, 2002), 57.
[63] Genêt (Janet Flanner), "Letter from Paris," 16 September 1939, *The New Yorker Book of War Pieces* (New York: Schocken, 1947), 6-7.
[64] Nigel Nicolson ed., *Harold Nicolson: Diaries and Letters, 1939-1945* (London: Collins, 1957), 36.
[65] Tom Harrison and Charles Madge eds., *War Begins at Home by Mass*

in a radio broadcast later that year, rebuked those who complained that the western front was too quiet. "The war is not being run to provide news. . . . Allied troops are not going to be thrown in haste, without due preparation, against a stone wall, or rather, a steel and concrete maze, bristling with every sort of gun."[66]

There will always be Monday-morning quarterbacks to deplore the refusal of the French general staff to order an attack on Germany early in September while the *Wehrmacht* was still engaged in Poland. Gamelin had indeed promised the Poles full military support within fifteen days of the French declaration of war – that is, no later than 18 September. French troops did advance into the Saar in the first week of the conflict. Some four hundred French soldiers died in this symbolic offensive, mainly from anti-personnel mines. Once Warsaw fell on 17 September, they were withdrawn. During the First World War, French commanders had repeatedly squandered their men in futile assaults against well-prepared defences. For every German soldier killed in these battles, the French lost two.[67] Remarkably, the proportion in September 1939 was the same: Germany announced 198 war dead on the western front.[68] (Not until 9 December was the first British soldier – a corporal on patrol near Metz – killed in action. He stepped on a mine.[69]) Gamelin was not going to repeat the errors of his predecessors. He knew that French rearmament was incomplete, with anti-tank and anti-aircraft guns particularly in short supply, and that Britain was not yet ready for war.[70] In his memoirs, he saw no reason, as he put it, "to

Observation (London: Chatto & Windus, 1940), 155-62.

[66] Charman, *Outbreak 1939*, 288.

[67] Fabre-Luce, *Journal de la France*, 141.

[68] William L. Shirer, *The Collapse of the Third Republic: An Inquiry into the Fall of France in 1940*, (New York: Simon and Schuster, 1969), 524.

[69] Major–General J.F.C. Fuller, *The Second World War, 1939-1945* (London: Eyre and Spottiswoode, 1948), 55.

[70] Martin S. Alexander, *The Republic in Danger: General Maurice Gamelin and the Politics of French Defence, 1933-1940* (Cambridge: Cambridge University Press, 1992), 356, 369.

shed French blood needlessly."[71] His half-hearted gesture has given rise to a myth that the French army, acting on its own, could have defeated Germany with little or no opposition. Two American authors, neither of whom is a professional historian, claim that Gamelin had only to give the order. "His troops could have marched into the *Ruhrgebiet*, the heartland of German industry, and the war would have been over."[72]

Really? A glance at the map shows that the shortest route from France to the *Ruhrgebiet* runs through Belgium and the Netherlands, both of which were neutral. Attacking Germany directly would entail a frontal assault on the Siegfried Line which, in the sector facing France, was complete by September 1939. Its 11,283 bunkers and gun emplacements now provided Germany with defence in depth.[73] The French lacked the heavy artillery necessary to destroy these fortifications. Gamelin had intended to send some army units on 17 September to test their strength, but by that time Poland was virtually conquered.[74] Field fortifications and minefields completed the German defences. The French army, moreover, was not yet fully mobilized.[75] In early September, the *Wehrmacht* deployed 35 divisions in the west. Of these, eleven were regular divisions of young, well-trained and well-equipped troops who, in the words of a British historian, "were more than a match for their French equivalents."[76] They would soon be reinforced by battle-hardened veterans fresh from their victory in the east. Germany began troop transfers from Poland to the French front on 20 September.[77] Gamelin had told Daladier and his cabinet

---

[71] General Maurice Gamelin, *Servir* (3 vols., Paris: Plon, 1947), I, 122.

[72] Manchester and Reid, *The Last Lion*, 36.

[73] Tooze, *The Wages of Destruction*, 316.

[74] J. R. M. Butler, *Grand Strategy*, (London: H. M. Stationary Office, 1948), II, 60.

[75] Nick Smart and Jeremy Black, *British Strategy and Politics during the Phony War: Before the Balloon Went Up* (Westport, CT: Praeger, 2003), 79.

[76] Brian Bond, "The Calm before the Storm: Britain and the 'Phoney War' 1939-1942," *The RUSI Journal*, Spring 1990, 62.

[77] *New York Times*, 21 September 1939.

colleagues on 7 September that Poland was finished in any case. The following day, he added that the French army was unable to extend its battle lines rapidly.[78] His views on Poland were shared by Harold Nicolson, who wrote on 6 September: "I feel perfectly certain that Germany will mop up Poland in a week or so. . . . Chamberlain did not want this war and is continually thinking of getting out of it. He may be right."[79]

The British government had promised to send 32 divisions to France by the end of the second year of war.[80] These were to replace the 34 Czechoslovak divisions lost at Munich. Until then, not much help could be expected from Britain; and without British participation, Gamelin was not going to engage in offensive action. Parliament enacted conscription on 27 April 1939 at the instigation of Chamberlain, who had earlier pledged not to introduce it. He sought primarily to reassure the French and impress Hitler. The measure encountered widespread opposition throughout the country, especially from the Labour Party.[81] Attlee claimed that it was not warranted by Britain's commitments to Poland, Greece and Romania.[82] He did not mention France. A leading British historian has since recognized that the bill was "little more than a gesture,"[83] since it added little to Britain's military potential. "Of course," wrote Churchill, "the introduction of conscription at this stage did not give us an army."[84] A single class of 200,000 men was registered in 1939. They were to be called up by waves. The first wave, drafted into service on 15 July,

---

[78] Élisabeth du Réau, "Édouard Daladier: The Conduct of the War and the Beginnings of Defeat," Blatt, *The French Defeat*, 106-7.

[79] Nicolson, *Diaries and Letters*, 31.

[80] Eleanor M. Gates, *End of the Affair: The Collapse of the Anglo-French Alliance, 1939-1940* (London: George Allen & Unwin, 1981), 27.

[81] Juliet Gardiner, *Wartime Britain, 1939-1945* (London: Headline Book Publishing, 2004), 78.

[82] 346 H C Deb., 27 April 1939, col. 1354.

[83] A.J.P. Taylor, *English History, 1914-1945* (Oxford: Clarendon Press, 1965), 444.

[84] Churchill, *The Gathering Storm*, 318.

amounted to 34,000.[85] Once war was declared, most men in their early twenties were still not in uniform. "Wait till we send for you" was the order of the day.[86]

By December 1939, four divisions of the British Expeditionary Force had arrived in France. As General Swinton admitted candidly, they were unprepared for real warfare. General Ironside concurred. Early in January he wrote in his diary: "The army we have in France is really largely a militia. It is untrained."[87] What training it did receive was with flags instead of artillery, trucks instead of tanks. Rifle parts often did not fit together properly because they were made by different companies.[88] Small wonder, then, that Gamelin was loath to expend his soldiers without adequate British support. On this point, he had the tacit approval of the Chamberlain government. As two British historians have observed, "His insistence that he would undertake no life-squandering offensives was entirely in accord with British strategic preferences."[89] In the spring of 1939, Liddell Hart had written that for France, "the strategic defensive is strongly indicated."[90] Given the paucity of Britain's eventual contribution on land, this was surely the wisest policy.

No sooner had Churchill entered the cabinet than he initiated a steady flow of military advice to Chamberlain. In a letter of 10 September, he referred to "the condition of our small Expeditionary Forces and their deficiencies in tanks, in trained trench mortar detachments, and above all in heavy artillery." He proposed "forming a British army of a texture and quality capable of taking its place beside our own regular divisions and the French troops, and thus worthily

[85] Jacques Benoist-Méchin, *Sixty Days That Shook the West: The Fall of France, 1940*, trans. Peter Wiles (New York: Putnam's, 1963), 26.

[86] E.S. Turner, *The Phoney War on the Home Front* (London: Michael Joseph, 1961), 18.

[87] *The Ironside Diaries,* 194.

[88] Tom Shachtman, *The Phony War, 1939-1940* (New York: Harper & Row, 1982), 65.

[89] Smart and Black, *British Strategy and Politics during the Phony* War, 76.

[90] Liddell Hart, *The Defence of Britain*, 311.

facing the enemy." This would entail raising fifty to fifty-five divisions, not just thirty-two. Chamberlain replied on 16 September that "fifty-five divisions would be beyond our capacity, taking into account the needs of the RAF." Churchill then gave ground, conceding that mobilizing an army that size might take 24 to 40 months. He did insist that the French be informed of Britain's intentions "because I doubt that [they] would acquiesce in a division of effort which gave us the sea and the air and left them to pay almost the whole blood tax on land."[91] Of course land operations were not Churchill's appointed bailiwick, and Chamberlain always had the last word.

The Supreme Inter-allied War Council, consisting of Chamberlain, Daladier and their military advisers, met for the first time in the northern French town of Abbeville on 12 September. Chamberlain spoke first, explaining that nothing could be done for the Poles, whose eventual liberation would have to wait until the allies were victorious in the west. For the time being, however, it was decided by both parties not to engage in important operations on land until they had the means to do so. They assumed that time was on their side.[92] Chamberlain reiterated his war policy in a secret telegram to Roosevelt on 14 September. "The time factor will work in favour of the allies and against Germany; consequently Anglo-French strategy should be adapted to a long war, beginning with a phase of defensive strategy, while building up resources and imposing the greatest measure of economic pressure." As for Poland, its fate "will depend on the ultimate outcome of the war; i.e. on our ability to defeat Germany, and not on our ability to relieve pressure on Poland at the outset. . . . A delay in the inception of the air war is all to the advantage of the defence of this country and of our sea-borne trade."[93]

---

[91] Chamberlain Papers, NC7/ 9/ 47-51.

[92] François Bédarida, *La stratégie secrète de la Drôle de Guerre. Le Conseil Suprême Interallié* (Paris: Presses de la Fondation Nationale des Sciences Politiques, 1979), 90-104.

[93] Colvin, *The Chamberlain Cabinet*, 256-8.

Chamberlain's conception of war was essentially passive. On announcing the fall of Poland to Parliament, he promised "not to rush into adventures that offer little prospect of success and are calculated to impair our resources and to postpone ultimate victory."[94] He would not have sanctioned a French offensive against Germany, since he was convinced that the allies had nothing to lose by waiting and that the German home front was about to collapse. Such fanciful hopes justified what Liddell Hart, who wanted above all to avoid the bloodbath of 1914-1918, had prescribed: a war of "limited liability."[95] A week after Britain declared war, the chancellor of the exchequer presented the war cabinet with a report showing that Britain's economic resources were considerably less than in 1914 and "extremely meagre for the financing of a long war."[96] To Chamberlain, the hard-headed businessman, only a war of "limited liability" made any sense.

Furthermore, there was public opinion to consider – especially when it coincided with official policy. As chancellor of the exchequer, Chamberlain had told the cabinet in May 1937 that the country would not tolerate a European conflict "on the same lines as the last war. . . . Our contribution on land should be on a limited scale." Britain's continental allies (i.e. France) would have to assume responsibility for most, if not all, the fighting on land. "I believe our resources will be more profitably employed in the air and on the sea than in building up great armies."[97] Once the Phoney War began, British rearmament was concentrated primarily on the navy and the air force. Although total defence expenditures more than doubled in 1939, the army's share did not exceed one third. Chamberlain, who had implicit faith in the RAF bomber command as a deterrent,[98] was confident that this was the

---

[94] 351 H C Deb, 20 September 1939, col. 983.

[95] Liddell Hart, *The Defence of Britain*, 44ff.

[96] Clive Ponting, *1940, Myth and Reality* (London: Sphere Books, 1990), 41.

[97] Self, *Neville Chamberlain, a Biography*, 254.

[98] G.C. Peden, "Neville Chamberlain, the British Army and the Continental Commitment, Malcolm Murfett ed., *Shaping British Foreign and Defence Policy in the Twentieth Century* (Basingstoke: Palgrave Macmillan, 2014), 91-3.

proper course. He wrote to his sister early in October: "My policy continues to be the same. Hold on tight. Keep up the economic pressure, push on with munitions production & military preparations with the utmost energy, take no offensive unless Hitler begins it. I reckon that if we are allowed to carry on this policy, we shall have won the war by the spring."[99]

"Limited liability" also characterized the prevailing mood of the British Dominions. Australia and New Zealand entered the war immediately after Britain, more out of loyalty to the mother country than out of conviction. In the words of New Zealand Premier Michael Savage, "Where she goes, we go; where she stands, we stand." Yet as recently as 26 August 1939, the government of New Zealand had expressed willingness to return Western Samoa to Germany, as long as it was not used as a naval base, if that could save the peace.[100] Prime Minister Robert Menzies of Australia did not even bother to declare war. He simply announced on the radio that Britain's declaration automatically drew Australia into the conflict. In September 1939 the Australian army numbered 3,000 men, who were equipped with weapons dating from the First World War; a civilian militia was authorized to fight only in defence of home territory. Both countries were concerned primarily with Japan, and even more so after the Japanese attack on Pearl Harbor.

Canada's position was somewhat different. The British guarantee of Polish independence had been poorly received in Ottawa. Addressing the Canadian House of Commons on 30 March 1939, Prime Minister Mackenzie King quoted approvingly Chamberlain's speech of 17 March, in which he refused to engage his country "by new and unspecified commitments, operating under conditions which cannot now be foreseen." Canada must look to its own concerns, he said. "We have tremendous tasks to do at home, in housing the people, in caring

---

[99] Chamberlain to Ida, 8 October 1939, *The Neville Chamberlain Diary Letters*, 456.

[100] Ritchie Ovendale, *"Appeasement" and the English Speaking World* (Cardiff: University of Wales Press, 1975), 286-7.

for the aged and helpless, in relieving drought and unemployment, in building roads, in meeting our heavy burden of debt, in making provision for Canada's defence." Canada's defence, not that of Europe. Moreover, he reminded his colleagues, geography tied Canada to the United States, a fact underlined by the opening of the Thousand Islands Bridge, linking the Province of Ontario and New York State, in August 1938. On that occasion, Roosevelt received an honorary doctorate from Queen's University in Kingston. His acceptance speech, which the Canadian premier quoted in part, included the assurance that "the people of the United States will not stand idly by if domination of Canadian soil is threatened by any other empire." This was taken to mean that Canada was in no direct danger, since it could always count on the United States as a potential ally.

The leader of the Conservative opposition, Dr. Robert Manion, expressed concern that Canada's involvement in another European war could tear the country apart, as nearly happened in the First World War. Many French Canadians had volunteered for service overseas, but the vast majority opposed conscription, which went into effect in 1917. Manion, whose wife was French-Canadian, insisted that whatever might happen in Europe, conscription for the Canadian army must be avoided at all cost. He quoted from a speech that Mackenzie King had made on 25 March 1937, in which he doubted that Britain would send an expeditionary force to Europe and that, *a fortiori*: "I think it is doubtful if any of the British dominions will ever send an expeditionary force to Europe."[101] No Canadian expeditionary force was in fact sent to continental Europe in 1939. When Canada declared war on 10 September, plans were made to raise a single Canadian army division of volunteers for service in Britain, not France. Canada's principal contribution was to be the training of pilots for the Royal Air Force. This was "limited liability" as official policy.

With the rapid defeat of Poland, it was only natural that many, not to say most, British subjects began to ask themselves whether the

---

[101] Dominion of Canada, Official Report of Debates: House of Commons, 1939, III, 2418-41.

inconveniences of even a phoney war were worth the effort. The blackout, the evacuation of children from large cities and the onset of rationing were justified only if the civilian population had a clear idea of what the war was all about. At the request of his publisher, Harold Nicolson dashed off a book, which was published in November 1939, to explain Britain's position. He began with Hitler, whose very presence as Germany's leader was seen as a threat to civilization. The horrid dictator had to be eliminated, but how did he attain power in the first place? "It is frequently stated," Nicolson wrote, "that Herr Hitler was put into power by the treaty of Versailles." Note the choice of words: stated, not claimed or asserted. So perhaps the much-maligned Versailles treaty did lead to war after all. Nicolson did not defend the treaty, but he could hardly denounce it since he had been a member of the British delegation at the Paris peace conference. No, he explained: the origins of Hitler's power lay elsewhere. "It would be more accurate to say that he owed his success to Raymond Poincaré. The German people as a whole had, by the end of 1922, accepted the peace treaty [sic]; it was Monsieur Poincaré's insistence, against the advice of his British allies, upon occupying the Ruhr . . . which drove the German public to a condition of despairing and inflamed resentment."[102] Never mind that the German people had never accepted defeat, let alone the Versailles treaty, or that the Ruhr occupation was followed in Germany by five years of prosperity, during which time only twelve Nazis managed to win seats in the Reichstag.

And now Britain had to endure the inconveniences of make-believe war on order to aid France, whose nationalistic premier had supposedly enabled Hitler. Nicolson's views were fully reflected in government circles, where it was widely assumed that Germany had been grievously wronged by France. If that were the case, the Nazis would surely be chomping at the bit to get even; yet Hitler neither sought nor initiated a war with the old enemy of 1914-1918. His quarrel was with the Soviet Union, which had no connection whatsoever with the Versailles treaty or the Ruhr occupation. But ingrained prejudices

---

[102] Harold Nicolson, *Why Britain is at War* (London: Penguin, 1939), 21-2.

are not easily eradicated. John Colville, the prime minister's assistant personal secretary, wrote in his diary on 31 October 1939 that French intransigence "had bred the bitterness and despair upon which Hitler rose to power."[103] Like Nicolson, he conveniently forgot the parliamentary crisis of 1930-1932 in Germany and the severe unemployment that led to the triumph of Nazism. It was so much simpler to blame the French for Hitler.

Obviously, such arguments could hardly encourage the British people to support the war effort. In early October, Chamberlain wrote to his sister that in three days during the preceding week, he had received 2,450 letters, of which 1,860 were pleas to "stop the war in one form or another."[104] It fell to Churchill, as the most bellicose member of Chamberlain's war cabinet, to drum up enthusiasm for the war. In a radio address of 1 October, he quickly set aside the question of Poland, whose defeat, he assured his listeners, was only temporary. "She will rise again like a rock which may for a spell be submerged by a tidal wave but remains a rock." This was cold comfort for the Poles, but Churchill was more interested in Russia, which he described as "a riddle wrapped in mystery inside an enigma." What mattered most was that with Poland gone, Germany now faced Russia directly. "An eastern front has been created which Nazi Germany does not dare assail."[105] So perhaps the Soviet Union would be the eventual undoing of Hitler's abject regime. In that case, did the British declaration of war make any sense?

George Bernard Shaw did not think so. Britain, he wrote, "did not care two hoots about Poland. . . . What in the devil's name is it [the war] all about now that we have let Poland go?" British war propaganda, noted Shaw sarcastically, implied that if Hitler were not

---

[103] John Colville, *The Fringes of Power: Downing Street Diaries, 1939-1955* (New York: Norton, 1985), 46.

[104] Chamberlain to Ida, 8 October 1939, *The Neville Chamberlain Diary Letters*, 454.

[105] Charles Eade, ed., *The War Speeches of the Rt. Hon. Winston S. Churchill* (3 vols., London: Cassell, 1951), I, 108.

sent to St. Helena, he would conquer the entire universe. "Stalin will see to it that nobody, not even our noble selves, will do anything of the sort; and Franklin Roosevelt will be surprised to find himself exactly of Stalin's opinion in this matter. Had we not better wait until Herr Hitler tries to do it, and then stop him with Stalin and Roosevelt at our back?"[106] Shaw was right, of course. Chamberlain never spoke of collective security; he may not even have thought about it. But his repeated allusions to Hitlerism as a blight on international relations and those of Halifax upholding the sanctity of treaties and the pledged word[107] indicate that collective security rather than self-defence was their sole justification – albeit unavowed and possibly unconscious – for having declared war. In that case, Britain and France would have been well advised to wait for the two dormant superpowers to get involved. Chamberlain refused to ally Britain with either one. As Harold Nicolson noted in 1938, "The P. M. is bitterly anti-Russian and also anti-American."[108] Besides, the die was cast. The allies had declared war and would forfeit their status as great powers if they stepped aside.

With Italy still officially a non-belligerent, Mussolini made a public speech on 23 September – his first since May – in which he noted that "with Poland liquidated, Europe is not yet actually at war." He praised the allies for their "wise" decision not to enlarge the conflict by declaring war on the Soviet Union, but added that they thereby forfeited their "moral justification" to continue hostilities against Germany. Since they had not reacted to Russia's *fait accompli* in occupying half of Poland, they should in all logic accept the occupation of the other half.[109] The following day, Lord Rothermere, proprietor of the *Daily Mail* and a noted Fascist sympathizer, wrote to Chamberlain urging him to negotiate a compromise peace. "If the major clash of armies and air forces now begins, Western civilisation in Europe must

---

[106] Bernard Shaw, "Uncommon Sense about the War," *The New Statesman and Nation*, 7 October 1939, 483-4.

[107] Cf. *infra*, 142-3.

[108] Nicolson, *Diaries and Letters* I, 329.

[109] *New York Times*, 24 September 1939.

be imperilled, if not, as President Roosevelt seemed to foreshadow, doomed. Should the democracies be victorious in such a war, they must emerge exhausted." The letter was never sent.[110]

Hitler availed himself of the military inactivity in the west to make a peace offer on 6 October. In a speech to Nazi militants who now formed the entire Reichstag, he proposed the cessation of hostilities on the western front, plus an end to the British naval blockade and German submarine operations. The *New York Times* correspondent in Berlin took Hitler's proposal seriously. "Herr Hitler did not mention an armistice. The tenor of his speech was self-assertive, yet free of aggressive emphasis, and it ended on a note that left full scope for diplomatic action or mediation."[111] In essence, Hitler was ready to conclude peace if Britain and France accepted Germany's domination of Central Europe and returned its colonies taken in 1919. He did not seek the destruction of the British Empire; the wreckage, he believed, would simply be taken up by "foreign or even hostile powers" – an obvious reference to Japan and the United States.[112] At the Guild Hall of Danzig on 19 September he had declared: "I do not pursue any war aims against either Britain or France."[113] Once again, in Berlin, he formally renounced Alsace-Lorraine. "I accepted the 1919 settlement. I declined to let a problem drive us into bloody war, a question which has no bearing on Germany's vital interests." Addressing himself to the allies, he asked rhetorically: "Why should there be war in the west? To restore Poland? The Poland of the Versailles treaty shall never rise again. Two of the world's greatest states guarantee that." And the allies might just as well forget any plans for regime change in Germany. "Should this war be waged only to give Germany a new regime, that is to say, to destroy the present Reich once more and thus create a new treaty of Versailles, then millions of human lives will be sacrificed in

---

[110] *Royal Historical Society Camden, Fifth Series,* December 1998, 291-2.

[111] *New York Times,* 7 October 1939.

[112] Joseph Goebbels, *The Goebbels Diaries, 1939-1941,* ed. and trans. Fred Taylor (New York: Putnam's, 1983), 123.

[113] Domarus, *Hitler Speeches and Proclamations,* III, 1809.

vain, for neither will the German Reich fall apart nor will a second treaty of Versailles be made."[114]

Whether sincere or not, Hitler's peace offer came at an opportune time. The German people, having rejoiced in their army's victory over Poland, now wanted to settle down and enjoy peace.[115] The British especially, and the French as well, showed little enthusiasm for war. Hitler played to the emotions of both sides. If the allied governments should reject his proposals, as appeared almost certain, he was confident that Germany would be victorious in the west. By claiming to be a man of peace, he knew that he could count on the support of his subjects in the event of further conflict.

Chamberlain, who admitted to his sister that Hitler had made a "clever speech,"[116] gave his response six days later, after the cabinet had examined the peace offer carefully. Some influential figures outside the government, such as Lloyd George and Sir Stafford Cripps, urged acceptance. Daladier, however, rejected the proposal out of hand.[117] France was not going to mobilize and then demobilize its entire army whenever it suited Hitler; and without France, Britain could not undertake a negotiated peace with Germany, at least not in 1939. So Chamberlain, who now claimed to distrust Hitler totally, had no choice but to refuse. "The plain truth," he explained to Parliament, "is that, after our past experience, it is no longer possible to rely upon the unsupported word of the present German government." He quoted approvingly Daladier's radio address of the previous day in which he said in part: "We have taken up arms against aggression; we shall not lay them down until we have sure guarantees of security – a security that cannot be called into question every six months."[118]

---

[114] *Ibid.*, 1830-48.

[115] Shirer, *Berlin Diary*, 230.

[116] Chamberlain to Ida, 8 October 1939, *The Neville Chamberlain Diary Letters*, 455.

[117] Esnouf, "British Government War Aims," 67-78.

[118] 352 H C Deb., 12 October 12 1939, series 5, cols. 565-567; cf. *Le Temps*, 12 October 1939.

Privately, however, the British government was less resolute. Ambassador Lothian met secretly with the German chargé d'affaires in Washington and urged Halifax not to reject Hitler's offer without due consideration.[119] Canadian Prime Minister Mackenzie King sent Chamberlain a telegram on 9 October in which he left the door open to a negotiated settlement, provided that Hitler did not dictate the terms. "I realize," he wrote, "how deeply you desire . . . to avoid if humanly possible the destruction of life and European civilisation which prolonged war could bring." Canada, being close to the United States and also the most important British Dominion, was taken very seriously in Whitehall, not least because Mackenzie King's position harmonized perfectly with that of Chamberlain. In his reply of 12 October, which was addressed to all Dominion governments, the British premier offered grounds for hope. "If . . . the German government have not yet closed their minds to the possibility of negotiation, Herr Hitler may be expected to reply to our statement. . . . In other words, if Herr Hitler wants to negotiate we have given him the chance to do so." [120] A month earlier, Chamberlain had called for Hitler's elimination.[121] Now he seemed ready to negotiate with the dreaded dictator – anything to avoid a real war. Since the German people had not yet overthrown the Nazi regime, as British propaganda strongly urged them to do, perhaps negotiation with Hitler was the only way out.

Soon thereafter, Nazi Germany gave Britain its answer. On 14 October the battleship *Royal Oak* was sunk by a German submarine, which had managed to slip into the naval base at Scapa Flow. The obsolete aircraft carrier *Courageous* had met with a similar fate on 17 September. In October and November 1939, over 200,000 tons of British merchant shipping were disabled or sent to the bottom by German magnetic mines. The war was now becoming increasingly real, at least at sea. Britain won a naval victory of sorts when three of its

---

[119] Norman Moss, *Nineteen Weeks: America, Britain, and the Fateful Summer of 1940* (Boston: Houghton Mifflin, 2003), 211.
[120] Esnouf, "British Government War Aims," 81-2, 103.
[121] Cf. *infra*, 151.

cruisers, two light and one heavy, severely damaged the German pocket battleship, the *Admiral Graf Spee*, in the South Atlantic on 13 December and forced it to seek temporary shelter in Montevideo harbour. Believing that a stronger British force was on the way, the German captain scuttled his ship and committed suicide. The crews of the three British cruisers were invited to hold a victory parade in London. As Amery noted, however, this meant nothing to the French, who had not tasted any military glory of their own but had to wait for the Germans to attack.[122]

A leading British authority on Hitler has written that since Britain and France did not recognize the conquest of Poland as final, they "forced a major campaign in the west."[123] By 9 October Hitler had lost patience with the allies for not having accepted his peace offer and decided to pursue the struggle on land as soon as possible.[124] The German generals balked. Many had fought in the First World War and respected the tenacity of the French soldier. "France is not Poland," they argued, adding that the autumn rains made the ground marshy, hampering the use of tanks.[125] Hitler replied, "It rains on the enemy too."[126] In a memorandum dated 10 October, he wrote that the German soldier, fresh from his victory in Poland, "is again the best in the world. His self-respect is as great as the respect he commands from others. Six months of delaying warfare and effective propaganda on the part of the enemy might cause these important qualities to weaken."[127] For once, however, he listened to his generals and agreed to postpone an offensive in the west until the spring. The delay served the German army well: it was able to replenish the fuel and arms expended in the Polish campaign. A vast retraining program, taking account of the

---

[122] Amery, *My Political Life*, III, 334.

[123] Trevor-Roper, *Hitler's War Directives*, xxiii.

[124] Domarus, *Hitler: Speeches and Proclamations*, III, 1849.

[125] Grenard, *La Drôle de Guerre*, 301.

[126] Ronald Atkin, *Pillar of Fire: Dunkirk 1940* (Edinburgh: Birlinn, 2000), 42.

[127] Brigadier-General Robert A. Doughty, *The Breaking Point: Sedan and the Fall of France, 1940* (New York: Archon Books, 1990), 14.

mistakes made in Poland, was initiated and brought to fruition by April.[128] The total number of divisions increased from 106 to 155. Enemy propaganda did not dampen German soldiers' morale, which remained high throughout the *Sitzkrieg*, as they called the war of waiting.[129] In their view, the British and French were the aggressors, having declared war for no apparent reason.

French morale, on the other hand, suffered greatly during the Phoney War. Pay in the French army was derisory. A private was paid 50 centimes, or 1.25 U.S. cents, a day. His counterpart in the British Expeditionary Force received 17 francs, or 43 cents a day. Base pay in the United States Army was 30 dollars a month, hence the term "buck private." This was raised to 50 dollars a month in 1941. French soldiers could be seen in public trying to sell their cigarette rations in the hope of making a little extra money.[130] In early March 1940, I.-F. Aubert, Daladier's *chargé de mission*, warned Arnold Toynbee that "there is a definite limit to the time for which French morale can stand a general mobilization unaccompanied by military activity."[131] Amery wrote that French conscripts had "nothing to do except to worry about their families and their neglected farms and shops."[132] A French historian adds: "Worst of all, the men did not understand why they were called up, and for how long, since there was no fighting."[133] Postal censorship in France revealed that, at the start of the Phoney War, French soldiers wanted to have it out with Germany once and for all.[134] By winter, the

---

[128] Frieser, *The Blitzkrieg Legend*, 26.

[129] Telford Taylor, *The March of Conquest: The German Victories in Western Europe, 1940* (London: Edward Hulton, 1959), 17-22.

[130] Frank C. Hanighen, "How France Is Taking the War," *The New Republic*, 20 December 1939, 255.

[131] Michael Dockrill, "The Foreign Office and France during the Phoney War, September 1939 – May 1940," Michael Dockrill and Brian McKercher, eds., *Diplomacy and World Power: Studies in British Foreign Policy, 1890-1950* (Cambridge: Cambridge University Press, 1996), 187.

[132] Amery, *My Political Life*, III, 335.

[133] Marc-Ednond Naegelen, *L'attente sous les armes ou la Drôle de Guerre* (Paris: Jérôme Martineau, 1970), 55.

weeks and months of boredom had largely dissipated their fighting spirit. Jean-Paul Sartre, who had been called up to serve in the army's meteorological service, wrote in his diary that the soldiers' morale was low: "The war machine is idling in neutral." He reproached the French general staff for its timidity. "What sort of war is it when the 'aggressor' does not attack?" he wondered.[135] With the general depression caused by boredom and extreme cold came a rash of suicides, accounting for nearly four percent of all French war dead. One soldier wrote home: "Why can't we have a real fight? If we have to die, at least it will be over, and we won't talk about it anymore."[136]

Among British troops in France, there was widespread boredom and much grousing about food, living conditions and lack of training.[137] At home, the mood was officially was one of optimism. In a radio address to the British people on 26 November, Chamberlain admitted that "the war has been carried out in a way very different from what we expected." But all was well. "The allies are bound to win in the end, and the only question is how long it will take them to achieve their purpose."[138] Chamberlain was in good company. A report of February 1939 by the chiefs of staff carried the warning that if war broke out that year, "the allies would have no means of winning quickly." Their superior economic potential would allow them to prevail in time.[139] A leading British economist had written the previous year that the Germany economy was stretched to the limit and could expand no

---

[134] Grenard, *La Drôle de Guerre,* 209.

[135] Jean-Paul Sartre, *Les carnets de la Drôle de Guerre* (Paris: Gallimard, 1983), 273.

[136] Maude Williams and Bernard Wilkin, *French Soldiers' Morale in the Phoney War, 1939-1940* (London: Routledge, 2019), 41-2.

[137] Brian Bond, The British Field Force in France and Belgium, 1939-1940," Paul Addison and Angus Calder eds., *Time to Kill: The Soldier's Experience of War in the West, 1939-1945* ((London: Pimlico, 1997), 42-43.

[138] *The Times,* 27 November 1939.

[139] F.H. Hinsley, *British Intelligence in the Second World War,* I (London: H. M. Stationary Office, 1979), 71.

further. "The intense activity, the incentive for which lies beyond the material sphere, must imply an increasing strain on the people, which will inevitably have its repercussions in the longer run."[140]

So with the German economy and society presumably near the breaking point, the allied long-war strategy seemed reasonable. Yet when the government told Britons in September to prepare for a war lasting three years, most people were dismayed. Some thought it was just a ruse to impress Hitler. Chamberlain's own credibility suffered: his highest approval rating in public opinion polls taken during the first few months of hostilities was 68 percent – not a particularly impressive score for a war leader.[141] By contrast, Churchill enjoyed an approval rating in October 1940 of 89 percent.[142]

In December, the Ministry of Information published a 32-page pamphlet entitled, *The Assurance of Victory*. Its title page carried Chamberlain's assertion that the allies would win in the end. "We do not have to defeat the Nazis on land," it explained, "but only to prevent them from defeating us." In this regard, the role assigned to France was capital. "On the western front the Germans are faced with the French army, the strongest and best trained military force in the world [*sic*]." In 1932, Lloyd George had begrudged France for maintaining a large army. Now the "five million fully trained men . . . protected by the Maginot Line" were the key to victory. Germany was said to be on the brink of economic and social collapse. "The Nazis must win quickly if they are to win at all." Britain's main strength "lies in our command of the sea."[143] So while the French army holds the Germans in check, Britain will win the war through a naval blockade, which economist L.P. Thompson compared to a stranglehold.[144] Presumably, the British

---

[140] Thomas Balogh, "The National Economy of Germany," *The Economic Journal*, September 1938, 496.

[141] Harrison and Madge, *War Begins at Home*, 420-1.

[142] Richard Lamb, *Churchill as War Leader* (New York: Carroll & Graf, 1991), 74.

[143] Great Britain, Ministry of Information, *The Assurance of Victory* (London: H. M. Stationary Office, 1939), *passim*.

people had only to sit tight, endure the blackout and wait patiently for the inevitable triumph. Such a prospect was not likely to stimulate their fighting spirit.

Reliance on a naval blockade to defeat Germany derives in large measure from a book by Liddell Hart, entitled *The Real War, 1914-1918*, which appeared in 1930. Most of this treatise is devoted to a blow-by-blow description of the land battles fought by the western allies; the eastern front receives scant attention. As for the only important naval engagement of the war, the battle of Jutland, the author claims that the opposing fleets merely "hailed each other in passing."[145] His emphasis changes radically in the book's conclusion: "The navy was to win no Trafalgar, but it was to do more than any other factor towards winning the war for the allies. For the navy was the instrument of the blockade, and as the fog of war disperses in the clearer light of these post-war years that blockade is seen to assume larger and larger proportions, to be more and more clearly the decisive agency in the struggle."[146] No evidence is cited to support this claim; but like Liddell Hart's other works, *The Real War* had a profound influence on the British government, which was only too content to let the navy, rather than the army, shoulder the burden of any future European conflict.

Toward the end of the First World War, the British blockade did contribute to Germany's defeat on the battlefield. Rubber, for example, was so scarce that German gas masks were no longer air-tight. The situation in 1939 was radically different from that of 1918, when the Germans were repulsed by the combined efforts of the French, British and American forces. During the Phoney War there was no real fighting on land; therefore no pressure was exerted on the German army. Thanks to the Nazi-Soviet pact, Germany could obtain most of the strategic materials it needed from the Soviet Union. What Russia

---

[144] L.P. Thompson, *Can Germany Stand the Strain?* (Oxford: Clarendon Press, 1939), 29.

[145] B. H. Liddell Hart, *The Real War, 1914-1918* (Boston: Little, Brown, 1930), 199.

[146] *Ibid.*, 471-2.

itself could not supply could be purchased elsewhere, shipped to Vladivostok and then transported by rail to Germany. The Scandinavian countries were not affected by the blockade and continued to trade with their southern neighbour. Italy, which was not blockaded because the British government hoped it would stay out of the war, also served as a transit point for German imports. Even if the blockade had been successful, the Nazi war effort could still function at full strength for another eighteen months.[147] So, as the socialist G.D.H. Cole noted, "Germany cannot be starved into surrender . . . and it is difficult to suppose that the infliction of privations will make the Germans readier to regard the allies as their potential deliverers."[148]

Even in 1918, Germany had not been starved into surrender. The German high command sued for an armistice in order to avoid total military defeat. The British blockade did contribute to a widespread food shortage, but mismanagement by the German authorities was the prime cause.[149] Only after the sailors at the Kiel naval base mutinied in November when ordered to mount a suicide attack on the British fleet was there a semblance of revolution in Germany, and it was Communist inspired. This was not the sort of revolution that Halifax, who lived in mortal fear of Bolshevism, hoped for. Like Chamberlain, his fellow Conservative, he wanted something more orderly, more reasonable – as reflected in the British propaganda leaflets of September 1939. Just get rid of Hitler's wicked regime, and we can do business once again.

Although the home front in Germany showed no signs of collapse, Chamberlain remained confident that his grand strategy was working. In a letter of 25 October to his cousin Arthur Chamberlain, he wrote: "Hitler's psychology is enough to baffle anybody, and this is not surprising seeing that he is quite abnormal. . . . If he had been

---

[147] Self, *Neville Chamberlain, a Biography*, 396-7.

[148] G D.H. Cole, "Thoughts on Blockade," *The New Statesman and Nation*, 4 November 1939, 637.

[149] W.K. Hancock and M.M. Gowing, *British War Economy* (London: H. M. Stationary Office, 1949), 97.

governed purely by military considerations, he would never have allowed France to mobilise or the B. E. F. to go to France. These were military blunders of the first magnitude. The agreement with Russia, into which he was led by Ribbentrop [*sic*] was a diplomatic blunder no less fatal. Now he has got himself into a complete jam and doesn't know what to do next; and if we can hold firm, he is done."[150] A few days later, he revelled in the dictator's presumed discomfiture. "The progress of the 'war' [his quotation marks] becomes more and more amazing. Hitler's silence seems incredible when you think how he has filled our eyes and ears during the last 18 months. It can only be explained I think by the state of 'abject depression' in which I believe he has been plunged owing to his inability to find any opportunity of doing anything. Indeed he has had no luck at all lately."[151]

Chamberlain's smug optimism seems to have been shared by a broad section of the British elite. In a dispatch of 24 November, Mollie Panter-Downes, *The New Yorker* correspondent in London, wrote: "Everyone [in her circle of friends] agrees that Hitler doesn't know what to do next." There seems to have been a consensus among such people that Britain and Germany, once rid of Hitler, should join in a war against the Soviet Union.[152] As the year 1939 drew to a close, Chamberlain confided to his sister: "I stick to the view I have always held that Hitler missed the bus in September 1938. He could have dealt France and ourselves a terrible, perhaps a mortal, blow then. The opportunity will not recur."[153]

In a conversation of early November with U. S. Ambassador Kennedy, Chamberlain held to the view that "nothing Hitler planned has gone the way he thought it would. . . ." The prime minister was

---

[150] Chamberlain papers, NC/7/6/29.

[151] Chamberlain to Ida, 5 November 1939, *The Neville Chamberlain Diary Letters*, 466.

[152] Mollie Panter-Downes, *London War Notes, 1939-1945* (New York: Farrar, Strauss and Giroux, 1971), 27.

[153] Chamberlain to Hilda, 30 December 1939, *The Neville Chamberlain Dairy Letters*, 483.

confident that the war would be over by the spring, but believed "that no peace proposal is practical just at this time. The German people have not suffered enough yet to be disgusted with the leadership."[154] Serious food and fuel shortages did, in fact, dampen civilian morale in Germany during the Phoney War. Coal deliveries from Britain ceased once hostilities were declared, and the blockade cut off imports of animal feed from North America. But any hope that popular discontent might threaten the regime was illusory. The German government had stockpiled huge reserves of canned goods, particularly ham. Ersatz foods, such as coffee, were in use since the last war; and German civilians, especially the poorer classes, had grown quite used to them.[155] "The Nazi police state," writes a British historian, "had more than enough power to maintain the dictatorship."[156] The army, the instrument of victory in 1940, remained well fed and well supplied.

Meanwhile, Europe had to endure its coldest winter in over 50 years. The Thames froze over. Allied troops in France were primarily occupied in keeping warm. A leading British periodical summarized the situation thus: "The allies are still waiting for Germany to pass from the defensive to the offensive."[157] The author was merely echoing his country's war plan, for which Ironside had little regard: (1) assuring the defence of Britain, (2) gradually building up an army in France and (3) "waiting to see what the Germans are going to do."[158]

---

[154] Kennedy to Hull, 8 November 1939, FRUS, vol. I General, 527.

[155] *The Spectator*, 16 February 1940, 6.

[156] Nicholas Stargardt, *The German War: A Nation Under Arms, 1939-1945* (New York: Basic Books, 2015), 56-60, 77.

[157] "The Situation," *The Nineteenth Century and After*, February 1940, 129.

[158] *The Ironside Diaries*, 5 January 1940, 194.

5 War Aims

The Phoney War got its name on 18 September 1939, when Senator William E. Borah of Idaho, a leading isolationist, told a group of reporters, "There is something phoney about this war."[1] A few days later, Oliver Harvey wrote in his diary that among the neutrals, and especially in the United States, "it is thought that we don't mean business." The leaflet-dropping campaign, he added, only made matters worse.[2] A British diplomat and sometime journalist visited the United States early in 1940, where he heard the following limerick, which may have originated in the British Foreign Office: "An elderly statesman with gout,/ When asked what the war was about,/ Replied with a sigh,/ My colleagues and I/ Are doing our best to find out."[3] By then, Roosevelt was truly appalled at the allies' inactivity and doubted that they knew what the war was about.[4]

During the eight months of waiting for Germany to attack in the west, the British government never quite managed to come up with a convincing reason for having declared war. In a dispatch to Lothian of late September, Halifax admitted that "the definition of our war aims for public consumption is difficult." It must include the liberation "in some form" of the Poles and Czechs, "but essentially it is a fight against a whole conception of policy, almost against a state of mind. We are fighting for intangibles and imponderables."[5] This was not

---

[1] *New York Times*, 19 September 1939.

[2] Harvey, *Diaries,* 322.

[3] R. H. Bruce Lockhart, *Comes the Reckoning* (London: Putnam, 1947), 78. Chamberlain suffered from gout.

[4] David Reynolds, *The Creation of the Anglo-American Alliance, 1937-41* (Chapel Hill, NC: The University of North Carolina Press, 1982), 69.

[5] Halifax to Lothian, 27 September 1939, FO 800/324 xc/A 1706.

likely to cut much ice with the Americans, or with the British for that matter. Not many people were willing to endure the privations of war for intangibles and imponderables. As for the Poles, liberating them would seemingly oblige Britain to declare war on the Soviet Union as well as Germany. Richard Stokes, a Labour MP and persistent campaigner against the war, sent a circular letter to his fellow parliamentarians on 4 October, which read in part: "Does anybody believe that we can force both Germany and Russia to give up a bit of the country they have divided between them?"[6] In a written statement to Parliament two weeks later, the government explained that the guarantee of Poland's independence applied to German aggression only.[7]

Before writing to Lothian, Halifax asked Sir Alexander Cadogan for his views on war aims. At first, Cadogan couldn't think of any, other than getting rid of Hitler; and even that might not solve anything. "I suppose the cry is 'abolish Hitlerism.' What if Hitler hands over to Göring?" Britain would still be at war, and Cadogan doubted that time was on the side of the allies. On further reflection, he added that the prime war aim must be "to deny to Germany the ever-increasing encroachment on the rights and liberties of others." But, as he admitted candidly, that could have been done the previous year in more favourable circumstances.[8]

Halifax made a radio broadcast on 7 November 1939 in an effort to drum up public support for the war. "We are fighting in defence of freedom; we are fighting for peace. . . . We are fighting against the substitution of brute force for law as the arbiter between nations, and against the violation of the sanctity of treaties and disregard for the pledged word." All this was rather vague, except for the reference to treaties. What treaties could he have been referring to except those of Versailles and Saint-Germain, whose sanctity had long since been called into question? As for the pledged word, Chamberlain

---

[6] Esnouf, "British Government War aims," 28.
[7] 352 H C Deb, 19 October 1939, col. 1082W.
[8] Cadogan *Diaries*, 219, 221-2.

had pledged to defend the rump of Czechoslovakia but failed to deliver on his promise. In any event, lack of public support can be explained by military inactivity, except occasionally at sea. Toward the end of his speech, Halifax recognized the debilitating effects of "paralysing boredom" and urged his listeners just to carry on. "The stimulus of great events is not there," he admitted.[9]

Harold Nicolson was in full agreement regarding the stimulus of great events – that is, battles. "The British people at the present moment are disheartened by the fact that they do not know what they are fighting for," he wrote in the fall of 1939. "The time will come, of course (and it will come with thunder and fire), when the British people will recognize that they are fighting for their very existence."[10] Until then, however, the question of war aims remained an enigma for most Britons. In a diary entry of 28 September, Chamberlain's assistant private secretary noted that public opinion, having failed "to appreciate the merits of a waiting policy . . . is already showing signs of impatience and is asking what we are fighting for."[11] With the defeat of Poland, many Britons wondered, as Ciano had predicted, whether the war still served any purpose.[12]

A few weeks into the Phoney War, Henry Wickham Steed, who had been editor of *The Times* from 1919 to 1922, wrote that the British people should know "exactly what we are fighting for, and why." They demand "that our war aims and peace aims should be set forth in such terms and such fashion that none can mistake them."[13] Since these were not forthcoming, he published a book in November 1939, giving his own war aims. First and foremost, Germany must return to its frontiers of 1919, leaving the Sudetenland to Czechoslovakia and the Corridor to Poland. This implied that Britons revise their negative opinion of the

---

[9] *The Times*, 8 November 1939.

[10] Nicolson, *Why Britain Is at War*, 150.

[11] Colville, *The Fringes of Power*, 28.

[12] Duff Cooper, *Old Men Forget*, 266.

[13] Wickham Steed, "Foreground and Background," *The Fortnightly*, October 1939, 361, 369.

peace settlement. "We listened with eager ears to the German propaganda which bade us believe that the treaty of Versailles was a monument of iniquity," whereas "it did set free in Europe 80,000,000 out of 100,000,000 people who were in bondage." Only victory on the battlefield, he argued, could achieve this end. "Without military victory we shall not destroy the false legend of German military invincibility from which Hitlerism drew much of its strength."[14] Wickham Steed's proposals do not appear to have influenced the government.

Memories of the First World War served to dampen public support for the Second. A student from Yorkshire, born in 1914 and not a pacifist, wrote: "I have not made up my mind about the about the present conflict. I cannot help thinking at times, drawing remembrances from the last war, that we are being led up the garden path again." He added that the "immense amount of anti-war propaganda to which we have been subject in the last 20 years has helped to produce the lack of enthusiasm for the [present] war," an enthusiasm "which was so pronounced in the 1914 struggle." Annual Armistice Day celebrations, whose chief purpose was to justify the sacrifices of the Great War for having secured the peace for future generations, were increasingly a source of disillusionment, as it became obvious that the peace had not been secured.[15] Germany's attack on Poland and the subsequent declarations of war by the Western allies were ample proof of that. For many Britons, the chief war aim during the Phoney War was simply to end it as soon as possible.

Apathy in Britain was replicated in the United States. Hugh Gibson, former U. S. ambassador to Poland and dean of the American diplomatic corps, addressed the Overseas Press Club at a New York hotel on 25 October, saying that the war was "curious" and "it's getting curiouser and curiouser." He quoted a recent headline in a British newspaper: "Are We at War?" The attitude of the average Briton, he

---

[14] Wickham Steed, *Our War Aims* (London: Secker and Warburg, 1939), 57, 189, 304.

[15] Joel Morley, "The Memory of the Great War and Morale during Britain's Phoney War," *The Historical Journal*, March 2020, 459-60.

believed, was expressed by an old lady who was quoted as saying, "I do wish that that man Hitler would marry and settle down." For Americans, "it is really very difficult to say how they [the allies] are going to keep the war going, and we are having a hard time finding out where the war is going to be fought."

Later that day and also in New York, Lothian spoke at The Pilgrims' annual dinner in an effort to explain why Britain was at war. He did admit that "our ultimate goal" (i.e. British war aims) was not yet "visible," but he claimed that it was not visible in 1914. After repeating the usual bromide that Britain sought "to prevent the hordes of paganism and barbarism from destroying what is left of civilized Europe," he got down to essentials. To his American hosts, Lothian waxed nostalgic for the period of 1815-1914, during which Europe enjoyed peace (save for a few regional conflicts) and ever increasing prosperity. Hitler, like Stalin, represented "economic nationalism" and "the break-up of the old order."[16] In essence, then, Britain was at war in order to restore the old order, otherwise known as the Concert of Europe.[17] Save for the Third Republic in France, the old order was fundamentally aristocratic.[18] The Concert of Europe included Tsarist Russia; and while British leaders might entertain the illusion of replacing Hitler with someone more amenable, regime change in the Soviet Union was totally out of the question. That was one obstacle to restoring the old order, of which Britain had been the chief beneficiary; but would Americans want to see it restored? And would the average British subject endure yet another war in order to prop up a society based on privilege?

War aims, as A.J.P. Taylor has shown, are weapons of war. They serve to motivate civilians and the military alike. Once the First World War broke out, the Entente powers knew what they were fighting for – because they were actually fighting. Britain sought to

---

[16] *New York Times*, 26 October 1939.

[17] Cf. *supra*, 29.

[18] See Arno J. Mayer, *The Persistence of the Old Regime: Europe to the Great War* (London: Croom Helm, 1981), 87-91 *et passim*.

restore the independence of Belgium and the balance of power on the Continent. France was fighting to liberate the areas of national territory occupied by Germany. Recovering Alsace-Lorraine did not become official policy until 22 December 1914.[19] Russia too had to defend itself. President Wilson, who had proposed "peace without victory" before the United States entered the war, was appalled by the terms imposed by Germany at Brest-Litovsk. In a speech given in Baltimore on 6 April 1918, he insisted that "force to the utmost, force without stint or limit" would decide the issue in favour of the democracies.[20]

Neville Chamberlain, on the other hand, wanted above all to avoid the use of armed force. In Parliament he was questioned early in October 1939 by independent MP and noted social reformer Eleanor Rathbone: "Is the right honourable gentlemen aware that there is a very strong and growing demand in the country for a more specific statement of war aims?" She was shouted down with cries of "No!"[21] Chamberlain did not reply, but the allies (and especially Britain, which had been the first to declare war) came under increasing pressure to state their war aims publicly. German propaganda held that with Poland conquered, they had no reason to continue the struggle unless it was for nationalistic reasons: to prevent Germany from assuming its rightful place in Europe.[22]

Public opinion in Britain, although largely ignored by the government throughout the Phoney War, did not remain silent on this issue. Early in November, the British illustrated weekly, *Picture Post*, published two articles prefaced by the statement: "Everyone is asking, 'What exactly are we fighting for?' Now is the time to tell us." The first article was devoted to the opinions of leading political and literary figures, who foretold, in necessarily vague terms, a brave new world of peace and international cooperation once Hitler was removed from

---

[19] A.J.P. Taylor, "The War Aims of the Allies in the First World War," *Politics in Wartime and Other Essays* (London: Hamish Hamilton 1964), 94-8.

[20] *New York Times*, 7 April 1918.

[21] 352 H C Deb., 9 October 1939, col. 2.

[22] *New York Times*, 29 October 1939.

power. How his overthrow might be accomplished was not explained. Only Lord Meston, president of the Liberal Party, argued that "our first and paramount aim is to defeat Nazi Germany," which would then have to surrender its weapons, disband its forces and release all political prisoners.[23]

In the second article, people from all walks of life were invited to express their views. Here some sceptics emerged. A gardener earning fifty shillings a week began: "Chamberlain states our war aims are 'to redeem Europe from the perpetual and recurring *German* aggression.' What about Italian aggression? And in the Far East we and the U. S. A. supply Japan with materials to carry on *her* aggression against China." (Emphasis in the original.) A reader from Edinburgh wrote that "this war is only the logical conclusion to the scheming of a bunch of conscienceless gangsters, aided and abetted by the majority of the German people. . . . We will change our tune about the kindly German people once this war is over." From Liverpool came the observation, "Americans view with suspicion our government's stubborn refusal to come out with a clear statement of war aims. . . . Many of us here have our suspicions too."[24]

Churchill tried to rouse the British public out of its lassitude in a radio address of 12 November, which he entitled, "After Ten Weeks of War" – that is, ten weeks of Phoney War. It was not his greatest speech and is rarely cited in history books, but it does provide a clear insight into Britain's predicament. "We are far stronger than we were ten weeks ago. We are far better prepared to endure the worst malice of Hitler and his Huns than we were at the beginning of September." This implies that Britain had declared a war for which it was not prepared. If Hitler had attacked the allies in September, as nearly everyone in Britain and France expected, the French would have had to do not most, but all, of the fighting on land. Churchill promised that "Hitler, the Nazi regime and the recurring German or Prussian menace to Europe will be broken and destroyed."[25] But Britain was neither willing nor able to

---

[23] "What Are Our War Aims?" *Picture Post*, 4 November 1939, 49.
[24] "What Are Our War Aims?" *Picture Post*, 11 November 1939, 44-5.

take the initiative. It would have to wait until Hitler and his Huns decided to wreak their worst malice.

Churchill's speech was poorly received by the British political class. R.A. Butler, under-secretary of state for foreign affairs, thought it "beyond words vulgar." Chamberlain withheld public comment, but his assistant personal secretary wrote that "Winston's speech made a very bad effect on No. 10."[26] Actually, much of what Churchill said was remarkably similar to Chamberlain's position. "I do not doubt myself that time is on our side. . . . I have this feeling that the Germany which assaults us today is a far less strongly built or solidly founded organism than that which the allies and the United States forced to beg for an armistice twenty-one years ago." The Germans "recoil from the steel front of the French army along the Maginot Line." Such optimism was entirely in keeping with official British war policy. But to see Hitler as simply the latest manifestation of a recurring German or Prussian menace was considered highly inappropriate. The expression "Hitler and his Huns" echoed British propaganda of the First World War, which no one wanted to repeat. This time, British war aims, to the extent that they existed, were directed at Hitler and not the good German people. A British historian notes that the Chamberlain government had declared war in a profoundly pro-German spirit, one which was widely shared by the public.[27]

It remained for Chamberlain to clarify the government's position, which he attempted to do in a radio address of 26 November. He had already broadcast to Germany, in German, on 4 September, saying: "In this war we are not fighting you, the German people, for whom we have no bitter feeling, but against a tyrannous, foresworn regime which has betrayed not only its own people but the whole of Western civilization and all that you and we hold dear."[28] To his fellow Britons he exuded an optimism derived from several weeks of military

[25] Churchill, *War Speeches*, I, 119-23.

[26] Colville, *The Fringes of Power*, 50-1.

[27] Ludlow, "Le débat sur les buts de paix en Grande-Bretagne," 93.

[28] *New York Times*, 5 September 1939.

inactivity. "We must be thankful that, so far, the war has brought no such casualty lists as those which overshadowed the early months of the war of 1914." He clearly hoped that future casualty lists, if any, would be minimal. "We are not losing anything by delay," he assured his listeners, "for time is on our side." Britain was at war to rid the world of "that aggressive bullying mentality" which defined Nazi Germany. If the German people can "abandon it without bloodshed, so much the better; but abandoned it must be." This was Britain's sole war aim, said Chamberlain in conclusion.[29] He apparently counted on the German people ("for whom we have no bitter feeling") to achieve it.

The most authoritative written statement of British government war aims came from Lord Lloyd of Dolobran, in a pamphlet which appeared in December 1939. It bore a preface by the foreign secretary, who explained that Britain was defending "the Christian conception of freedom." For Lord Lloyd, an Anglo-Catholic, the primary threat to Christian civilization came from the Soviet Union, whose agents and money "were busy all over Europe." In reaction to Communist subversion, he explained, right-wing nationalist movements had taken power in various countries. Lord Lloyd was particularly fond of Salazar, the Portuguese dictator, whose "wise but authoritarian government" had brought "greater prosperity than ever before" to his country. He warmly endorsed Franco's overthrow of the Spanish republic and claimed that "there is much in the Italian labour charter which we should, and do, admire." The problem with Hitler was that he had allied himself with godless Communism to conquer Poland, "the natural bastion of European defence against Oriental incursions." The Nazi-Soviet pact was "Herr Hitler's final apostasy," and it led inevitably to the British declaration of war.[30]

There is no evidence that Lord Lloyd's pamphlet rallied the British public around a war to defend the Christian conception of freedom. A survey taken in late November 1939 revealed that the

---

[29] *The Times*, 27 November 1939.
[30] Lord Lloyd of Dolobran, *The British Case* (London: Eyre & Spottiswoode, 1939), 9-10, 37, 39, 48, 53.

largest group of respondents, 32 percent, could not come up with a single reason for being at war. Another 17 percent were decidedly negative, claiming that it was a war "to save the capitalists' money" or "for the Jews." One observer concluded: "There seems to be a strong feeling in the country that the wretched war is not worth going on with." People grumbled "against the utter futility and absurdity of having to fight these old battles all over again." Even those who wanted to get rid of Hitler and thought it possible were sceptical about the final outcome. A diarist wrote in November, "The government keeps repeating, 'We are going to smash Hitlerism'. . . . And then what?" Chamberlain himself admitted publicly on 28 November that since nothing seemed to be happening, the population was "a little restive."[31]

And for good reason. Chamberlain's war address to Parliament ended with the phrase, "I trust I may see the day when Hitlerism [not Nazism] has been destroyed and a liberated Europe re-established."[32] Yes, but when? How long would the British people tolerate a war of make-believe? Privately, the prime minister equated "Hitlerism," a term of his own devising, with Hitler himself. "Until he disappears and his system collapses," he explained to his sister early in September, "there can be no peace."[33] Brimming with self-confidence, he returned to this theme two months later: "To my mind it is essential to get rid of Hitler. He must either die or go to St. Helena or become a real public works architect, preferably in a 'home.' His entourage must also go, with the possible exception of Göring, who might have some ornamental position in a transitional government. Having once got rid of the Nazis, I don't think we should find any serious difficulty in Germany over Poland, Czecho-Slovakia, Jews, disarmament &c. Our real trouble is much more likely to be with France."[34]

---

[31] Harrison and Madge, *War Begins at Home,*, 11, 165, 183, 422.

[32] H C Deb, 3 September 1939, 351, col. 292.

[33] Chamberlain to Ida, 10 September 1939, *The Neville Chamberlain Diary Letters,* 445.

[34] Chamberlain to Ida, 5 November 1939, *Ibid.,* 467.

So Britain was at war to eliminate Hitler, or better still, to have him and his government eliminated by the German people themselves, as was proposed in the propaganda leaflet of 7 September 1939.[35] W.H. Dawson, a specialist in German affairs, had no use for Hitler, but he did take issue with government policy on this crucial point. The German nation, he wrote, "is not even credited with the elementary virtue of patriotism. Hence we see leaflets by the million showered upon the German landscape urging the Germans to disown Hitler and his government, though the least professional of psychologists could have said that the effect must be the precise opposite of that wished." He added that the blockade could only encourage the spirit of anti-British resistance within Germany.[36] Among ordinary Britons, the leaflet-dropping campaign was greeted with considerable scepticism. A Red Cross nurse asked: "Will that have any more effect than if they dropped them on us? We would just burn them. No doubt they will do likewise."[37]

A few British voices were raised in opposition to Chamberlain's tactic of inciting the Germans to overthrow Hitler, but they all came from outside the government. In November 1939 G.D.H. Cole published a pamphlet which read in part: "The German people are not burning to rise and throw off the Nazi yoke. Hitler is not merely a hated tyrant, shielded only by a mercenary bodyguard from the vengeance of his people. His is also, in a sense we must never forget, a national hero."[38] An editorial in a prestigious liberal weekly noted that Hitler's prestige among his people was enhanced by his easy victories over Czechoslovakia and Poland. "About the fighting spirit of the Germans there can be no doubt. . . . There is no reason to believe that German prowess has deteriorated and that the spirit of the German army in the present is at all inferior to the spirit of the German Imperial

---

[35] Cf. *supra*, 117.

[36] *The Times*, 23 January 1940.

[37] Gardiner, *Wartime Britain*, 16.

[38] G.D.H. Cole, *War Aims* (London: The New Statesman and Nation, 1939), 29.

army in the last war." A negotiated peace based on compromise "will not remain a peace and will become a German victory. To win the war it is not enough to 'overthrow Hitlerism.' The war cannot be won unless Germany's armed might is destroyed."[39] This opinion, which was similar to the French position, was not openly shared by most British politicians and journalists during the Phoney War.

A Liberal critic denounced the government's war aims as "dangerously vague,"[40] and from the start, they were meant to be vague. At a cabinet meeting of 9 September 1939, Chamberlain announced that he was "unwilling to attempt to define our war aims, as this might have the effect of tying us down too rigidly and might prejudice an eventual settlement."[41] A peaceful settlement was uppermost in his mind, as in that of Halifax, both of whom hoped for a speedy conclusion to the war. The foreign secretary confided to U. S. Ambassador Kennedy in early October "that if this war continues it will mean Bolshevism all over Europe."[42] His fear of the "red menace" was widely shared. Arthur Rucker, Chamberlain's principal private secretary, expressed the view in October that Communism was a greater threat than Nazism. First, Hitler had to go; then Britain could unite "with a new German government against the common danger."[43] Once it became evident that Hitler was not going to be overthrown, elements of the British establishment proposed dealing with the existing German regime. On 8 January 1940, Chamberlain received a memorandum from ten members of the House of Lords, who warned: "It is now widely held that, in the long view, the weakening or dismemberment of Germany would destroy the natural barrier against the western march of Bolshevism. We would suggest to you that this is

---

[39] "The Situation," *The Nineteenth Century*, February 1940, 131-4.
[40] Andrew McFaydean, "War Aims and Peace Terms," *The Contemporary Review*, November 1939, 524.
[41] Cab. 65/1, W. M. 9 (39), 68.
[42] Kennedy to Hull, 4 October 1939, FRUS, General (1939), 502.
[43] Colville, *The Fringes of Power*, 40-1.

a strong reason in favour of an early peace."[44] In France, Britain's policy was described as "diplomacy under arms."[45]

The government's feeble attempts to explain why Britain was at war left the field open to self-appointed pundits of various persuasions. Among the most prominent was Sir Walter Layton, who, as editor of *The Economist* from 1922 to 1938, had enabled that venerable journal to attain a worldwide circulation. The allies, he explained, had taken up arms because the present German regime had violated all the accepted norms of civilised behaviour. "In the six years of Nazi rule the rights and freedoms of small nations have been ruthlessly trampled under foot in the supposed interest of the German race; the persecution of the Jews has created for other countries a refugee problem on a scale hitherto unknown to history." A Germany that can be trusted will be welcome in the leadership of Europe; but first, it must renounce autarchy. In a postwar settlement (assuming, of course, an allied victory) Germany's position will be one of "equality, not encirclement."[46]

On one issue there was near-total agreement: postwar Germany must be treated by the victorious allies with civility and understanding. The mistakes of the last war would not be repeated, since it was widely held in Britain that Germany had been humiliated and was left to find solace in Nazism. In 1918, President Wilson had imposed on the vanquished foe a republican form of government as a precondition for armistice. The next peace settlement would allow the good German people to choose whatever regime they found suitable. In the words of a leading conservative weekly, "Germany can remain totalitarian, she can return to democracy, she can revert to monarchy; we do not aspire to prescribe her constitution. Nothing will be taken from her. Even the

---

[44] Richard Collier, *1940, the World in Flames* (London: Hamish Hamilton, 1979), 4.

[45] C. Hartley Grattan, "The Struggle for Peace," *Harper's Magazine*, February 1940, 297.

[46] Sir Walter Layton, "Allied War Aims: A Plan for European Peace," *News Chronicle*, 2 November 1939.

German character of Danzig will still be recognized. . . . There is only one condition: Hitlerism, damned irrevocably, must go. . . . Without Hitlerism Germany can have peace and freedom and even friendship."[47] The government had tried to steel the population for a long war, lasting perhaps three years, but privately both Chamberlain and Halifax hoped that it would be over by spring, once the good German people got rid of Hitler. In the event, the Phoney War – Chamberlain's war – *was* over by spring, but not in the way he had anticipated.

As regards Hitler and the German people, the Labour Party, which had rejected Chamberlain's invitation to join a coalition government, was in essential accord with the prime minister. An official statement made public in February 1940 began with the pledge: "Democracy must defeat Hitlerism. Victory for democracy must be achieved either by arms or economic pressure or – better still – by a victory of the German people over the Hitler regime, resulting in the birth of a new Germany." After that, the allies can negotiate peace terms, including freedom for the Poles and Czechs, with a non-Nazi government. "Germany must be invited to co-operate as an *equal*." [emphasis in the original][48] On peace aims (again assuming an allied victory), the Labour Party agreed with Chamberlain, who, in rejecting Hitler's peace offer of 6 October 1939, explained: "It is no part of our policy to exclude from her rightful place in Europe a Germany which will live in amity and confidence with other nations."[49]

For Sir Stafford Cripps, there could be but one war aim: "Our enemy is Hitler and the Nazi regime, and not the German people." Once Hitler is defeated, the British people will be "only too anxious to co-operate with the true German people."[50] In a book explaining Labour's position, Arthur Greenwood referred to his radio address of 3 September 1939, in which he declared: "We do not want to destroy the

---

[47] "Three Years' War - and Why," *The Spectator*, 15 September 1939, 364-5.
[48] *Daily Herald*, 9 February 1940; cf. Ben Pimlott ed., The *Political Diary of Hugh Dalton, 1918-1940, 1945-1960* (London: Jonathan Cape, 1986), 295.
[49] 352 H C Deb, 12 October 1939, col. 566.
[50] "What We Are Fighting For," *Tribune*, 15 September 1939.

German people." Like Halifax, he looked forward to a just peace, in which "force ceases to be an instrument of national policy."[51] Only Dalton, among leading Labour MPs, was at all sceptical. In a diary entry of 18 October, he expressed doubt that "there is always a 'good old Germany' just round the corner." But he preferred not to vent his opinion on that score publicly.[52]

The Labour Party's peace aims, once Hitler was eliminated from power, were not fundamentally different from those of the government. "What it desires," wrote Lord Snell in the spring of 1940, "is that the German nation should once more take her proper place in the councils of Europe . . . as a good European neighbour." As for Czechoslovakia, Attlee did not propose to restore its original boundaries, but insisted on "the withdrawal of [German] troops and police from the territory which even at Munich was held to belong" to that country. This was similar to the liberation "in some form" that Halifax envisaged. In his contribution to Labour's manifesto, Dalton overcame the suspicion of Germany that he had expressed privately. "We do not seek the humiliation or the dismemberment of your country. We wholeheartedly desire to welcome you without delay into the peaceful collaboration of civilised nations." But first, Hitler must go. "If you establish a government sincerely willing that Germany shall be a good neighbour and a good European, then there shall be no humiliation or revenge."[53]

No British commentator was more sympathetic to Germany during the Phoney War period than Arthur Bryant, whose book, *Unfinished Victory*, appeared in January 1940. Bryant was no marginal crank but the chauvinistic writer of popular tub-thumping books depicting Britain's past glories. He was knighted in 1954. Among his most devoted readers were Winston Churchill and Clement Attlee.[54]

---

[51] Arthur Greenwood, *Why We Fight, Labour's Case* (London: Routledge, 1940), 29, 215.

[52] Dalton, *Political Diary*, 307.

[53] C.R. Attlee *et al.*, *Labour's Aims in War and Peace* (London: Lincolns-Prager, n. d. [1940]), 7, 103, 139.

Since he also edited Chamberlain's speeches and had them published,[55] it is a fair assumption that the two men were in agreement on most issues. Bryant claimed that the allied victory of 1918 was unfinished, because "it did not endure," and it did not endure because "an injured and revengeful Germany" was bound to rise from its defeat. He laid particular stress on the alleged violations of German maidens' chastity committed during the allied occupation of the Rhineland by Negro troops from the French Empire. It would seem that being raped by a Negro is worse than being raped by anyone else, but was Britain totally without fault in this regard? Marc Bloch, who was more of a historian than Bryant could ever hope to be, wrote in 1940 that the average British soldier was "a looter and a lecher" (*pillard et paillard*).[56] The undocumented accusations against Negroes appear to be a case of the pot calling the kettle black. Adding to Germany's humiliation, according to Bryant, were the sharp business practices of Jewish "newcomers from the eastern ghettos."[57] So maybe Hitler's anti-Jewish measures were justified after all. Bryant establishes no causal connection between Germany's defeat and the influx of Eastern European Jews, many of whom had entered Germany before 1914. Nor does he cite any evidence that they were more unscrupulous than other businessmen; but of course as a pop historian, he didn't have to. The moral of his pamphlet, in any case, was clear: we mustn't be beastly to the Germans.

Although *Unfinished Victory* was well reviewed in the *Sunday Times* and the *Times Literary Supplement*, it encountered fierce opposition among leading academic historians. A.J.P. Taylor called the author "a Nazi apologist."[58] Hugh Trevor-Roper was "nauseated" by

---

[54] Andrew Roberts, *Eminent Churchillians* (London: Weidenfeld & Nicolson, 1994), 287.

[55] Chamberlain to Hilda, 19 February 1939, *The Neville Chamberlain Diary Letters*, 383.

[56] Marc Bloch, *L'étrange défaite* (Paris: Albin Michel, 1951), 100.

[57] Arthur Bryant, *Unfinished Victory* (London: Macmilllan, 1940), xii-xiii, 121-2, 150-1.

the book. This was not, he wrote, "a plea for political realism but a plea for Nazism itself." Once Nazi sympathisers in Britain began to be interned in May 1940, Bryant quickly bought as many copies of his polemic as he could find, with the result that it has since become a collector's item.[59]

The pundits could foresee a just peace (i.e. one scrupulously fair to the good German people) because they were assured of victory. Only a killjoy like George Bernard Shaw could evoke the possibility that Germany might win. He was not at all sanguine about the outcome. If the allies lost, they would be saddled with a crushing indemnity "and if we win we shall have to bleed ourselves white."[60] Shaw was in the minority, since optimism was the order of the day. Brigadier-General Sir Henry Croft, a Conservative MP, expressed total "confidence in the fact that the French army cannot be destroyed."[61] Sir Henry was in good company, since Winston Churchill and the British Ministry of Information had pronounced the French army to be the finest in the world. In 1938, Churchill described it as "the most perfectly trained and faithful mobile force in Europe."[62] Yet an ordinary Briton might well ask: if the French army is invincible, why do we have to send troops to France?

Norman Angell added to the confusion by noting: "Germany is not attacking us – any more than she was attacking us in 1914." Given the disillusionment in Britain over having to commit a mass army to France in the First World War, this was not likely to arouse much enthusiasm for the Second. Nor could any enthusiasm be expected from his observation: "We entered the war to 'stop Germany.' She has been stopped – by Russia."[63] So what was Britain fighting for? Many, not to

---

[58] Richard Griffiths, *What Did You Do During the War? The Last Throes of the British pro-Nazi Right, 1940-1945* (London: Routledge, 2017), 41.

[59] Roberts, *Eminent Churchillians*, 314-15.

[60] G. Bernard Shaw, "Peace Aims," *The New Statesman and Nation*, 18 November 1939, 711-12.

[61] 355 H C Deb, 30 November 30, 1939, col. 336.

[62] Liddell Hart, "The Military Strategist," Taylor ed., *Churchill Revised*, 206.

say most, British subjects would have been at a loss to answer that question. George Buchanan, an independent Labour MP from Scotland, reported to the House of Commons that, having met with his constituents on a weekly basis, "I cannot find this great unanimous desire for the war. Frankly speaking, I find the reverse. . . . In 1914 I never saw anything like the hostility to the war that I find today." The only way out, he believed, was a negotiated peace – and soon. "You say: 'We cannot negotiate with Hitler.' With whom can you negotiate? Suppose that he is shot to-morrow and is dead; is there any guarantee that the next man is any better than Hitler?" Buchanan deftly refuted the official argument that Britain was at war with Hitler and not the German people. "I do not believe that Hitler, even if he were a greater man than he is, could to-morrow arm millions of people in Germany and lead them into war unless they want to go."[64]

Lloyd George did not propose direct negotiations with Hitler, but rather an international conference which would include the three nominal belligerents, plus Italy, the Soviet Union and the United States. "Phrases about the overthrow of Hitlerism are not enough. What kind of peace settlement have we in mind?"[65] In the fall of 1939, British parliamentarians all received an appeal from an *ad hoc* association calling itself The National Peace Council, which included the chief rabbi and Vera Brittain, a leading pacifist, whose recollections of the First World War, *Testament of Youth*, became a best seller throughout the 1930s. It called on the government, after consultation with the French government, to declare its terms of peace publicly and make them known in Germany.[66] The inclusion of France in such deliberations was a rarity at the time. Most proposals from British pacifists ignored France altogether. They wanted Britain to conclude an immediate settlement with the Nazi regime. That this would leave

---

[63] Angell, *For What Do We Fight?*, 39, 260.
[64] 351 H C Deb., 3 October 1939, cols. 1885-1888.
[65] *Manchester Guardian*, 23 October 1939.
[66] FO 371/22947 17569.

France to face Germany alone (as was largely the case after Dunkirk) apparently never occurred to them.

Throughout much of the Phoney War, British agents made informal contacts with German aristocrats, such as Von Papen and Prince Max von Hohenlohe, who were known to oppose Hitler, in the hope of replacing him and arriving at a negotiated settlement. "It seems," wrote Colville on 29 October, "that the upper classes and high military authorities in Germany are anxious to avoid the outbreak of a real war, since they believe that Bolshevism in Germany would be the final and inevitable outcome." (It was, at least in the Soviet zone.) Prince Max stipulated that Britain must state its war aims in such a way as to reassure the German people that it did not plan to partition or humiliate their country. The Foreign Office recognized that the French had to be consulted first. Chamberlain, however, was ready to enter into negotiations immediately as long as Hitler was eliminated from power. "In return for a change of regime (or at least a modification), restoration of frontiers and disarmament," wrote Colville, "the P. M. would be prepared to agree to economic assistance for Germany, to no demand for reparations, and to colonial discussions."[67]

France, having contributed nearly all the ground forces to the allied cause in 1939, still had an important say in the matter. From the start, French war aims were markedly different from those of Britain. In a note of 8 September to the war committee of the French cabinet, Gamelin explained that the destruction of the Nazi regime was only a part of the war effort. "We must destroy utterly Germany's power to set Europe ablaze periodically."[68] Comments in the press reflected this view. The French, with few exceptions (chiefly intellectuals), knew why they were at war: it was to defeat Germany, not just Hitler.[69] They did not need treatises, such as those published in Britain, explaining their country's position. Paul Bastid, a French parliamentarian and

---

[67] Colville, *The Fringes of Power*, 45.
[68] France, Fondation Nationale des Sciences Politiques, fonds Daladier, 3 DA 1 Dr 1.
[69] Charpentier, *La Drôle de Guerre des intellectuels français*, 87-94.

former minister of commerce in the government of Léon Blum, was highly sceptical of British propaganda leaflets urging the German people to overthrow their government. Bastid, who was later to serve under de Gaulle in the National Resistance Council, wrote: "If we think that everything will be settled by getting rid of Hitler, we are in for some very cruel disappointments. The present policies of Germany do not emanate from one man. Even if he were to go, the entire structure of the Reich would remain. We cannot afford the luxury of a war in every generation. The danger we face is constant and cannot be conjured away by humanitarian homilies."[70]

Daladier, who had deferred to his ally by dismissing Bonnet as foreign minister, now asked Ambassador Corbin early in October to summarize British war aims. In his reply, Corbin did not mince words. British policy, he wrote, was clear enough: "A fight to the finish against Hitlerism; peace and sympathy for the good German people." Such war aims, he added, were narrow and essentially negative. "I hardly need emphasize the dangers of such a program. . . . It is analogous to the spirit of the Anglo-Saxon negotiators at Versailles, from which arose the many misunderstandings that have since poisoned Anglo-French relations." The British people, he added, were confused by their government's moralizing. They needed some clear-cut reason for going to war.[71]

To avoid further misunderstandings, Daladier sent an aide-mémoire on 23 October to the Foreign Office explaining France's position. "The government of the Republic believes that the essential war aim should be . . . to make it impossible for Germany once again to imperil the peace of Europe. A change of government in Berlin will not suffice. . . . The security of France, and with it that of Great Britain and all of Europe, can no longer depend on German good will. . . . Only effective material guarantees can prevent a recrudescence of German imperialism." It may be useful, for propaganda purposes, to concentrate on Hitler, but that should not prevent the two allied

---

[70] Paul Bastid, "La propagande par tracts," *La Dépêche*, 14 September 1939.
[71] Corbin to Daladier, 5 October 1939, fonds Daladier, 3 DA 2 Dr 3 sdra.

governments to examine in secret the safeguards that, one day, will be necessary to impose on the enemy.[72]

Accordingly, the Foreign Office sent a telegram the following day to the governments of Canada, Australia, New Zealand and South Africa, informing them of the French position, with which it obviously disagreed. "We must be careful in presenting our objectives lest we reunite [sic] the Germans behind Hitler by threatening the unity or integrity of the Reich or by calling in question the very existence of the regime."[73] The fear of reuniting the Germans behind Hitler reveals a remarkable ignorance among British politicians of the true situation in Germany. Thanks to an easy victory over Poland, the Nazi regime was more popular than ever among Hitler's subjects.[74]

The Australian government, in its reply of 14 November, expressed total agreement with the British position regarding Germany. "We are profoundly apprehensive," wrote Prime Minister Menzies, "of any artificial attempt to disrupt German unity, for we feel that such a suggestion would not only have the present effect of rallying German people behind Hitler but would have the ultimate effect of laying the foundations for a future nationalistic movement of an aggressive kind which would inevitably produce another war."[75] His views reflected the general consensus in Britain itself. The prestigious *Economist* offered only two possibilities of solving "the German problem," as it was called. "One is to parcel Germany into a number of small states, permanently garrisoned by and subjected to the allies. The other is to treat Germany purged of the Nazis as an equal. The Versailles policy of humiliating and penalizing Germany without successfully holding her down runs the maximum risk of provoking a war every generation." The journal foresaw a generous peace settlement with the vanquished foe: Austria would remain in the Reich, and the allies would pay for the reconstruction of Warsaw. As for disarmament, "Germany must not

---

[72] FO 371/22946, 17569.
[73] FO 800/325 XC/A17606.
[74] Tooze, *The Wages of Destruction*, 327.
[75] FO 800/325, XC/A17606.

again be expected to remain indefinitely in a state of permanent inequality."[76]

In Ottawa, the reaction to French war aims was even sharper. Oscar D. Skelton, Canada's permanent undersecretary for External Affairs, wrote that "we cannot permit France to fill up a blank cheque." As usual, the treaty of Versailles was trotted out for more abuse. "Evidently those now in authority in France have learned nothing and forgotten everything. They apparently desire to revive the Versailles tactics in the most stringent form."[77] Halifax recognized that there were "fundamental differences of opinion" between Britain and France on this vital question, but he hoped that "we may gradually (and privately) be able to wean the French from their worst fallacies."[78]

On this, as on other matters concerning the war, the foreign secretary was clearly over-confident. He had received a dispatch late in October from Sir Eric Phipps, the British ambassador to France, who was about to retire after 40 years of public service. Phipps passed on to his chief reports from British consular offices throughout France that "Frenchmen of every political colour" made no distinction between Hitler and the German people. British refusal to accept French war aims could not only cause "a rift between our two countries . . . but it might lead to a lowering of French moral[e]" particularly among the troops. Many French people, he noted, were "suspicious of British Policy." They had not forgotten that British and American loans during the inter-war period allowed Germany to modernize and expand its industrial base, including the arms industry. They also recall "misplaced British fears after the war of French 'hegemony.' I could quote other instances but I will not weary Your Lordship." In conclusion, Phipps warned that "there are already signs, which it would be imprudent to ignore, that many of them doubt whether Great Britain will do what is necessary to win a lasting peace."[79]

---

[76] "War Aims," *The Economist*, 21 October 1939, 77-8.
[77] Skelton to King, 25 October 1939, Canada, *Documents on Canadian External Relations, 1939-1941*, I, part 3, 185.
[78] Halifax to Lothian, 21 November 1939, FO 800/311 XCA 1987.

Sir Ronald Hugh Campbell, who succeeded Phipps as British ambassador, confirmed his predecessor's findings. The British consul in Strasbourg, he noted, reported that "what are considered to be the generous illusions of Great Britain about Germany continue to be the subject of persistent but never unfriendly comment in the local press. . . ." Apart from some intellectuals, the general consensus in France was that Germany must be divided into its component parts. When British correspondents visited French army headquarters, General Prételat, who commanded one army group at the front, repeated this aim, saying: "I speak not only for the whole of the army but for the whole of France."[80] A delegation of British MPs visiting Paris was told by their French counterparts that, as part of eventual peace terms, France would demand the left bank of the Rhine.[81]

The French aide-mémoire elicited a diplomatically worded draft reply which Halifax submitted to the cabinet in December. Britain and France, it read, "must, unless a German government can be found which is willing and able voluntarily to accept their terms, secure the defeat of Germany. . . ." The British government recognized, in principle, that certain material guarantees would be necessary to forestall further German aggression, but these "may perhaps be left for further consideration." As for the eventual dismemberment of Germany, Halifax repeated that any such suggestion "would have the immediate effect of rallying the German people behind their present leaders."[82] Despite the conciliatory tone of the document, it is evident that the Foreign Office had not modified its policy regarding war aims. In the mistaken belief that the German people were not already united behind Hitler and that a more compliant government could somehow be found in Berlin, it refused to give serious consideration to France's need for safeguards against future German aggression.

---

[79] Phipps to Halifax, 23 October 1939, FO 371/22946 17569.
[80] Campbell to Halifax, 6 November, 1939, FO 371/226946 1769.
[81] Hanighen, "How France is Taking the War," 256.
[82] FO 371/22947 1759.

Distrust of Britain was widespread in France during the Phoney War period, and even more so thereafter. French literary critic Victor Giraud reproached successive British governments for having dissipated the fruits of victory in 1918. They "preached and practised unilateral disarmament, refused to accompany us in the Ruhr, and accepted with tranquil serenity successive violations of the Versailles treaty."[83] Giraud, who had written a Franco-centric history of the First World War, may be dismissed as an extreme chauvinist, but his views were largely shared by Théodore Ruyssen, the pacifist former secretary-general of the International Union of Associations for the League of Nations. Ruyssen vigorously defended the treaty of Versailles, which he considered "a solid and well balanced construction. . . . What led to the present crisis was not the generally humane and moderate clauses of the Versailles treaty, but the hesitant and incoherent postwar policies of the allies." In a future settlement, "certain aspects of the Versailles treaty should be maintained and pursued with increased vigour." He ridiculed "the sheer blindness of the British government, which feared the restoration of German power far less than the prestige of its ally, France."[84]

As the Phoney War dragged on, some appreciation of the French position began to appear among the more educated elements of British society. The *Economist*, which had previously disparaged the Versailles treaty, admitted that "there is probably more straight thinking [in France] than in this country, perhaps because the war is physically nearer to the French, perhaps because they have a shaper memory than we of the sacrifices that were necessary in 1914-1918." A peace settlement "must include full material guarantees of French immunity from German aggression . . . if the French are to consider their sacrifices fully justified."[85] The conservative *Spectator* explained that,

---

[83] Victor Giraud, "Devant l'éternelle Allemagne," *Revue des Deux Mondes*, November-December 1939, 59.

[84] Théodore Ruyssen, "Pour la reconstruction de la Paix: Quelques écueils à éviter," *La Grande Revue*, September-December 1939, 362-3.

[85] "War Aims," *The Economist*, 3 February 1940, 191.

in the eyes of the French, "our great fault . . . is that we do not realize with sufficient clarity that war is an immensely serious thing. We persist in imagining that war is peace in a more inconvenient form."[86]

Even more supportive of the French position (and critical of the British) was Labour MP R.H.S. Crossman, who wrote: "The French, with justification, regard the Left and Right in this country as in sentiment isolationist." He recalled that "whereas the French wanted collective security, the British Left seemed content with a collective pacifism." So the French were right to say to their ally, in effect: "If you are going to pull out once again and sit moralising on your island, we shall be forced to ignore your protests and knock Germany into a shape from which it will take generations to recover." The least that Britain could do at this stage would be to convince the French that "we mean business."[87]

As subsequent events were to show, France alone was in no position to "knock Germany into shape." Germany was finally knocked into shape by the Soviet Union, with help from the United States, Britain and Canada. A renascent French army also contributed to the victory. After surrendering unconditionally to the allies, the prostrate Reich was divided into four zones of occupation, shorn of its eastern provinces and dotted with foreign garrisons that were to remain in place for nearly half a century. Denis Saurat, professor of French at King's College, Oxford, explained to British readers in the spring of 1940 that his compatriots sought "complete victory," followed by "a severe but benevolent military occupation lasting long enough to convince the German masses that they have been misled by their leaders."[88] This is in fact what finally happened, thus vindicating France's war aims – but only after four years of Nazi occupation. France in 1940 lacked the military strength to achieve its goal.

---

[86] *The Spectator*, 22 March 1940, 15.

[87] R.H.S. Crossman, "British War Aims and French Security," *The New Statesman and Nation*, 20 January 1940, 65-6.

[88] Denis Saurat, "French Aims," *The Fortnightly Review*, April 1940, 357-9.

Harold Nicolson recognized that the French approached the question of war aims with a greater sense of realism than the British. "I imagine that, at the end of this war, the British people will want to obtain certain material guarantees for the future security of the West." His comments were published in a French periodical and remained unknown to British readers. Nicolson asked the French to be patient with the British in their moralistic attitude. He hoped that his compatriots would eventually show more understanding of the French position, so that the two peoples might find a common ground on war and peace aims.[89] Nicolson made no such exhortations in a British journal. His only published statement on the origins of the war in English blamed Raymond Poincaré for the rise of Hitler.

The British people did in fact come around to the French position, on their own and only after having to fight Germany in a real war. Gallup polls of September 1939 revealed that 90 percent believed that the enemy was Hitler and not the German people; by 1945, the reverse was true. In surveys taken by Mass Observation at the war's end, a third of the respondents proposed imposing severe reparation payments on the vanquished foe. Another third wanted to see Germany rendered impotent, totally incapable of making war again – the preferred method being to dismantle the Reich into its individual component states.[90]

In March 1940, Dalton published a short book in which he cast doubt on the common theme in Britain that security for France must be reconciled with equality for Germany. He tried to dispel the fear of France hegemony, a fear often expressed by British politicians during the inter-war years. "Nowadays, I believe, the French claim to security is sincere and final. France has outgrown aggression. She demands only, but very firmly, that she shall not be perpetually menaced from beyond her eastern frontier." The German claim to equality, on the

---

[89] Harold Nicolson, "Divergences possibles entre les buts de guerre entre la France et l'Angleterre," *Les Nouveaux Cahiers*, 1 February 1940, 3.
[90] Richard Weight, *Patriots: National Identity in Britain, 1940-2000* (London: Macmillan, 2002), 104.

other hand, "only cloaked the will to mastery." Equality for Germany can be achieved "only within a political order guaranteeing general security."[91] Such a political order was created after the war as the North Atlantic Treaty Organization, whose first secretary-general, Lord Ismay, stated privately that its purpose was to "keep the Soviet Union out, the Americans in, and the Germans down."[92]

Chamberlain tried to paper over the differences with France in a speech on peace aims (not war aims), which he delivered in Birmingham on 24 February 1940.[93] The two allies, he assured his audience, enjoy "complete identity of purpose." They "think and act as one." The "great and growing" British Expeditionary Force "keeps watch and ward over the western front side by side with the magnificent soldiers of France." Other than independence for the Poles and Czechs, however, he made no concrete proposals. There must be an end to militarism; and for this, the present German government cannot be trusted. "It is therefore for Germany to take the next step and show us that she has once and for all abandoned the thesis that might is right." Only then can a lasting peace be established.

Reconciliation between Britain and France was the object of a joint declaration signed on 28 March that neither will conclude a separate peace with Germany. The two allies, it read, "undertake not to discuss peace terms before reaching complete agreement on the conditions necessary to ensure to each of them an effective and lasting guarantee of their security." Of course, this presupposes that they will both be victorious. In presenting the agreement to Parliament, Chamberlain emphasized "any proposals for peace, whatever their source, would not even be discussed before this country and France had reached full agreement on the requirements for a true peace safeguarding their own security and that of other free nations in

---

[91] Hugh Dalton, *Hitler's War, Before and After* (London: Penguin, 1940), 143-5.
[92] http://www.nato.int/cps/us/natohq/declassified_137930.htm
[93] *Britain's Peace Aims* (pamphlet),
https://utdr.utoledo.edu/islandora/object/utoledo.5348.

Europe."[94] In effect, the prime minister acknowledged tacitly that they had not yet reached full agreement.

The British government's official deference toward France was not reflected in public discourse. As historian H.A.L. Fisher noted, "scheme after scheme is put out in this country, one more charming, attractive and ingenious than the other, but having all this common feature that they leave France out of account."[95] A certain neglect of France is perceptible in contemporary British historiography. In the words of Donald Cameron Watt, the Second World War "was in the beginning a war between the British and German peoples."[96] Never mind that the French army was fully mobilized from September 1939 until its defeat in June 1940. The French people, who had to endure serious privations throughout the Phoney War, simply do not enter the picture. "The Third Republic," he writes in an afterthought, "was in its penultimate stage of decay" and therefore does not merit our attention.[97] Professor Watt exaggerates. In the crucial arms sector, the Third Republic proved to be remarkably resilient. The French military budget, as a percentage of national revenue, exceeded that of Britain throughout the 1930s. The largest share went to the navy, the fourth most important in the world. In 1938, French military shipyards were the *third* most active, surpassing those of Japan.[98] Besides, if the Third Republic was in its death throes, as he claims, did it make any sense for Britain to threaten Germany with war and then drag France into it? *Gouverner, c'est prévoir.*

---

[94] 359 H C Deb, 2 April 1940, cols. 40-1.

[95] H.A.L. Fisher, "Beyond the War," *The Fortnightly*, February 1940, 119. Fisher himself was a victim of the Phoney War. In April 1940, he was run over by a bus while crossing the street at night during the blackout.

[96] Donald Cameron Watt, *How War Came: The Immediate Origins of the Second World War, 1938-1939* (New York: Pantheon Books, 1989), 385.

[97] *Ibid*, 617.

[98] Robert Frankenstein, *Le prix du réarmement français, 1935-1939* (Paris: Publications de la Sorbonne, 1982), 35, 223 *et passim*.

No account of France was taken at a peace rally held in Kingsway Hall, London, on 3 April 1940. It was presided over by Lord Tavistock, an open admirer of Hitler and his system, who shared the platform with John McGovern, an Independent Labour MP from Scotland. McGovern referred to the Nazi social program as "miles ahead of ours." The meeting, which bore the slogan "Peace is possible now," was held in connection with an organisation which called itself The British Council for Christian Settlement in Europe. Some two thousand people attended. Lord Tavistock announced that he had recently visited the German legation in Dublin and was told that Hitler was ready to re-establish Poland and a Czech state and to help the Jews attain a national home. A woman in the audience asked, "How does it happen that Hitler, who destroyed Poland and Czechoslovakia and persecuted the Jews, has changed his mind at your request?" Lord Tavistock replied that the Poles and Czechs had provoked Germany into attacking them (!), but that Hitler was willing to offer generous terms. Despite a few critical questions, those in attendance seemed generally sympathetic to this prospect.[99]

British neglect, not to say dismissal, of France during the Phoney War period stems in part from a failure to understand why France was at war. To read some comments, one might think that the French wanted nothing better than to assert their hegemony over Europe as in the time of Louis XIV. Most misunderstood was the wartime watchword in France, *"Il faut en finir."* (Let's get it over with.) A reporter for the *Times* who visited France early in March 1940 to assess the feelings of its people, explained what it meant. He interviewed, among others, Madame Leroy, the owner of a small farm. Her husband had been killed in the First World War, and now her son was called up. Both she and the French leaders who were also interviewed agreed on one thing: France cannot endure a war at every generation. Here, then, was the true meaning of *"Il faut en finir."*[100]

---

[99] *Manchester Guardian*, 4 April 1940.
[100] *The Times*, 5 March 1940.

Not to understand the French attitude was, for the British public, bad enough; not to understand Britain's involvement was worse. "After six months, the people of this country are puzzled," wrote *The Economist* in March. They "have ceased to believe, not in the cause for which we are fighting, but in the war itself." There was "some sense of frustration," but no sense of defeat. "Only a negligible few doubt that an allied victory is assured."[101] Optimism was the order of the day, at least among the British elite. Even Harold Nicolson, who had expressed doubts about the war in September, confided to his diary in March, "Three things are now apparent: (1) The Germans dare not attack the Maginot Line, (2) We have won the war at sea, (3) In the air our pilots are superior to the German pilots."[102]

In his weekly newsletter of early April, Commander Stephen King-Hall, MP, exuded such confidence in the final outcome that he sent a copy to the prime minister. "We are absolutely secure against a *Blitzkrieg*," he wrote. "Behind our [*sic*] Maginot Line, behind the defences of our sea power and the potential striking power of the air force, and keeping the blockade in being, we should organise our resources so as to live as full a life, as civilised a life as possible." In an accompanying letter, King-Hall informed Chamberlain that this particular issue was banned in France because it postulated a conflict lasting three years. The French government did not believe that the public could endure the war of waiting for another winter.[103] Paul Reynaud, who by then had replaced Daladier as premier, was particularly insistent that the war be brought to a speedy (and presumably successful) conclusion.[104]

For all his usual optimism, Chamberlain, in a letter to his sister a week before real fighting began in Norway, did evoke the possibility that Hitler might win. "To try the offensive [in the west] is to gamble

---

[101] "War of Nerves," *The Economist*, 16 March 1940, 454.

[102] Nicolson, *Diaries and Letters*, II, 64

[103] Stephen King-Hall, "On Winning the War," 5 April 1940. Prem 1/436 xc/A17612.

[104] Cf. *infra*, 186, 190.

on a single throw. If he succeeds, well & good; he has won the war. But if he doesn't succeed, he has lost it, for he will never have another chance as good."[105] Well and good? One can only marvel at Chamberlain's insouciance. Hitler did gamble on a single throw; and he won the Phoney War, as Chamberlain had speculated he might. With Bohemia and Moravia now firmly annexed to the Reich, it would soon be the turn of Western, democratic Europe to experience Nazi tyranny.

British strategists did not anticipate a major land war on the European continent in the near future. Oliver Stanley, who had replaced Hore-Belisha as war secretary, visited France in February 1940 and informed General Brooke that he was "very doubtful whether the Germans would attack" in the west that year.[106] On 4 May, the cabinet received a report from the chiefs of staff as to how Germany might unleash a real war against the allies. It began: "The most likely method by which she might attempt to achieve this object is by a major offensive against Great Britain" – presumably by sea and air. But this, they added, was a mere "supposition," since "Germany is not seeking a very rapid decision." The "104 allied divisions" in France (of which 10 were British) made that country "reasonably secure against land attack."[107]

So Britain presumably did not have to raise a mass army anytime soon. The chiefs made it quite clear that Churchill's projected 55 British divisions, which were intended primarily to improve French morale, could wait. In the spring of 1940, they existed only in his imagination. Yet a French strategic survey, presented to the Allied Military Committee on 16 April, noted that "the Reich appears to have suffered little wear and tear during the first six months of war, and that mainly as a result of the allied blockade. Meanwhile, it has profited

---

[105] Chamberlain to Ida, 30 March 1940, *The Neville Chamberlain Diary Letters*, 514.

[106] Edward Smalley, *The British Expeditionary Force, 1939-40* (London: Palgrave Macmillan, 2015), 25.

[107] Esnouf, "British Government War Aims," 182-3.

from the interval to perfect the degree of equipment of its land and air forces, to increase officer strength and complete the training of its troops, and to add further divisions to those already in the field."[108] Throughout the Phoney War period, and especially since November 1939, British strategists tended to minimize the importance of the French front. And if perchance they were mistaken and Hitler did try the offensive, the French army would surely hold, would it not?

In a dispatch of April 1938, Ambassador Corbin wrote that "certain [British] political figures, in particular Mr. Winston Churchill, believe that the French army, being the only force capable of stopping a German advance on the continent, is the true army of Great Britain."[109] Churchill had asserted in Parliament that Anglo-French relations were "founded upon the power of the French army and the power of the British fleet."[110] From this logic, it followed that Britain could avoid the bloodletting of 1914-1918. Both Chamberlain and Churchill based their strategy on the premise that Hitler's war machine could not possibly defeat "the magnificent soldiers of France," protected by their supposedly impregnable fortifications. Churchill visited the Maginot Line in August 1939 and pronounced it a guarantee of "absolute security." He was especially impressed by "the alert and intelligent appearance of the French soldiers."[111] Corbin wrote to Daladier in October that the British displayed "such confidence in the French army that they are tempted to consider their military contribution as [merely] a token of solidarity instead of as a vital necessity."[112] Less than a week after the chiefs of staff presented their report, the facile assumptions underlying British war policy would be put to the test.

---

[108] Murray, "The Strategy of the 'Phoney War': a Re-evaluation," 16

[109] Corbin to Paul-Boncour, 7 April 1938, DDF, 2nd series, IX, 256.

[110] 330 H C Deb., 21 December 1937, col. 1833.

[111] John Lukacs, *The Duel, 10 May – 31 July 1940: The Eighty-Day Struggle Between Churchill and Hitler* (New York: Ticknor & Fields, 1991), 63.

[112] Martin S. Alexander "'Fighting to the last Frenchman'?, Reflections on the BEF Deployment to France and the Strains in the Franco-British Alliance," *Historical Reflections/Réflexions Historiques*, Winter 1996, 254

6 Dénouement, 1940

The 20 February 1939 issue of *Life*, the popular illustrated weekly, bore on its front cover a photograph of General Maurice Gamelin, the French army chief of staff, with a typically American title: "France's No. 1 Soldier." A brief editorial explained his importance and that of his army. "Whether war comes in Europe will depend in large part on whether Germany thinks she can defeat France. The French army is smaller than the German but better trained and better officered, and many experts still rate it invincible in defense. . . . Because the peace of the world may hang on the French army and its commander, LIFE herewith presents an estimate of both by the greatest living journalist of military strategy, Captain B.H. Liddell Hart." Two years earlier, this renowned specialist in the art of war had pronounced the French army to be "almost the most backward in ideas among the armies of the great powers."[1] To his American readers he was more reassuring.

Liddell Hart was no Pollyanna. He recognized that the loss to France and Britain of 34 Czechoslovak divisions (whose number he put at 40) had modified the military balance in favour of Germany. France, moreover, had to prepare for a war on two, and possibly three, fronts – against Germany, Italy, and even Spain, where Franco's troops had recently defeated the republican army, whereas "Germany is free to throw her whole weight against France." The French air force and aircraft industry, formerly the finest in the world, were by 1939 in a sorry state. Yet he maintained a guarded optimism. On land, he asserted, the defence has definite advantages, thanks in large measure to the Maginot Line. He was confident that the many veterans in the French army would show greater staying power than the raw German

---

[1] B. H. Liddell Hart, *Europe in Arms* (London: Faber & Faber, 1937), 42.

recruits facing them. As defenders of their own soil, they will surely be more motivated than any invading force. (In the event, which Liddell Hart could not possibly foresee, the Germans were to acquire combat experience in Poland. By 1940, they were no longer raw recruits.) Photographs accompanying the text showed cadets at the French military academy of Saint Cyr – some at drill, others fencing – with a caption explaining that they "will uphold the French army's reputation for having the best-trained officers in the world."[2]

Such a rose-coloured vision reflected not only the views of Henry R. Luce, the publisher of *Life*, but also the position of the British government. Inasmuch as the French army was deemed to be "invincible" in defence, Britain could pursue a policy dear to both Liddell Hart and Neville Chamberlain, that of "limited liability," which left the lion's share of the fighting on land to France. Americans could bask in their comfortable isolation, secure in the belief that the French army, virtually unaided, would preserve world peace. During the First World War, the U. S. Army had few weapons of its own, other than rifles and some machine guns. Most of its artillery, especially the famous 75-millimetre field piece, and combat aircraft, such as the Spad 13 fighter, had to be procured from France. The mainstay of the American tank corps in 1918 was the Renault FT 17. Twenty years later, most Americans tended to assume that French weaponry, and by extension the French army itself, were still first-rate.

The French government was more circumspect. Unlike Chamberlain, who prided himself on having brought peace to Europe, Daladier knew that France had to prepare for war. French strategy after Munich, like that of Britain, was based on the postulate of a long war, in which the allies would eventually gain the upper hand thanks to their superior resources. French military intelligence reasoned that their army did not have to conquer Germany – a task for which it was totally unsuited – but simply deny the enemy a quick victory. Underlying the long-war strategy were three tacit assumptions: first, that there would be, from the very start, some real fighting in the west and that the

---

[2] "Gamelin," *Life*, 20 February 1939, 56-63.

174

French army would hold; second, that France would receive tangible military and economic assistance from Britain; and third, that the Soviet Union could be counted upon to provide a second front in Poland. In the best-case scenario, an alliance between France and Russia might deter Hitler and make war unnecessary.[3]

When news of the impending Nazi-Soviet pact reached Paris late in the afternoon of 22 August, Daladier realized that war with Germany was imminent and that France would have to bear the brunt of the fighting on land. The Polish army, he explained to U. S. Ambassador Bullitt, could not hold out for more than two months. (In fact, it was crushed in three weeks.) Britain would not be able to muster a serious army for two years. "Furthermore," Bullitt reported, "he believed that as soon as England and France should become engaged in Europe, Japan would begin taking over French, British and Dutch possessions in the Pacific. . . . He felt that the Poles had been guilty of criminal folly in not replying in the affirmative to the Russians' proposal for active assistance to Poland." Daladier was loath to sacrifice the lives of able-bodied Frenchmen in a war "the outcome of which was, to say the least, doubtful;" but what could he do? To renege on France's commitments to Poland would be a blow to French public opinion and would encourage further German aggression.

Bullitt then spoke with Alexis Léger, who "said that a war now would begin at an exceedingly bad moment for France and England." He too blamed the Poles for having rejected the Soviet Union's offer of military assistance. "Throughout our conversation," Bullitt wrote, "politicians kept calling him on the telephone urging that it would be folly to go to war in support of Poland in view of the agreement between the Soviet Union and Germany." Léger replied that France had to fight lest all of Eastern Europe and the Balkans fall into Hitler's hands. To Bullitt he confided: "It was exceedingly doubtful, to put it mildly, that France and England would be able to win the war."[4]

---

[3] Peter Jackson, *France and the Nazi Menace: Intelligence and Policy Making, 1933-1939* (Oxford: Oxford University Press, 2000, 342, 371.
[4] Bullitt to Hull, 22 August 1939, FRUS, I (1939), 301-4.

Several French generals shared this view,[5] and for good reason. General Alphonse Georges, commander of the north-eastern front and perhaps the ablest military strategist in France, recognized in August 1939 that Germany had benefitted most from the cold peace that followed Munich. Among other advantages, it had acquired the Czechoslovak arms industry. Even Churchill, who often sang the praises of the French army, admitted that German rearmament had proceeded faster during this period than that of France or Britain.[6]

Once war was declared, the French government issued the usual public exhortations designed to sustain civilian morale. In a radio address of 10 September, Finance Minister Paul Reynaud made the cheery prediction: "We will win because we are the strongest." (*Nous vaincrons parce que nous sommes les plus forts.*) A poster with this message, urging French citizens to buy war bonds, soon appeared throughout the country. In the background was a Mercator projection map of the world, highlighting the British and French empires, whose area was considerably larger than that of greater Germany. Although such propaganda was basically no different from the British, Reynaud was later taken to task for making such a glib statement; but he defended himself, noting that no government would ever declare: "We will be defeated because we are the weakest."[7]

The Nazi-Soviet pact had effectively undermined the western allies' initial strategy of a prolonged stalemate on land coupled with a naval blockade capable of slowly strangling Germany.[8] Both Chamberlain and his military advisers remained convinced nonetheless

---

[5] Jean-Louis Crémieux-Brilhac, *Les Français de l'an 40*, I: *La guerre oui ou non* (Paris: Gallimard, 1990), 115-16.

[6] Major-General Sir Edward Spears, *Assignment to Catastrophe* (London: Heinemann, 1954), I, 15-17.

[7] Paul Reynaud, *Au cœur de la mêlée, 1930-1945* (Paris: Flammarion, 1951), 342-3.

[8] Michael Jabara Carley, "'A Situation of Delicacy and Danger,' Anglo-Soviet Relations, August 1939 – March 1940," *Central European History*, July 1999, 176

that Britain and France would eventually prevail thanks to the superior economic resources of their respective empires.[9] He remained wedded to the long-war strategy longer than most, but had to give it up for political reasons. Despite the best efforts of his government in preparing its citizens for a three-year war, it was apparent after a few weeks that the British public had already had its fill. By early October, 1939, Chamberlain expressed confidence privately that the allies would be victorious in the spring of 1940.[10] Halifax feared that a long war would allow Bolshevism to dominate Europe.[11]

Daladier recognized early on that the long-war strategy had little chance of success. In his first wartime cabinet meeting on 9 September, he announced a fundamental change: France must "make war and win with as few losses as possible and as quickly as possible."[12] Whether he realized it or not, these two imperatives were contradictory. To keep casualties to a minimum, France could not take the initiative, but had to wait for the 32 divisions promised by Britain. Daladier soon realized that these were not forthcoming. To General Armengaud he commented on 3 October: "The English, behind the Channel, have the advantage of conserving their strength . . . to wait for the Americans and perhaps the Russians. But we risk becoming, after the Czechs and the Poles, the prey of the Reich." Unlike Chamberlain, he had no illusions about Germany's military might. "The German war instrument is very strong, as recent events have shown. It is more adept at manoeuvre than ours. Can our army withstand its assault?"[13] On 14 October, he lamented: "France is waging the war alone." He briefly toyed with the idea of making a separate peace with Hitler over the heads of the British. "In any case, I will not wait until two million

---

[9] Joe Maiolo, "'To Gamble on a Single Throw': Neville Chamberlain and the Strategy of the Phoney War," *Britain in Global Politics*, I, 221.

[10] Chamberlain to Ida, 8 October 1939, *The Neville Chamberlain Diary Letters*, 456.

[11] Cf. *supra*, 152.

[12] Jackson, *France and the Nazi Menace*, 387.

[13] Crémieux-Brilhac, *La guerre oui ou non*, 140-1.

French soldiers are killed before ending the conflict. Besides, even if the war continued without fighting (*sous une forme blanche*), the prolongation would be a disaster for the country."[14] His successor, Paul Reynaud, also sought a quick end to the conflict; he knew that France could not sustain a long war.

Daladier had only himself to blame if France was obliged to wage war alone. He had struck a bad bargain at Munich, sacrificing Czechoslovakia, a loyal ally with a modern, well-equipped army, in order to preserve an embryonic entente with Britain, a traditional rival without a credible land force. Now he found his country tied to a power that was determined not to repeat the experience of 1914-1918, when it had been totally committed to an alliance with France, and whose current engagement on the European continent was one of "limited liability." From London Ambassador Corbin presented him with a grim assessment of Britain's war policy. In a dispatch dated 25 September, he wrote: "Churchill is the most open-minded and imaginative of British ministers . . . but even he has trouble grasping that however effective the blockade, the war's final decision will always depend on armies on the ground . . . and I hardly need add that Churchill's colleagues are even more inclined to relegate land operations to secondary importance, relying on the Maginot Line's impregnable solidity."[15]

Whatever economic potential the allies may have had, their finances were weaker than in 1914 and grossly inadequate for waging a long war. "In terms of finance," writes a Canadian historian, "time was more an enemy than a friend to Britain."[16] French government finances were even more fragile. The human and material losses of the First World War, inter-allied war debts and inadequate reparations payments left France deeply in debt by 1939. Some British ministers, such as Halifax, could look forward eventually to financial assistance from the

---

[14] Paul de Villelume, *Journal d'une défaite, 26 août 1939-16 juin 1940* (Paris: Fayard, 1970), 65.
[15] Alexander, "'Fighting to the Last Frenchman'?", 244.
[16] Imlay, *Facing the Second World War*, 104.

United States. Their French counterparts had few such hopes. Small wonder that Reynaud, who had been finance minister before becoming premier, enthusiastically supported an allied campaign in Scandinavia, or any other operation designed to end the war speedily.

As the apparent stalemate wore on, some less optimistic assessments than Reynaud's radio broadcast of 10 September managed to filter through official French censorship. General Raymond Duval, one of his country's more perspicacious military leaders, wrote late in 1939: "We went to war with an army weaker (*moins solide*) than in 1914." He was especially critical of officers from the rank of colonel and above, who were too far removed, geographically and mentally, from the troops. As a result, "our larger units are poorly trained for a war of movement." Conscript soldiers and junior officers in an extremely hierarchical army were often left to their own resources, with little guidance from their commanders.[17] Duval proved to be remarkably prescient. A British historian notes that in May and June 1940, "the German commanders were closely involved in battle, while their French counterparts usually remained in the rear."[18] The latter were encouraged to do so by the army high command, which did not want them to be drawn into the fighting.[19] Yet no less a figure than Napoleon Bonaparte had insisted that high-ranking officers bivouac at the front.[20]

In a more political vein, Jean Mistler, chairman of the French Chamber's foreign affairs committee, wrote in March 1940: "I know of nothing more stupid than those newspaper articles which portray Germany as a country on the verge of political, economic and military collapse. Whatever German émigrés may claim, such a débâcle can occur only after a prolonged famine or a serious military reversal.

---

[17] General Duval, "La situation militaire: l'attente," *Revue des Deux Mondes*, 1 December 1939, 430-1.
[18] Julian Jackson, *The Fall of France: The Nazi Invasion of 1940* (Oxford: Oxford University Press, 2003), 221.
[19] Doughty, *The Breaking Point*, 25.
[20] Dorgelès, *La Drôle de Guerre*, 232.

These conditions do not exist at present." Mistler doubted that the naval blockade alone could win the war.[21] His critique was apparently directed at articles in the British press. It was Chamberlain who based his war policy on the premise that Germany could not stand the strain and would eventually succumb to internal disorder. He was not alone in this belief. On the eve of war, Shirer detected what he called "almost a defeatism" among the German populace.[22] Some German businessmen assured French consular officials that Hitler would not survive a war. Gestapo archives reveal that even among committed Nazis only a hard core was truly bellicose.[23]

Such hesitations manifested themselves before war had actually been declared. Once it began, Hitler proved to be very much in charge. Daladier had no illusions about the enemy's presumed weakness. "It would be puerile," he told the cabinet in November 1939, "to hope for an impending collapse of Germany under the weight of its economic difficulties."[24] Reynaud too recognized the power of the German war economy. He reported to the cabinet in December that the Nazi regime "has prepared to perfection . . . a highly efficient economic and financial machine that allows it to direct all the energy and resources of its people to the war effort."[25] That same month, he warned the Chamber of Deputies that if the French people do not accept the necessary sacrifices, "we may easily, very easily, lose the war."[26] The letters he received from other parliamentarians, one of whom had been mobilized for military service, indicate that the possibility of defeat was taken quite seriously.[27] The British political class, secure in the belief

---

[21] Jean Mistler, "Après six mois de guerre," *Revue de Paris*, 15 March 1940, 133-5.

[22] Shirer, *Berlin Diary*, 189.

[23] Crémieux-Brilhac, *La guerre oui ou non*, 338.

[24] Talbot C. Imlay, "France and the Phoney War," Robert Boyce ed., *French Foreign and Defense Policy, 1918-1940: The Decline of a Great Power* (London: Routledge, 1998). 266.

[25] Imlay, *Facing the Second World War*, 57.

[26] J O C Débats, 13 December 1939, 2263.

[27] Reynaud, *Au cœur de la mêlée*, 347-9.

that the French army was invincible in defence, did not even contemplate such an outcome.

In fact French citizens, and not only those in uniform, *were* making the necessary sacrifices, as Reynaud himself was well aware. He had introduced drastic measures, including heavy taxation of war profits above six percent. Anything in excess of ten percent was simply confiscated. Factory workers were especially hard hit: they no longer received extra pay for overtime and were subject to a levy of forty percent on all earnings for hours worked above forty a week.[28] As of 6 September, the work week in defence industries was officially set at sixty hours.[29] These decrees, along with rationing, family separations, inflation, shortages, the meagre pay of conscript soldiers and the general disruption of peacetime life were the lot of the average French citizen.[30] On New Year's day 1940 the Foreign Office received a report from the Ministry of Information which stated: "As a result of the war, the standard of living in France has fallen very sharply, while in England conditions are practically untouched."[31] For the British, the most serious inconvenience of the Phoney War was the blackout, which claimed more lives due to road accidents that all military operations undertaken during that period.[32]

As a direct result of the forty percent levy, morale in a particularly strategic sector of the work force suffered greatly, as was widely recognized by management. *Le Réveil économique*, a leading business journal, explained that no worker can understand why he/she should receive less pay for overtime. The steel magnate and former governor of the Bank of France, François de Wendel, in an impassioned

---

[28] William Henry Chamberlin, "France at War," *The Yale Review*, March 1940, 496.

[29] Pertinax (André Géraud), *Les fossoyeurs* (New York: Éditions de la Maison Française, 1943), 1, 150.

[30] Grenard, *La Drôle de Guerre*, 139-94.

[31] Quoted in Gates. *End of the Affair*, 39-40.

[32] Barry Turner, *Waiting for War: Britain 1939-1940* (London: Icon Books, 2019), 220.

speech to the Senate, denounced the measure as counter-productive. Raoul Dautry, minister of armaments and the only business executive in the cabinet, wrote to Daladier on 12 March, demanding its repeal.[33] Daladier could hardly oblige, since he was about to be replaced as premier by Reynaud. In the meantime, arms production stagnated, and even declined in some cases. That of the Somua S35 tank, France's best armoured vehicle, was less in April 1940 than during each of the previous four months. The output of antitank guns and munitions that month was less than half the average monthly production for the September-December 1939 period.[34] By contrast, German arms production doubled between January and July 1940.[35]

There were structural problems as well. In 1936, Reynaud noted that metal manufacture in France had decreased globally by 31 percent since 1928. Production of cast iron was 40 percent of Germany's and that of steel only a third. The following year he added that the monthly output of military aircraft in France had fallen from 65 to 35, while German production was ten times as great.[36] The last estimate was certainly exaggerated, but it was obvious by then that Germany was out-producing France in military goods. Daladier too recognized his country's industrial weakness. In a speech to war veterans on 12 November 1938, he emphasized that total industrial production had increased by 17 percent in Germany from 1929 to 1937 and 24 percent in Britain, while that of France had fallen by 25 percent.[37] Yet even if France had managed to keep pace in percentage terms with its powerful neighbour, the fact remains that the workforce in French industry was only 5.5 million as against 14 million in Germany. Worse still, the French were not as well trained as their German counterparts in the use of modern machinery.[38]

---

[33] Crémieux-Brilhac, *Les Français de l'an 40*, II: *Ouvriers et soldats*, 252-3.
[34] Talbot C. Imlay, "Paul Reynaud and France's Response to Nazi Germany, 1938-1940," *French Historical Studies*, Summer 2003, 510.
[35] Touze, *The Wages of Destruction*, 346.
[36] Benoist-Méchin, *Sixty Days That Shook the West*, 28.
[37] Daladier, *Défense du pays*, 91.

With the realization that France was not about to be invaded in the autumn of 1939, the French government resolved to pursue the war actively, to make it less "phoney," while avoiding a direct confrontation on its eastern frontier. Not to fight at all, with the French army fully mobilized, could only depress the morale of civilians and soldiers alike. As early as 12 September, Gamelin proposed to open a front in the Balkans. During the First World War, an allied force deployed in Macedonia under French command had relieved the hard-pressed Serbian army and eventually compelled Bulgaria to surrender. This time, however, the Chamberlain government opposed the venture. Britain lacked the necessary military resources and was afraid of provoking Italy.[39]

Britain and France were prodded into action by the Soviet invasion of Finland on 30 November 1939. At first, the allies were reluctant to intervene, believing that the Russians would win easily.[40] This was certainly the view in Moscow. As Nikita Khrushchev recalled, "All we had to do was raise our voice a little, and the Finns would obey. If that didn't work, we could fire one shot and the Finns would put up their hands and surrender. Or so we thought."[41] Stout Finnish resistance soon disabused them of this notion. Neither Britain nor France had a treaty of alliance with Finland, but the sight of a small, democratic country being assaulted by the Soviet colossus aroused widespread sympathy for the Finns. In Britain, the tone poem by Jean Sibelius, *Finlandia*, was broadcast daily on the BBC Home Service. Anti-Communism, which was never far beneath the surface, also contributed to the growing pro-Finnish sentiment.

As he would do throughout the war, Winston Churchill set the tone in a radio address of 20 January 1940, which was relayed

---

[38] Grenard, *La Drôle de Guerre,* 114.

[39] Bédarida, *La stratégie secrète,* 115-20, 202-13.

[40] John H. Wuorinen ed., *Finland and World War II, 1939-1944* (New York: Ronald Press, 1948), 69.

[41] Edward Crankshaw, ed., *Khrushchev Remembers* (Boston: Little, Brown, 1970), 152.

throughout the world by short-wave. "The service rendered by Finland to mankind is excellent. They have exposed, for all the world to see, the military incapacity of the Red Army and of the Red Air Force. . . . Everyone can see how Communism rots the soul of a nation; how it makes it abject and hungry in peace, and proves it base and abominable in war."[42] In his diary entry of 29 January, John Colville recorded that "for the first time," there was "a feeling that we may have to start the fighting."[43] In the context of Chamberlain's war policy, this was surely a novel idea. Leopold Amery, a close friend of Churchill, told Halifax, "We [i.e. the French] can hardly beat her [Germany] on the Western Front." So he recommended a foray into Scandinavia.[44] Under the guise of aiding Finland, the allies could conceivably cut off Germany's supply of iron ore from Sweden.

On 5 February, the allies agreed on a plan to send a few thousand "volunteers" to Finland under Finnish command. The line of supply was to begin at the Norwegian port of Narvik, from which the allies would advance to the iron ore deposits in Sweden. It was proposed to send some 100,000 British and 50,000 French troops to Norway, but only the "volunteers" would actually fight in Finland, thus avoiding a direct conflict with the Soviet Union. To make the plan operable, the Finns would first have to request such assistance, while the Swedes and Norwegians would have to accept the passage of allied troops on their territory.[45] Ironside, who approved of this strategy in principle, wrote in his diary: "One is almost frightened at the boldness of the plan, knowing what slender means one has at the moment to carry it out."[46]

---

[42] Churchill, *War Speeches* I, 137.

[43] Colville, *The Fringes of Power*, 76.

[44] Patrick R. Osborn, *Operation Pike: Britain Versus the Soviet Union, 1939-1941* (Westport, CT: Greenwood Press, 2000), 31.

[45] Anthony F. Upton, *Finland 1939-1940* (Newark, DE: University of Delaware Press, 1974), 103-5.

[46] *The Ironside Diaries*, 216.

The means were slender indeed. The Finns soon realized that the allied commitment to their country's defence was inadequate, if not actually fraudulent. By February, the Soviet army had regrouped and began to mount a renewed assault on Finnish lines, using heavy artillery. Marshal Gustav Mannerheim, the Finnish commander-in-chief, notified the allies that he needed 50,000 additional troops immediately. Since they failed to arrive, he urged his government to seek a peace settlement with Moscow.[47] In the end, the Soviet Union annexed more Finnish territory that it had initially demanded, but did not attempt to occupy the entire country. To do so would risk war with Britain and France, something that Stalin was most anxious to avoid. The U. S. ambassador in Moscow, Laurence Steinhardt, praised him for "the policy of realism and prudence which has on the whole been characteristic of his conduct of Soviet foreign relations."[48]

Finland did not formally request allied aid; Norway and Sweden, anxious to preserve their neutrality, refused passage of foreign troops on their territory. So in theory, Britain and France were absolved of any responsibility. Both governments, however, had to answer to parliamentary opposition for their inaction. In London, Sir Archibald Sinclair wondered if his fellow MPs "realized how greatly this fiasco has affected our prestige abroad." He quoted the Finnish prime minister as saying: "Help was offered too late to be of any use." Then he questioned the government's entire war policy. To play for a draw, as Chamberlain seemed to be doing, was tantamount to accepting defeat. "It is time we stopped saying, 'What is Hitler going to do? What is Mussolini going to do? What is Stalin going to do?' It is about time we asked, 'What is Chamberlain going to do?'"[49]

In France as in Britain, the Finnish defeat laid bare the paucity of allied strategy. The mood of French parliamentarians was so sombre that they had to meet in secret session. No one asked what Daladier was going to do. Rather, he was rebuked for what he had already done.

---

[47] Wuorinen, *Finland and World War II,* 71-2.
[48] Steinhardt to Hull, 20 March 1940, FRUS, III (1940), 189.
[49] 368 H C Deb., 19 March 1940, series 5, cols. 1859-60.

Leading the charge was Pierre Laval, who recalled that France had declared war, in principle, to save Poland; and now Poland was destroyed. In spite of allied claims to defend small nations against aggression, Finland was left to fight alone. "We see that Germany has seized the initiative, for its own gain and that of the Soviets." The naval blockade, he added, was only partly effective and necessitated a long war which France, already deeply in debt, could not afford. The people's morale was sorely tried by the endless waiting. An allied victory, therefore, must come quickly, or not at all. Addressing himself directly to Daladier, Laval concluded, "You have committed us without due consideration to a fearsome adventure."[50] Here can be seen the origins of the collaborationist policy that Laval was soon to pursue.

Daladier was replaced as premier by Paul Reynaud, who pledged to prosecute the war with renewed vigour. Gamelin planned to undertake a direct offensive against Germany in the spring or fall of 1941, by which time the French army would presumably have adequate British support, especially in heavy artillery. Reynaud, however, knew that his compatriots could not endure another winter of military make-believe. In his first appearance before the Supreme Inter-allied War Council, he reported that public opinion in France was well aware of the allies' inability to protect small countries from aggression. Everywhere, people were asking: "How can the allies win the war?" The number of divisions, "despite the arrival of British contingents," was increasing faster on the German side than on theirs.[51] A quick victory was essential, but how and where? After the fiasco over Finland, British strategists concocted a hare-brained scheme called Operation Pike, which entailed the bombing of Soviet oilfields and refineries in the Caucasus. They assumed that the Soviet Union was the weaker partner in the pact with Nazi Germany and could not put up any sustained resistance. Destroying the Soviet oil industry, it was believed, would weaken Germany's military strength by cutting off its main source of fuel.[52] The French government supported the plan

---

[50] J O Sénat, Comité secret, 14 March 1940, 5-9.

[51] Bédarida, *La stratégie secrete*, 325; cf. Churchill, *The Gathering Storm*, 521.

enthusiastically because it would involve major British participation. Moreover, as de Gaulle noted somewhat cynically, some French politicians were more eager to fight Stalin than Hitler. Air strikes against Russia, mainly by the RAF, suited them perfectly.[53]

A few days before Finland's defeat, Chamberlain had promised Parliament that military aid to that country, in accordance with the League of Nations covenant, would be forthcoming. The Soviet Union had already been expelled from the League, largely on the initiative of France. A Labour MP asked him: "Is this not tantamount to our going to war with Russia?" Chamberlain replied simply: "We have not arrived at that yet."[54] Fortunately, they never did. To his credit, the prime minister was extremely reluctant to undertake an air offensive in the Caucasus, since it would involve the allies in a war with the Soviet Union.[55] Operation Pike remained on the agenda, however. It was not abandoned until the German conquest of France, thereby saving Britain the fate of having to fight both Germany and Russia.

There remained Norway. In a memorandum to the cabinet on 29 September 1939, Churchill warned that "drastic action would be needed" if iron ore from Sweden was exported to Germany through Narvik. He was even more emphatic on 16 December, proposing the stoppage of iron ore supplies "as a major offensive operation of war. No other measure is open to us for many months to come which gives so good a chance of abridging the waste and destruction of the conflict, or of perhaps preventing the vast slaughters which will attend the grapple of the main armies."[56] Here then was an ingenious way to carry the war to Germany while maintaining "limited liability" in France. A foray into Scandinavia was the logical consequence of Phoney War strategy.[57] The allied expeditionary force, which had been disbanded

---

[52] Osborn, *Operation Pike*, 51, 139.

[53] De Gaulle, *Mémoires de guerre*, I, 36.

[54] 358 H C Deb., 11 March 1940, series 5, col. 837.

[55] Bédarida, *La Stratégie secrète*, 336.

[56] Nigel Knight, *Churchill: The Greatest Briton Unmasked* (Cincinnati, OH: David and Charles, 2008), 97.

after the Russo-Finnish war, was hastily reconstituted. On 8 April 1940, the Royal Navy began to lay mines in Norwegian waters, in open violation of that country's neutrality.

Four days earlier, Chamberlain had given a partisan speech in high spirits to the National Union of Conservative and Unionist Associations. "After seven months of war," he began, "I feel ten times as confident of victory as I did at the beginning." When war broke out, he recalled, "German preparations were far ahead of our own." But now Britain had caught up – or so it seemed. He admitted that he did not understand why Hitler had not taken advantage of his earlier military superiority – "however, one thing is certain: he missed the bus."[58] For Chamberlain, everything seemed to be going according to plan. In July 1939, he had explained to his sister, "What you want are defensive forces sufficiently strong to make it impossible for the other side to win except at such a cost as to make it not worth while." Once the Germans realize that a war against Britain and France is not worth while, "Then we can talk."[59] In December 1939, he asked General Montgomery, at the time a division commander in France: "I don't think the Germans have any intentions of attacking us. Do you?" Montgomery disagreed, believing that Germany would attack in its own good time; but Chamberlain was unmoved.[60] Ironside too rejected the official complacency. On 2 April he confided to his diary: "Perhaps the most dangerous thing of all is this idea amongst so many people that this war can be won without a battle and that we are not going to have any casualties. Are we going to win the war . . . just by proving to the Boches that they cannot win? I very much doubt it."[61]

---

[57] Thomas Munch-Petersen, *The Strategy of Phoney War: Britain, Sweden and the Iron Ore Question, 1939-1940* (Stockholm: Militarhistoriska Förlaget, 1981), 259.

[58] Churchill, *The Gathering Storm*, 526.

[59] Chamberlain to Ida, 23 July 1939, *The Neville Chamberlain Diary Letters*, 431.

[60] *The Memoirs of Field-Marshal the Viscount Montgomery of Alamein, K. G.* (London: Collins, 1958), 58.

The German government was hardly intimidated by Chamberlain's posturing. On 5 April, Goebbels told a select group of journalists that the British and French missed their chance to crush Nazi Germany when it was weak. "They left us alone . . . and when we were done, and well armed, better than they, then they started the war!"[62] Allied designs on Scandinavia did not remain secret for long. Until early in 1940, Hitler considered "the maintenance of Norway's neutrality to be the best course for Germany." By February, he changed his mind: "The English intend to land there, and I want to be there before them."[63] There is evidence to suggest that Nazi sympathisers in Britain leaked military secrets to Germany, including plans for the venture into Scandinavia.[64] The British, on the other hand, were totally unaware of Hitler's intentions. On 1 April, the cabinet decided to limit the allied effort to naval warfare and not to commit ground forces unless "the Germans set foot on Norwegian soil, or there is clear evidence that they intend to do so."[65] Eight days later, the German navy slipped through the minefield and landed troops in several places along the Norwegian coast.

As operations got under way, Churchill addressed the House of Commons in terms that were hardly less optimistic than Chamberlain's recent speech. "In my view, which is shared by my skilled advisers, Herr Hitler has committed a grave strategic error in spreading the war so far to the north and in forcing the Scandinavian people, or peoples, out of their attitude of neutrality." Hitler will have to fight "if necessary during the whole summer, against powers possessing vastly superior naval forces and able to transport them to the scenes of action more easily than he can."[66] This is precisely what Reynaud expected. He

---

[61] *Ironside Diaries*, 243.

[62] Paul Johnson, *Modern Times: The World from the Twenties to the Eighties* (New York, Harper & Row, 1983), 341.

[63] Liddell Hart, "The Military Strategist," Taylor ed., *Churchill Revised*, 207.

[64] Newnan, *Profits of Peace*, 169.

[65] Hinsley, *British Intelligence in the Second World War*, 121.

[66] 359 H C Deb. 11 April 1940, series 5, cols. 747-8.

enthusiastically supported the Norwegian venture because it would involve the Royal Navy. France sent some of its best troops, the *chasseurs alpins*, to Norway, but the main effort was to be borne by Britain.

A day earlier, and before addressing the French people on radio, Reynaud gave an exclusive interview to Anne O'Hare McCormick, the doyenne of American foreign correspondents. He emphasized that the allies were now engaged in serious fighting. The Americans may well have derided the war as "phoney," but this was no longer the case. "You must therefore allow us to conduct this fight in our own way. We cannot be concerned to supply drama for the audience." Reynaud noted that the war had engulfed two countries that had heretofore been neutral. Other neutrals may eventually find themselves involved. "I am confident that we can win without your active help. But you must recognize that we face a powerful and desperate enemy with enormous manpower, a mighty military machine and great reserve forces for a comeback, as recent years have demonstrated."[67] Herein lay France's dilemma: although Reynaud knew his country to be inferior to Germany in both military and economic terms, the government could not maintain the confidence of its own people, let alone win new allies, without some kind of success in battle.[68]

The hopes of both Churchill and Reynaud were soon dashed. Allied troops were landed in small ports without adequate supplies or lines of communication, away from strategically important zones. The Germans had already captured most airfields in Norway, from which they strafed and bombed the opposing naval and ground forces at will.[69] So Hitler hadn't missed the bus after all; he took the airplane instead. The entire Norwegian operation, undertaken against the advice of German military strategists, was his idea.[70] Naval losses were about the

---

[67] *New York Times*, 11 April 1940.

[68] Fabre-Luce, *Journal de la France*, 185.

[69] Correlli Barnett, *Britain and Her Army, 1509-1970* (London: Allen Lane, 1970), 428.

[70] Johnson, *Modern Times*, 363.

same on both sides, but Germany suffered more because it had fewer ships to begin with.[71] Still, the allied thrust into Scandinavia can hardly be counted as a victory for the Royal Navy, since it failed to intercept German ships ferrying troops to the Norwegian coast.[72] On land the Germans were victorious everywhere except in Narvik, where a combined British, French, Polish and Norwegian force pushed back the numerically inferior enemy garrison almost to the Swedish border on 28 May. By then, however, there were more urgent matters awaiting the allies in France. Their troops in Narvik were withdrawn on 8 June; British forces elsewhere in Norway had already been evacuated five weeks earlier.

News of the retreat shocked British MPs. Whereas the Dunkirk evacuation was soon to be hailed as a brilliant exploit, the withdrawal from Norway could only be called a defeat. On 7 May, Chamberlain had to face hecklers in Parliament over his earlier contention that Hitler had missed the bus. He had explained to his cabinet colleagues that "the operations in Scandinavia were in some measure in the eyes of the world, a test of allied strength."[73] They soon became a test of *his* strength: the entire conduct, or rather misconduct, of the war was now laid at his doorstep. "It is not Norway alone," said Attlee. The country's leaders "have had an almost uninterrupted career of failure. Norway follows Czecho-Slovakia and Poland. Everywhere the story is 'Too late'." Amery administered the *coup de grâce*: "Somehow or other we must get into government men who can match our enemies in fighting spirit, in daring, in resolution and in thirst for victory." Then, quoting Oliver Cromwell, he uttered the stinging indictment: "You have sat too long here for any good you have been doing. Depart, I say, and let us have done with you. In the same of God, go."[74]

---

[71] Geirr H. Haarr, *The Battle for Norway: April-June 1940* (Annapolis, MD: Naval Institute Press, 2010), 367.

[72] Richard Charles Mee, "The Foreign Policy of the Chamberlain Wartime Administration, September 1939 – May 1940," unpublished Pd.D. thesis, University of Birmingham, 1998, 260.

[73] *Ibid.*, 272.

Chamberlain won a vote of confidence by 281 to 200; but 41 MPs who usually voted with the government now opposed it, and another 60 abstained. Churchill loyally defended the government against what he called "abuse" from the opposition benches.[75] He was, of course, defending his own reputation, since the entire Norwegian affair was his idea. Yet it was Churchill who was called to the premiership, not because of his role in the recent fiasco, but because he seemed to have the fighting spirit that was now so obviously needed. For Chamberlain, Britain's defeat in Norway was perhaps the beginning of wisdom: it exposed the frailty of his entire war policy. In early May, he admitted to his sister that "we are not yet strong enough. . . . We have plenty of manpower, but it is neither trained nor equipped. We are short of many weapons of offence and defence."[76] Privately, he mused that "perhaps it was providential that the revolution which overturned me coincided with the entry of the real thing."[77] Prior to leaving office, he recognized publicly that "Germany, with her vast and well equipped armies, is so well placed that she can at any moment attack at any one or a number of different points."[78] Just how well placed would become painfully evident within a few days.

The German offensive in the west began with the Netherlands, which that had been neutral in the First World War and tried to remain so in the Second. The Dutch army had no tanks, except one French model of 1918 vintage. But it did have anti-aircraft guns and managed to destroy most of the German transport fleet. In proportion to their numbers, the Dutch inflicted more casualties on the invading force than any other power in the spring of 1940. For a country that had not been at war since the age of the musket, this was a respectable showing.[79]

---

[74] 359 H C Deb. 7 May 1940, series 5, cols. 1081, 1093, 1150.

[75] *Ibid.*, col. 1360.

[76] Chamberlain to Hilda, 4 May 1940, *The Neville Chamberlain Diary Letters*, 526.

[77] Iain Macleod, *Neville Chamberlain* (London: Frederick Muller, 1961), 282.

[78] 359 H C Deb. 7 May 1940, series 5, col. 1081.

[79] John Mosier, *The Blitzkrieg Myth: How Hitler and the Allies Misread the*

Nonetheless, Holland was overrun in five days, even as the Germans were occupied elsewhere.

Belgium was next. This time, the allies were ready – or thought they were. On 10 January 1940, a light plane carrying two German staff officers to a high-level meeting in Cologne was blown off course and had to make a forced landing in Belgium. They were carrying plans for the spring offensive, which were essentially a replica of the old Schlieffen plan plus a sweep through Holland. The Germans tried to burn the plans, but were stopped by the Belgian police, who turned them over to the allies. When Hitler heard of the mishap, he abandoned the Schlieffen strategy and chose instead that of General von Manstein, who had proposed attacking France through the Ardennes, using tanks as a spearhead. The allied commanders assumed that the captured plans were still in effect.

As soon as fighting broke out on 10 May, the British Expeditionary Force plus the best trained and fully mechanized units of the French army entered Belgium, with the French vanguard reaching Breda in the Netherlands. British soldiers had built pill-boxes along the Franco-Belgian border, but they had to leave these defensive positions in order to participate in the advance ordered by the French army command. It had long been French strategy to keep the enemy as far away from Paris as possible, and the move into the Low Countries was intended to incorporate the Dutch and Belgian armies into the allied coalition.[80] By 15 May, however, the allies realized their error, as the Germans penetrated French defences at Sedan, the scene of a decisive French defeat in the Franco-Prussian War of 1870. The French defenders in that sector included many elderly reservists, who had already had their fill of fighting in 1918. Their units were last in line for the allocation of modern equipment.[81] There were retreads from the last war in the German army as well, but they were usually kept well away from the front. As the Germans advanced toward the Channel, the allied

---

Strategic Realities of World War II (New York: HarperCollins, 2003), 121-2.

[80] Alexander, *The Republic in Danger*, 398.

[81] Jackson, *The Fall of France*, 35.

forces in Belgium began to withdraw. They soon found themselves cut off from the main body of the French army.

Obviously, serious mistakes were made. In retrospect, a purely defensive strategy in northern France would seem more appropriate; but this was not politically feasible, since the allies were duty-bound to come to the aid of Belgium. The French *chasseurs ardennais* failed to plant antitank mines and fell trees along the route taken by German armour in the thick forest.[82] Their commanders insisted on keeping the roads open for the cavalry. In the event, French cavalry did mount an offensive through the forest, but was repulsed by German tanks.[83] Keeping the roads open may explain why the allies did not deploy tactical aircraft to bomb the veritable traffic jam of enemy tanks in the Ardennes. Worst of all, the French high command disregarded a warning from their military attaché in Berne that the initial German thrust would be directed at Sedan on 8 to 10 May.[84] For this negligence there can be no logical explanation.

Ground attacks by allied aviation in open terrain failed utterly. The Advance Air Striking Force of the RAF based in France included early model Hurricanes with two-bladed fixed-pitch propellers, the later versions being reserved for the defence of Britain. They failed to provide adequate support for the bombers,[85] obsolete Blenheims and the infamous Fairey Battle, a single-engine, slow moving aircraft without self-sealing fuel tanks. Five Battles flying a reconnaissance mission over Saarbrucken on 30 September were all shot down by Messerschmitt fighters.[86] Despite its dismal performance, this misbegotten machine remained in service the following spring. On 10 May 1940, thirty-two Battles were sent out to harass German infantry

---

[82] Collier, *1940, the World in Flames*, 96.

[83] Liddell Hart, *Memoirs*, II, 281.

[84] Naegelen, *L'attente sous les armes*, 91.

[85] David French, *Raising Churchill's Army: The British Army and the War Against Germany, 1919-1945* (New York: Oxford University Press, 2000), 176.

[86] Allport, *Britain at Bay*, 208-9.

columns. Thirteen were brought down by enemy fighters and ground fire. All the survivors returned damaged. On 12 May, seven out of nine Blenheims were destroyed by Messerschmitts. The following day, light bombers of the French air force tried to attack German troops crossing the Meuse but were so badly mauled that they made no further sorties that day. Late that afternoon, seventy-one Battles and Blenheims attacked in the same sector. Forty never returned – the highest loss rate that the RAF had ever experienced, indeed its worst defeat of the entire war.[87] Night bombing of the Ruhr district by the RAF did little damage.[88] In its January 1940 issue, *The Engineer*, a British periodical, claimed that "our aircraft have, so far, proved beyond doubt superior to those of Germany."[89] Unfortunately, not the aircraft sent to France. In the seven weeks of the French campaign, the RAF sustained more losses than during the entire battle of Britain.[90]

The Germans, on the other hand, had perfected a ground-support aircraft that was largely instrumental in bringing them victory: the dive-bomber. Neither the RAF nor the French air force had a similar, ground-based weapon. The French single-seat dive-bomber was reserved for the navy and played no part in the campaign of 1940. Allied light bombers could manage at best a shallow dive, which still left them vulnerable to anti-aircraft fire.[91] The Junkers model 87, known as the Stuka, was effective only when Germany had mastery of the skies, as was indeed the case over France. It could dive at an 80-degree angle and release its bomb load of 1,500 kilograms with uncanny accuracy. Many French tanks were destroyed from the air, including elements of de Gaulle's force at Montcornet on 17 May.[92]

---

[87] Chaz Bowyer, *History of the RAF* (London: Bison Books, 1986), 74; cf. Shachtman, *The Phony War*, 209.

[88] Shirer, *Berlin Diary*, 347.

[89] David Edgerton, *Britain's War Machine: Weapons, Resources, and Experts in the Second World War* (New York: Oxford University Press, 2011), 14.

[90] R. J. Overy, *The Air War, 1939-1945* (London: Europa, 1980), 34.

[91]Rocolle, *La guerre de 1940*, I, 226.

[92]Schactman, *The Phony War*, 217.

Their armour plating and guns gave them no protection against the Stuka, whose siren also terrified French infantrymen. The French army had few modern anti-aircraft guns and had to rely on the standard French machine gun of 1914 vintage, which was too cumbersome to serve in an anti-aircraft role.[93] As de Gaulle recalls: "Throughout the afternoon, the Stukas, swooping down from the sky and returning constantly, bombed our tanks and trucks. We had nothing with which to oppose them."[94] Unlike Britain and Germany, France in 1940 had no radar to guide interceptors to their target. At the outset of the war, its slim fighter force was divided into five different types, ranging from good (the Curtis P-36) to obsolete. The sixth type was the Dewoitine 520, France's best fighter. It had just begun to enter service when the Germans attacked.[95]

The Stuka proved its effectiveness against the British army as well. The *Luftwaffe*, which could provide direct air support within 45 minutes of a request from ground troops, sent dive bombers regularly to drop incendiary bombs on units of the B. E. F. A British infantryman whose battalion was bombed by fifty Stukas in fifteen minutes, later wrote: "An attack by Stukas in these numbers cannot be described; it is entirely beyond the comprehension of anyone who has not experienced it. The noise alone strikes such terror that the body becomes paralysed; the still active mind is convinced that each and every aircraft is coming for you personally; you feel that you have grown so large that they cannot possibly miss."[96]

In armour, France and Germany are said to have been evenly matched. The French could field 2,946 tanks against 2,977 German. Many historians claim that the French models were superior.[97] Such a

---

[93] Eric Deroo and Pierre de Taillac, *Carnets de déroute, 1939-1940. Lettres et récits inédits* (Paris: Tallandier, 2010), 153; cf. Mosier, *The Blitzkrieg Myth*, 135.

[94] De Gaullle, *Mémoirs de guerre* I, 43.

[95] David Isby, *The Decisive Duel: Spitfire vs 109* (London: Abacus 2013), 98.

[96] French, *Raising Churchill's Army*, 177.

[97] For example, Jean-Baptiste Duroselle, *L'abîme, 1939-1945* (Paris:

blanket assertion requires closer examination. Some 600 French tanks then in service were the Renault FT 17, which had served in the First World War. They were, of course, renovated, but still vastly inferior in speed, defensive armour and firepower to more recent models.[98] France's best tanks, the Somua and the Char B-2, were available in only 305 and 160 units respectively.[99] The FT 17 was worse than useless, since it required fuel, maintenance and crews, all of which would have better served elsewhere. The others are presumed to be superior to German models because of their thicker armour plating and bigger main guns.[100] Here too, a closer examination is warranted.

The Char B, France's heavy tank, had a high silhouette and a 75-millimetre gun mounted in its hull. The gun had only a 15-degree traverse ratio. To fire it, the entire tank had to be directed toward its target and exposed to enemy fire. The Char B's thick defensive armour came at a heavy cost: it was slower than comparable German models and had a range of only 17 kilometres, as against 100 kilometres for German and Czech tanks. Refuelling was difficult at best and nearly impossible under aerial bombardment, causing many tank crews to abandon their mounts once they ran dry. Alone among French tanks, the Char B was equipped with radio, which transmitted in Morse code because the noise of the engine precluded voice transmission. On other models, radio transceivers were retrofitted, belatedly, in 1939. That of the Somua was perched atop the shell casing ejection port and stopped working once the tank went into battle.[101] Most communication between French tank commanders was done with flash flags. All

---

Imprimerie Nationale, 1982), 201.

[98] Liddell Hart, *Europe in Arms*, 51.

[99] Colonel Ulrich Liss, *Westfront 1939/40: Erinnerung des Feldarbeiters im OKH* (Neckargemünd: Vowinkel, 1959), 28.

[100] Ernest R. May, *Strange Victory: Hitler's Conquest of France* (New York: Hill and Wang, 2000). 478.

[101] Stephen A. Schuker, "Seeking a Scapegoat. Intelligence and Grand Strategy in France, 1939-1940," Jonathan Haslam and Karina Urbach, *Secret Intelligence in the European States System, 1918-1989* (Stanford, CA: Stanford University Press, 2014), 110.

French tanks suffered from having a one-man turret: the gunner, who was usually the tank commander, had to load and fire while directing operations. When Churchill visited Paris on 16 May, his French hosts told him that their armour was "totally inadequate."[102]

Nor was British armour any better. "Tank crews were half-trained," notes a British historian. "Tanks lacked radios, sighting telescopes and even armour-piercing ammunition."[103] He adds that "throughout the war, there was never a well designed British tank." American models were more reliable.[104] Only 23 tanks in the British Expeditionary Force had a gun that could fire armour-piercing ammunition.[105] In 1940, German tank crews had already acquired experience in Poland. Their tanks, including the Czech models impressed into the German army, all had two- and even three-man turrets. All had radio. Most importantly, German tactics were more effective than those of the allies. Whereas the French dispersed their armour to support the infantry, as in the First World War, the Germans used tanks as a battering ram to break through the enemy's defences.[106] They also had the 88-millimetre cannon, which had originally been designed as an anti-aircraft weapon. During the Spanish civil war, it was used against armour and proved to be the best anti-tank gun of the Second World War.

Tanks can destroy fortifications, buildings, bridges and other tanks; but they cannot occupy enemy terrain or take prisoners. Only the infantry can do that, and throughout the Second World War, German infantry was the best in the world. "They were better," asserts a British historian. "Man for man, German soldiers fought more effectively in World War II than their allied counterparts did."[107] In 1940, writes

---

[102] Butler, *Grand Strategy*, 184.

[103] Len Deighton, *Blood, Tears and Folly* ((London: Vintage Books, 2007), 193.

[104] *Ibid.*, 211.

[105] Allport, *Britain at Bay*, 204.

[106] Michel, *La défaite de la France*, 49.

[107] Max Hastings, "Botch on the Rhine," *The New York Review of Books*, 28

another, "the German army . . . proved itself devastatingly effective."[108] Churchill himself recognized their superiority. Referring to the allied fiasco in Norway, he wrote that "some of our best troops, the Scots and Irish guards, were baffled by the vigour, enterprise and training of Hitler's young men."[109] If Britain's finest soldiers were baffled, how much more so were the poorly paid French conscripts, many of whom were veterans of the First World War, whose fighting spirit had been dampened by eight months of enforced idleness as they waited for the Germans to attack.

This is not to excuse the atrocities committed by German soldiers, such the total destruction in July 1944 of Oradour-sur-Glane, a French village near Limoges, and the wanton massacre of its inhabitants. German infantry was simply better organized and better equipped than its adversaries. The squad was organized around the MG 34 machine gun, an air-cooled weapon whose cyclic rate of fire was 900 rounds a minute. Since the barrel often overheated, the gunner's second, who fed the ammunition, provided a spare. Each squad member carried an ammunition belt. Other armies had automatic weapons at the squad level, but none with the firepower of the MG 34. The French automatic rifle, which had been adopted in 1924, could fire 450 rounds a minute and had a 25-round magazine. The British Bren gun had a 30-round magazine and could fire 500 rounds a minute. The American Browning Automatic Rifle, which had entered service in 1918, had two rates of fire: 350 and 550 rounds a minute. Its magazine held only 20 rounds. Of all the automatic weapons used by the allies only the Bren gun had a quick-change barrel.

The standard French machine gun in 1940 was the antiquated 1914 model Hotchkiss, whose cyclic rate of fire was only 450 rounds a minute. Although air-cooled, the Hotchkiss was extremely heavy and could be carried only over short distances by a crew of three. It was mounted on a tripod, making the sitting gunner an easy target. By

May 2020.
[108] Tooze, *The Wages of Destruction*, 401.
[109] Churchill, *The Gathering Storm*, 583.

contrast, the MG 34, with its bipod, could be carried by one man who, being close to the ground, enjoyed better concealment. Even older than the Hotchkiss was the Lebel rifle, which still standard issue in 1940. When adopted in 1886, the Lebel was truly revolutionary because it was the first rifle to fire a cartridge using smokeless powder as a propellant. The Lebel had a higher muzzle velocity than any other infantry weapon of the day, and the rifleman no longer had to wait until the smoke cleared before firing again. Like all other European rifles recycled from the First World War, the Lebel was a bolt-action repeater. But whereas the German Mauser was fed from a five-round clip, which was easily replaced, the Lebel had an eight-round tubular magazine under the barrel. Once it was empty, the rifleman had to load each cartridge individually from a box, losing precious time in a war of movement.

In 1936, the French army adopted a bolt-action repeater fed by a five-round clip, but it was available only in small quantities by 1940. Most French soldiers had to fight with museum pieces. The new rifle, like the automatic rifle of 1924, fired a 7.5-millimetre cartridge. The Lebel and the Hotchkiss used the older 8-millimetre round. It doesn't take much imagination to envision the confusion that could occur in the heat of battle, with the 7.5-millimetre round being issued to units equipped with the older weapons and the 8-millimetre going to the newer. France was the only major belligerent in the Second World War to send its army into combat using rifle cartridges of two different calibres. It lacked the financial resources to equip totally its land and air forces with modern weapons. The French navy absorbed a disproportionate share of what military credits were available.[110] Daladier admitted that France could not afford a modern army, navy and air force all at once.[111]

French military communications were woefully inadequate. General Gamelin's headquarters at Vincennes, near Paris, lacked radio, telephone or even carrier pigeons. The supreme commander maintained

[110] Jackson, *France and the Nazi Menace*, 386.
[111] Henri Michel, *La Drôle de Guerre* (Paris: Hachette, 1971), 269.

contact with his subordinates in the field solely through messengers. Whereas the Germans made full use of radio, the French and British armies relied primarily on field telephones, as in the First World War. The cables connecting them were vulnerable to artillery fire, and German artillery was excellent. Once the fighting began, French and British communications broke down altogether. Battlefield liaison between the two allies was poor from the start.[112]

So in the final analysis, the French defeat was military, not political or moral, and had nothing to do with any presumed "decadence" in French society. The theory that France had lost the battle because of some deep-seated moral failings implies that Nazi Germany won because it was somehow morally superior. Was it? The reader may want to provide an answer to that question. It is commonplace to attribute any defeat, in any war, to "defeatism." Here, the position taken by Paul Reynaud should give us pause. He wanted victory wholeheartedly and remained in office as long as it remained even remotely possible. But he also knew that France had fewer than half as many men of military age as Germany, and a smaller industrial base. In a dispatch of 26 April to Ambassador Corbin, he wrote: "We have to act quickly or lose the war."[113] But it was already too late; the situation in Norway favoured the Germans from the start. Concerning the fall of France, Liddell Hart put it best when he wrote that "the collapse started at the *front* [emphasis in the original], not in the rear."[114] By the same token, the German victory also started, and finished, at the front. However reticent many German civilians may have been initially at the prospect of war, it was their army that won the battle. Morale on the home front, either in France or in Germany, during the brief campaign of 1940 was not a determinant. On 16 May, following the German breakthrough at Sedan, General Spears had dinner with Léon Blum, to whom he put the question: would the Maginot Line hold?

---

[112] Smalley, *The British Expeditionary Force*, 132-3.

[113] Imlay, "France and the Phoney War," 263.

[114] Preface to Colonel Alphonse Goutard, *The Battle of France, 1940*, trans A.R.P. Burgess (New York: Ives Washburn, 1959), 10.

Blum answered that the Maginot Line was a shield, and a shield does not cover the whole body. A knight's best defence is his sword.[115] In his memoirs, Churchill recognized "that the quality of the French army was allowed to deteriorate during the winter, and that it would have fought better in the autumn than in the spring."[116] After eight months of phoney war, the sword had grown rusty with disuse.

So it was with the British army. Throughout the war of waiting, it lacked the intensive training and the combat experience of the opposing Germans. Lord Gort, the British commander in France, was concerned "that conditions in the B. E. F., in the absence of actual hostilities, have been, to a certain extent unreal, and more similar to peacetime training than to warfare; there is a danger that those who have no war experience may not readily clear their minds of peacetime conditions where fire was represented by tokens."[117] The French defeat of 1940 was also a British defeat. Fortunately for Britain, the bulk of its army was rescued after only thirteen days of actual fighting.

The French fought bravely, inflicting nearly twice as many casualties daily on the German invaders after the Dunkirk evacuation as before. From 5 to 24 June, official Nazi government statistics established the daily toll of Germans killed, wounded or missing at 4,762. In the first phase of the Russian campaign, 22 June – 10 December 1941, German losses averaged 4,506 per day.[118] Goebbels recognized the enemy's valour in a diary entry of 16 June: "The French are resisting very stubbornly."[119] After Dunkirk they were fighting virtually alone, supported by only one British division, the 51st Highland, which was cut off and taken prisoner.[120] And their ally had

---

[115] General Sir Edward Spears. *Assignment to Catastrophe* (London: Heinemann, 1954), I, 144.

[116] Churchill, *The Gathering Storm*, 503.

[117] Smalley, *The British Expeditionary Force*, 80-1.

[118] Eddy Bauer, *La guerre des blindés*, I (Paris: Payot, 1962), 139-40. Bauer was a major in the Swiss army.

[119] *The Goebbels Diaries*, 122.

[120] Barnett, *Britain and Her Army*, 431.

not made matters easier for them. To cover their retreat, British troops blew up over 500 bridges in France, leaving French army units stranded and without any possibility of re-supply. Over the protests of the French engineer in charge, the B. E. F. destroyed the long-distance telephone switchboard at Lille, thereby depriving the French first army of all external communication.[121]

Just as the French army rallied belatedly to the defence of the homeland, so did the civilian population. The desultory performance of the French arms industry changed overnight once the war began in earnest. From 10 May on, factory workers toiled as they had never done since the battle of Verdun in 1916. They put in eleven hours a day (twelve hours a day in the aircraft industry) seven days a week. The government quickly eliminated the levy on overtime pay. Production of the Dewoitine 520, France's most advanced fighter (still slightly inferior to the older Messerschmitt 109 in top speed and rate of climb), increased from 51 in April to 136 in May.[122] The output of aero engines at the Gnôme and Rhône works attained a record of 1000 in May, as against 225 in September and 370 in December. Manufacture of the Somua tank was hindered by the loss of the metallurgical industry in northern France to Hitler's troops. German advances in June further disrupted French war production.[123] Nonetheless, the production figures for May lead to the inescapable conclusion that lack of urgency on the factory floor was a prime factor in limiting arms manufacture when it was most needed. During the Phoney War there was little sense of urgency in Britain, where arms production suffered in part as a result of the blackout, which was more strictly enforced than in France or Germany.[124] So the months-long waiting period was itself largely responsible for the French defeat.

---

[121] Bloch, L'étrange défaite, 107; Smalley, The British Expeditionary Force, 163.
[122] General (Charles) Christienne, "L'industrie aéronautique française de septembre 1939 à juin 1940," Français et Britanniques dans la Drôle de Guerre, 400, 406.
[123] Crémieux-Brilhac, Ouvriers et soldats, 337-60.

The defeat was not total. In the short war against Italy, the French "Army of the Alps" – some 185,000 men – yielded little territory to an Italian force of 450,000, despite having to defend its rear against the Germans coming from the north. The French, in well-fortified positions, held the high ground, while the Italians had to trudge through narrow mountain passes, as they led donkeys carrying pack artillery captured from the Austrians in 1918. In the air, the French were clearly victorious. On 15 June, French air ace Pierre Le Gloan shot down five Italian warplanes – four fighters and one bomber – in less than half an hour.[125] He was flying a Dewoitine 520, examples of which had been delivered to his squadron on 1 June. On the ground, Italian losses numbered 642 killed, 2,631 wounded, 2,151 frostbitten and 642 missing. The French suffered 37 killed, 62 wounded and 155 captured.[126] The morale of French soldiers on the Italian front was good. Italy was the aggressor; they were fighting to defend France, not Poland or some exalted ideal such as Christian civilisation. Historians generally focus on the fall of France and tend to ignore the Italian campaign since France did not fall to Italy, but to Germany.

Admittedly, the German forces enjoyed amazing good luck. The "sickle-cut" strategy of using tanks as the spearhead of a rapid but narrowly-based offensive left their army's flanks exposed. But it succeeded. When German tanks ran low on fuel, their crews had only to stop at the nearest French filling station, whose owner could hardly refuse them service, or at a captured fuel depot.[127] French tank crews had to respect private property and await refuelling by the army. The national highways of France (*routes nationales*), which had been designed to allow the French army to advance expeditiously to the

---

[124] Amery, *My Political Life*, III, 331n.

[125] Henri Azeau, *La guerre franco-italienne* (Paris: Presses de la Cité, 1967), 81-2.

[126] Georgio Rochat, "La campagne italienne de juin 1940 dans les Alpes occidentales," *Revue historique des armées*, 250 (2008), 77-84.

[127] Spears, *Assignment to Catastrophe*, I, 219.

front, were not bombed by the *Luftwaffe* so that they could serve the Germans in the opposite direction.

Superior tactics defined the German army of 1940. The taking of Eben Emael, the redoubtable Belgian fortress, in less than 30 hours, was a masterstroke. Combat engineers, ferried in by glider, landed on the roof and dropped grenades into the ventilation shafts. In the field, junior officers were allowed considerable discretion: a platoon leader or company commander could act according to the needs of the moment, even ignoring a directive, in order to accomplish his unit's mission.[128] The British chain of command, by contrast, retained the rigidity of the First World War. Only after Dunkirk did it become more flexible.[129] Surveying the legacy of 1918, Marshal Foch had predicted that France would fall behind. "We will achieve a paradoxical state wherein Germany, which is not supposed to have an army, will develop within its cadres a new organization which will correspond to the war of the future, while we, who have an army, will continue with an existing model which will no longer be of any use."[130] Marc Bloch, who detested Nazism, admitted that Hitler's social revolution had brought to the fore "fresh minds . . . capable of understanding the new and the unexpected."[131] The German army of 1940 was far more egalitarian than its Imperial predecessor. Officers were chosen on the basis of ability and no longer represented a caste. They usually ate at the same field kitchens as the troops, whose morale was excellent. Hitler, who had been a corporal in 1918, issued detailed instructions for German officers on taking an interest in the personal problems of their men.[132]

Not only was the German army larger, better armed, better trained and better led than those of the allies. The French in 1940

---

[128] Doughty, *The Breaking Point*, 149.

[129] Smalley, *The British Expeditionary Force*, 54-5.

[130] Pierre Cot, *Triumph of Treason* (Chicago: Ziff-Davis, 1944), 57.

[131] Bloch, *L'étrange défaite*, 204. In this he anticipated by a generation David Schoenbaum's magisterial treatise, *Hitler's Social Revolution: Class and Status in Nazi Germany* (New York: Doubleday, 1966).

[132] Shirer, *Berlin Diary*, 440-1.

lacked the outside support that had propelled them to victory in 1918. In a radio address to the French people on 20 June, Marshal Pétain recalled that in 1918 France had on its side 85 British and Imperial divisions, as against only 10 in 1940, plus 58 Italian divisions and 42 American.[133] Whatever one may think of Pétain's subsequent policy, on this point he was substantially correct. Reynaud had made similar calculations in a conversation with Churchill *prior* to the German offensive in the west.[134] Pétain might have added that in 1914 Germany had to fight on two fronts. In 1940, France had to fight on two fronts. Of course the French, largely on their own in the brief campaign, could have done better; but their defeat, like the German victory, was hardly strange. Professor May, after wrongly attributing superior arms to France (such as bombers that could exceed 400 miles per hour – that is, faster than best fighters of the day, the Spitfire at 362 mph or the Messerschmitt 109 at 357 mph), reverses course somewhat toward the end of his book. France "was not doomed to lose the entire war, and certainly not in a matter of weeks." He then brings in Britain, whose modest army had already evacuated French territory: "French and British leaders might have been able to halt or at least check the German offensive. . . ."[135] Yes, perhaps they might have, but for how long? And did the British want to be mired in another prolonged slugfest on the Continent?

In recent years, a small army of historians has analyzed the German war machine and found it deficient in many respects, especially as to resources. Professor Paul Kennedy acknowledges these deficiencies, but adds a note of caution. "It may be unwise to go all the way with recent revisionist literature about Germany's unreadiness for

---

[133] Auguste Laure, *Pétain* (Paris: Berger-Levrault, 1941), 435-6. By 1918, allied divisions were down to 14,000 men each; an American division had twice that number.

[134] Churchill, *The Gathering Storm*, 573.

[135] May, *Strange Victory*, 137, 450, 698. The Potez 63-11, of which the author thinks so highly, had a top speed of 264 miles per hour. See David Donald ed., *Encyclopedia of World Aircraft* (Etobicoke, ON: Prospero Books, 1990), 763.

war in 1939." In 1939, yes – but it was better prepared in 1940. As noted earlier, German generals used the eight months of make-believe war to improve their troops' fighting potential.[136] "At the end of the day," he continues, "military effectiveness is relative. Few, if any, armed services claim that all their needs are satisfied; and the German weaknesses have to be measured against those of their foes. When that is done, the picture seems far more favourable to Berlin, especially because of the efficiency of its armed services in *operational doctrine* [emphasis in the original]: its army was prepared to concentrate its tank forces, and then to allow them initiative on the battlefield, keeping in touch by radio; its air force . . . was trained to give assistance to the army's thrusts. . . . All this was important compensation for, say, meagre stocks of rubber."[137] In other words, the *Wehrmacht* of May-June 1940 was not all-powerful, but it was more powerful than its adversaries. Gamelin's verdict on the French defeat is probably the most accurate: "Inferiority of numbers, inferiority of equipment, inferiority of method."[138]

The victory in the west instilled pride in the hearts of nearly all Germans. "The war in Europe developed into a patriotic affair as soon as the old foe France was surprisingly beaten so quickly," writes a German historian. "The bond between Hitler, the military, and the whole nation was never stronger."[139] Hitler ordered church bells to be rung for seven days.[140] It was his finest hour.

---

[136] Cf. *supra*, 133-4.

[137] Paul Kennedy, *The Rise and Fall of the Great Powers* (London: Unwin Hyman, 1988), 308.

[138] Winston S. Churchill, *The Second World War*, II: *Their Finest Hour* (London: The Reprint Society, 1951), 55.

[139] Jürgen Förster, "Motivation and Indoctrination in the Wehrmacht, 1933-1945," *Time to Kill*, 269.

[140] Domarus, *Hitler, Speeches and Proclamations*, III, 2033.

7 Winston Churchill's War

On taking office as prime minister, Winston Churchill set forth his intentions to the House of Commons in a short address which is remembered chiefly for one of his more celebrated rhetorical flourishes: "I have nothing to offer but blood, toil, tears and sweat." These were stirring words indeed, but they hardly constituted a plan of action. As befits an incoming head of government, he presented his program a few sentences further on. "You ask, what is our aim? I can answer in one word: It is victory, victory at all costs, victory in spite of all the terror, victory, however long and hard the road may be; for without victory, there is no survival." A resolution welcoming the formation of a government that was resolved "to prosecute the war with Germany to a victorious conclusion" passed by a vote of 381 to 0.[1]

Although no one openly opposed the resolution, there were many abstentions, especially among the Conservatives. Not everyone wanted victory at all costs, since the costs were almost certain to be borne in large measure by the propertied classes. Neville Chamberlain was still the leader of the Conservative Party, and most of its members remained loyal to him. He had tried to avoid total war, which he knew would ruin Britain financially. When he entered the legislative chamber on 13 May, he was greeted with sustained cheers from the Conservative benches. What acclaim Churchill received came almost entirely from Labour. Churchill's inner cabinet included the party's leader Clement Attlee and his chief lieutenant, Arthur Greenwood. Wisely, the new premier retained the two leading Conservatives: Chamberlain as lord president of the Council and Halifax as foreign secretary. The Conservatives had won a landslide victory in the general elections of

---

[1] 360 H C Deb., 13 May 1940, series 5, cols. 1501-1502, 1525.

1935; and since Parliament decided that no elections would be held in wartime, they continued to dominate British politics. The Labour Party supported the new government, as did the Liberals, but Churchill needed the Conservatives in order to maintain his parliamentary majority.

Churchill's participation in the war cabinet as first lord of the Admiralty had done little to allay the fears of his fellow Tories. Chamberlain had brought him into the cabinet because "he would have been a most troublesome thorn in our flesh if he had been outside."[2] Churchill's radio address of 20 January, in which he claimed that the war at sea was going splendidly for Britain, had encountered considerable scepticism at home, since it was followed a few days later by the sinking of two British destroyers by German submarines. In the same speech he tried to enlist the support of the neutral states of Western Europe in the war against Germany. His appeal was poorly received in the Netherlands and Belgium, whose sovereigns had offered in November to mediate between the belligerents. Most British Conservatives found a public exhortation of this kind, which had not been vetted by the prime minister, to be in extremely poor taste. Throughout the Phoney War, Churchill was widely viewed in his own party as a loose cannon.[3]

Within two days of having committed himself and his country to victory, the new head of government had to face the possibility of defeat. On 15 May, he received a telephone call from Reynaud informing him that the Germans had penetrated French defences at Sedan, the scene of a decisive Prussian victory in 1870. Ever the realist, the French premier concluded: "We have lost the battle." Churchill was incredulous. How could the French army, which he had pronounced the finest in world, be defeated so easily? The following day, he dashed off to Paris to assess the situation and perhaps give Reynaud some moral support. "Winston," writes Oliver Harvey, "arrived at five full of fire

---

[2] Chamberlain to Hilda, 17 September 1939, *The Neville Chamberlain Diary Letters*, 448.

[3] Andrew Roberts, *Churchill: Embattled Hero* (London: Phoenix, 1995), 7.

and fury, saying the French were lily-livered and must fight."[4] He calmed down somewhat when he realized that they *were* fighting but had been outclassed in the critical Ardennes sector. His initial reaction is understandable, given his prior conviction that the French army was supreme. If the French were invincible, how could they possibly be defeated unless they refused to fight? They could hardly expect much help from Britain. A British historian writes that "Churchill had nothing to offer but rhetoric" to Reynaud and his ministers.[5] He left the daily administration of government to his predecessor, to whom he gave the following instructions: "Neville, please mind the shop!" With Chamberlain presiding, the first item of cabinet business on 17 May was to determine what logistical problems would arise if the British Expeditionary Force had to leave France.[6]

In a diary entry of 27 May, Harvey consoled himself with the long-war strategy, which was already beginning to wear thin. "We know that Germany cannot face a long war, that their resources of petrol, material and technical troops must be severely tried. They cannot carry on an offensive for long. . . . "[7] That day, the Dunkirk evacuation began, and it surpassed even the most optimistic expectations. Once it was completed on 4 June, Churchill admitted to his fellow parliamentarians: "I feared it would be my hard lot to announce the greatest military disaster in our long history."[8] He had initially assumed that only 20,000 or 30,000 soldiers would be re-embarked; instead, four-fifths of the B. E. F. returned home. But they left behind nearly all their weapons and equipment. Dunkirk was certainly not the British army's greatest defeat, but it was a defeat all the same. Still, if Britain was to continue the fight at home, the B. E. F.

---

[4] Harvey, *Diaries*, 359.

[5] Barnett, *The Collapse of British Power*, 582.

[6] David Dilks, "The Twilight War and the Fall of France: Chamberlain and Churchill in 1940," *Transactions of the Royal Historical Society*, 28 (1978), 81.

[7] Harvey, *Diaries*, 369.

[8] 361 H C Deb., 4 June 1940, series 5, col. 788.

could not be held responsible, lest the public fall prey to defeatism. On 28 May, General Mason-Macfarlaine, who had recently served as British military attaché in Berlin, summoned elements of the local press corps to the Berkeley Hotel in London and instructed them to blame the French. "It is now no secret," he explained, "that on several fronts, the French failed to withstand the assault. . . . In fairness to the British army and its commanders, it cannot be too highly emphasized that . . . the armies of the French have been outfought - not the B. E. F."[9]

Field-Marshal Montgomery did not share this view. "In September 1939," he wrote in his memoirs, "the British army was totally unfit to fight a first class war on the continent of Europe." Its weapons and equipment "were quite inadequate, and we had only ourselves to blame for the disasters which early overtook us in the field when fighting began in 1940."[10] A modern researcher adds that, as an imperial police force, the British army in the inter-war years stressed mobility over firepower. Training was not adapted to the exigencies of modern warfare until 1942.[11] General Pownall, writing in June 1940, admitted that "the B. E. F. did not suffer the same violence and scale of attack as is reported to have fallen on the French Ninth Army, or even the First Army."[12] Churchill agreed, confiding to Ismay after the defeat that "our contribution to the battle in France had been niggardly."[13] On New-Year's eve 1939, Anne Chamberlain, the prime minister's wife, had spoken to the women of France on radio, assuring them that the four British divisions already landed there were "only the vanguard of the great army now being formed."[14] She understood that the French expected more from their ally.

---

[9] Nicholas Harman, *Dunkirk: The Patriotic Myth* (New York: Simon and Schuster, 1980), 237-8.

[10] Montgomery, *Memoirs*, 49-50.

[11] Smalley, *The British Expeditionary Force*, 38-9.

[12] Pownall, *Diaries*, 360.

[13] Ismay, *Memoirs*, 141.

[14] Chamberlain Papers, NC11/11/1.

For many propagandists, however, the temptation to heap all the blame on France was too great. Arthur Bryant, in whose eyes Britain could do no wrong, paid homage to "the young men who, ill equipped and abandoned by their allies, triumphantly and in the face of all expectations, fought their way intact to Dunkirk. . . ."[15] In reality, the British were not abandoned by their allies, rather the reverse. British commanders had not given their French counterparts prior notice of the planned evacuation.[16] The French fought on, as best they could. By defending Lille until their food and ammunition were exhausted, soldiers of the First French Army tied up a German force which would otherwise have advanced on Dunkirk. A senior British naval officer, Captain W.G. Tennant, recognized that it was the stubborn French defence of the Dunkirk perimeter that enabled the British to escape.[17] French soldiers, whose evacuation had to wait until most of the B. E. F. was rescued, were sent back to France within a week to oppose the German advance. Between 30,000 and 40,000 were left to be taken prisoner. "The vital role of the French rearguard," writes a British historian, "is recognized in all responsible British accounts of Dunkirk, without somehow sinking into the national consciousness."[18]

Churchill, to his credit, avoided holding France publicly responsible for Britain's predicament, although he did blame the King of the Belgians for ordering his army to capitulate on 28 May. The beleaguered monarch did so only after the B. E. F. had begun its retreat, and his pleas for help from Britain and France had gone unanswered.[19] Lloyd George, in a newspaper article of 2 June, called the Belgian surrender "a squalid example of perfidy," and Reynaud claimed in a radio address that "there has never been such a betrayal in history."[20]

---

[15] Arthur Bryant, *English Saga, 1840-1840* (London: Fontana, 1940), 371.

[16] Allport, *Britain at Bay*, 259.

[17] Harman, *Dunkirk: The Patriotic myth*, 145.

[18] P.M.H. Bell, "The Breakdown of the Alliance in 1940," Waites ed., *Troubled Neighbours*, 203.

[19] Mosier, *The Blitzkrieg Myth*, 145.

The Belgians had, in fact, fought bravely. Two companies of Belgian *chasseurs ardennais* held up Germany's First Panzer Division on 12 May for more than twelve hours.[21] Between Roulers and Ypres, Belgian troops improvised an anti-tank barrier by piling some 2,000 railway cars end to end. But by 27 May they had reached the limit of their endurance.[22] Belgian artillery proved effective despite bombardment by the *Luftwaffe*. A German staff officer wrote: "It was astonishing to see that the Belgians fought with increasing tenacity the nearer the end approached."[23] In this context it is worth recalling that Chamberlain had not consulted the Belgians (or the Dutch or the Danes or the Norwegians) before issuing his guarantee to Poland. A British historian notes that during the First World War, most of Belgium was occupied by a hostile power, and the rest was a battlefield. "A patriotic Belgian could reasonably ask whether his country would have fared better if King Albert had been less heroic, and the Germans had been permitted to enter with no more than a formal protest."[24]

For most Britons, the loss of Belgium, like that of Holland, was a peripheral concern; the prospect of a German victory in France was far more crucial. Several days before the Dunkirk evacuation got under way, Churchill asked the chiefs of staff to evaluate Britain's chances of continuing the war on its own. Their report, entitled "British Strategy in a Certain Eventuality" (the eventuality of a French defeat), was presented to the cabinet on 26 May. Inasmuch as the top brass could hardly throw in the towel at this point, they were guardedly optimistic. If the morale of the troops and the civilian population held, they wrote in conclusion, Germany's immediate military advantages could

---

[20] Jackson, *The Fall of France*, 91.

[21] Williamson Murray, *A War to Be Won: Fighting the Second World War* (Cambridge, MA: Belknap Press, 200), 70.

[22] Hanson W. Baldwin, *The Crucial Years, 1939-1941* (New York: Harper & Row, 1976), 131.

[23] Telford Taylor, *The March of Conquest*, 252.

[24] Roy Douglas, *The Advent of War. 1939-1940* (New York: St. Martin's Press, 1978), 139.

eventually be overcome. The political question of whether Britain *should* continue the war was left to the politicians. From 26 to 28 May, the cabinet was locked in a debate as to the advisability of seeking a compromise peace. The main point of contention was timing. Halifax asserted that it would be best to negotiate with Hitler while France was still in the fight.[25] Churchill answered that if France could not defend itself, it should leave the war rather than drag Britain into a settlement under impossible conditions.[26] He did not oppose negotiation in principle, but insisted that if Britain was ever to negotiate, it should be from a position of strength. Like Chamberlain, he assumed that the German economy was brittle and could not stand the strain of a long war. At some point, therefore, the German people would, of their own volition, throw off the dreaded Nazi regime.[27] In this, he was gravely mistaken. Flush with captured gold and resources from the newly occupied countries, plus the oil of Romania, which joined the Axis on 23 November 1940, Germany managed to attain self-sufficiency in strategic materials. It often obtained Romanian grain and oil by bartering arms taken from Czechoslovakia.[28] German civilians were not subject to serious restrictions until 1944.[29] "If only we could stick things out for another three months," Churchill argued, "the position would be entirely different." The cabinet generally concurred.[30]

With the impending defeat of France, the British people had to face the fact that their home territory was in danger. They no longer needed an explanation as to why their country was at war: it was now self-defence, pure and simple. Churchill's allusion to survival in his inaugural address to Parliament of 13 May was quickly taken up by the

---

[25] Esnouf, "British Government War Aims," 199-202, 227-8.

[26] Sir Llewellyn Woodward, *British Foreign Policy in the Second World War* (London: H. M .Stationary Office, 1962), I, 5.

[27] Walter Reid, *Churchill 1940-1945: Under Friendly Fire* (Edinburgh: Birlinn, 2008), 36.

[28] Murray, *The Change in the European Balance of Power*, 292.

[29] Charmley, *Churchill: The End of Glory*, 422.

[30] Esnouf, "British Government War Aims," 243-5.

press. "The British people are fighting for survival," asserted one weekly a few days later.[31] Another raised the possibility that the British Isles might soon be invaded.[32] In his speech of 4 June to the House of Commons, Churchill vowed that Britons would repel any invasion attempt – on the beaches and the landing grounds, in the fields, streets and hills – and concluded: "We shall never surrender." Why this master of the English language used the declarative "shall" rather the more emphatic "will" is unclear. He was probably addressing himself to Roosevelt, to whom he had given his word earlier not to surrender.[33] The president had to be convinced that any military aid to Britain would not be wasted. Actually, no one was asking the British to surrender, but at least they had finally awakened from their eight-month slumber. Colville, in a diary entry of 6 June, wrote: "The war has now for the first time become the question of paramount importance to the average Englishman."[34]

Churchill could assure Parliament and the public that Britain would fight on if invaded, but the sad fact is that it had very little to fight with. After his rousing speech, he is said to have remarked in an aside: "And we'll fight them with the butt ends of broken beer bottles because that's bloody well all we've got!"[35] Although apocryphal, this comment was painfully close to the mark. Under Chamberlain, the country had been in a Phoney War economy. Strategic materials continued to be absorbed in large measure by the civilian market. Copper was still used in the production of jewellery, bedsteads and curtain rods; half the lead production went to civilian use.[36] Britain had the industrial base necessary to make war, but did not mobilize it soon

---

[31] "Survival," *The New Statesman and Nation*, 18 May 1940, 635.

[32] "The Invasion of Britain," *The Spectator*, 7 June 1940, 769.

[33] Cf. *infra*, 229.

[34] Colville, *The Fringes of Power*, 149.

[35] Another version holds that he made the remark to American commentator Edward R. Murrow following a radio speech. Collier, *1940, the World in Flames*, 91.

[36] Hancock and Gowing, *British War Economy*, 177.

enough. Commander Stephen King-Hall wrote in March that "the democracies are mobilizing their superior economic resources" and that "the Nazis are now beginning their death struggle."[37] Such unbridled optimism was clearly premature. The following month, the French financial attaché in London viewed the British war budget as inadequate.[38] At that time, a million Britons were still unemployed. Churchill complained on 4 May that manpower in the munitions industry had increased by only eleven percent since September.[39] Small wonder, then, that he turned to the United States for arms.

France could no longer defend itself and soon left the war. At the last meetings of the Supreme Inter-allied War Council on 11 and 12 June, Churchill urged the French to engage in guerrilla warfare throughout the length and breadth of their country. This was the sort of rhetoric he had to offer, and it met with a unanimous rejection.[40] General Weygand, who had replaced Gamelin as commander-in-chief, was indignant. He dismissed the proposal as pure fantasy. ("*C'est du roman!*")[41] Two weeks earlier, Churchill had told his cabinet colleagues that the French should probably cease fighting.[42] Now he wanted to turn all of France into a battlefield. Marshal Pétain objected that the Germans would wreak vengeance on civilians and their property throughout the country.[43] During the First World War, many Belgian civilians were killed by German troops, who suspected them of being real or potential *francs-tireurs*. (Actually, very few were.) Pétain wanted France to avoid a similar fate – or worse. General Spears, who had little faith in guerrilla warfare, called it the prime minister's

---

[37] Edgerton, *Britain's War Machine*, 11.

[38] Imlay, "France and the Phoney War," 266.

[39] Taylor, *English History*, 465.

[40] Azéma, *1940, l'année noire*, 141.

[41] François Bédarida, "La rupture franco-britannique de 1940. Le Conseil Suprême Interallié, de l'invasion à la défaite de la France, " *Vingtième Siècle. Revue d'histoire*, January-March 1990, 45.

[42] Cf. *supra*, 215.

[43] Villelume, *Journal d'une défaite*, 411.

"favourite hobby-horse."[44] When Reynaud asked permission to conclude a separate armistice with Germany, Churchill offered more rhetoric. He acknowledged that "France has been sacrificed in the struggle against the common enemy," but promised that "Great Britain will in any event restore her to power and greatness." In an effort to delay an armistice, he held out hope that the United States would soon enter the war.[45]

With the French army in retreat everywhere except on the Italian front, Churchill made one last desperate effort to keep France in the fight. On 16 June, he proposed a union between France and Britain, which would include joint citizenship, associated parliaments and – most important of all – a single war cabinet to direct all military operations. He had a strategic interest in keeping the French fleet active and in mobilizing France's colonial resources against a common enemy. Reynaud accepted the proposal; but it was opposed by most of his ministers, who argued that it would make France totally subservient to Britain and leave their country open to devastation by the Germans. Practical considerations also entered the picture. A political union implying the loss of French sovereignty could not be validated by the cabinet alone but would require parliamentary sanction. The proposal quickly expired and was never revived.[46]

In Britain, the fall of France was widely greeted first with expressions of shock and then with sighs of relief. After the Munich conference, Halifax had written: "It is one thing to allow German expansion in Central Europe, which to my mind is a normal & natural thing, but we must be able to resist German expansion in Western Europe or else our whole position is undermined."[47] And now it was.

---

[44] Spears, *Assignment to Catastrophe*, II, 155.

[45] John Costello, *Ten Days That Saved the West* (London: Bantam Press, 1991), 281-2.

[46] Avi Shlaim, "Prelude to Downfall: The British Offer of Union to France, June 1940," *Journal of Contemporary History*, July 1979, 49

[47] Goldstein , "Neville Chamberlain, the British Official Mind and the Munich Crisis," 286.

In his diary, he bemoaned the reversals suffered by the French army, "the one firm rock on which everyone [in Britain] was willing to build for the last two years."[48] Yet no one in the British government (and hardly anyone outside it) wanted France to *conquer* Germany. Shades of Louis XIV and Napoleon! The "firm rock" was expected simply to hold until the good German people realized that they could not win. A Canadian historian has noted that "British planners possessed no clear idea of how to defeat Germany."[49] And for good reason: they were not encouraged to find one by their political leaders. Chamberlain believed that "Germany's defeat was neither necessary nor desirable."[50] Churchill promised victory whatever the cost; but not until June 1940, when Britain itself was threatened, was there a national consensus in favour of defeating Germany. Ever since 1919, successive British governments had done everything possible to prevent French hegemony on the continent of Europe; and in this, they were remarkably successful – if anything, too successful. The Russian-born wife of J.M. Keynes grasped intuitively the nature of the problem. On 14 June she asked: "If the British and the French were not ready for war, then why did they declare it?"[51] Why indeed? That is the essential question of the Phoney War.

Ever complacent, Chamberlain had written to his sister late in March, "After all, if the Germans can annihilate us so completely, why haven't they done it?"[52] Now he had his answer. On receiving news of the German breakthrough at Sedan and on the Meuse, he was taken aback: "All my world has tumbled to bits in a moment."[53] He had hoped to "live to see the day when Hitlerism has been destroyed and a liberated Europe has been re-established." Instead, as noted by a

---

[48] Roberts, *"The Holy Fox"*, 211.
[49] Imlay, *Facing the Second World War*, 357.
[50] *Ibid.*, 217.
[51] *The Maisky Diaries*, 286.
[52] Chamberlain to Ida, 30 March 1940, *The Neville Chamberlain Diary Letters*, 514.
[53] Chamberlain to Hilda, 17 May 1940, *ibid.*, 531.

biographer, "he lived only to see Hitlerism triumphant and the greater part of Europe held in thrall."[54] In a diary entry of 8 June, he shifted responsibility for the disaster onto the French: "The French are terrible allies."[55] They were terrible allies because they were defeated in battle, and they were defeated because they had no body of water, such as the English Channel, to protect them. But what sort of ally was Chamberlain? Later that month, he confided to his sister: "We are in fact alone, and we are in any case free of our obligations to the French who have been nothing but a liability to us. It would have been far better if they had been neutral from the beginning."[56] (Whatever happened to "the magnificent soldiers of France," whose praises he had sung only a few weeks earlier?[57]) That the French should not have gone to war in 1939 is a reasonable proposition, but Chamberlain needed France as a co-belligerent in order to save his government and his political career. Fearing a parliamentary revolt, he pleaded with Daladier on the evening of 2 September to declare war immediately.[58] Now he blamed the French for the tragic outcome of *his* war, the war he had initiated and lost. From his narrow Anglo-centric point of view, he failed to see that Britain, which had provided only a token military contribution to the war effort on land, was a liability to France.

So Britain was now alone. Well, not quite alone, since it could count on support from the Dominions; but it was free of continental commitments. For this, King George VI, like most of his subjects, was truly thankful. In a letter to his mother, Queen Mary, he wrote: "Personally I feel happier now that we have no more allies to be polite to & to pamper."[59] In truth, France was hardly pampered, since it had

---

[54] Macleod, *Neville Chamberlain*, 277.
[55] Peter W. Ludlow, "The Unwinding of Appeasement," Lothar Kettenacker ed., *Das "Andere Deutschland" im Zweiten Weltkrieg* (Stuttgart: Ernst Klett Verlag, 1977), 43-4.
[56] Chamberlain to Hilda, 29 June 1940, *The Neville Chamberlain Diary Letters*, 546.
[57] Cf. *supra*, 168.
[58] Cf. *supra*, 105-6.
[59] Harman, *Dunkirk: The Patriotic Myth*, 242.

to bear the brunt of the fighting on land; but at least it was out of the way. Britain did have to be polite to its allies during the First World War, an experience that neither the king nor any of his subjects wanted to relive.[60] Churchill had to be polite to Reynaud, who pleaded for Britain to send more fighters to France. In a letter of 16 May, Air Marshal Hugh Dowding vigorously opposed the move since it would deplete the squadrons needed to defend British airspace. He later confessed to Halifax: "I don't mind telling you that when I heard of the French collapse, I went down on my knees and thanked God."[61]

Dorothy Sayers rose to the occasion by writing a poem which began, "Praise God, now for an English war."[62] (It would not remain solely English for long, since Churchill desperately needed American participation in some form.) Among ordinary Britons, "No more bloody allies!" was a common refrain.[63] Even Greenwood, who was minister without portfolio in Churchill's war cabinet, referred to the French as "these bloody gallant allies" less than a week after real fighting in the west had begun. He had warmly welcomed Britain's declaration of war; but on learning of Poland's defeat, he admitted that "it lies on my conscience . . . that we did not do more for her . . . ." The lesson to be drawn, he explained, was "that in future such help as we give to our friends should be quick, certain and generous."[64] Now he blamed everything on the French. Ironside corrected him: "I told him that we had depended upon the French army. That we had no army and that therefore it was not right to say, 'these bloody allies.' It was for them to say that of us."[65] "The fall of France," writes a British historian,

---

[60] Bond, "The British Field Force in France and Belgium, 1939-1940," *Time to Kill*, 49.

[61] Quoted in Brian Bond, "Dunkirk: Myths and Lessons," *The RUSI Journal*, September 1982, 3.

[62] The full text can be found in Wheeler-Bennett, *King George VI*, 461.

[63] Nick Hayes, "An 'English War', Wartime Culture and 'Millions Like Us'," Nick Hayes and Jeff Hill eds., *"Millions Like Us"? British Culture in the Second World War* (Liverpool University Press, 1999), 1

[64] 351 H C Deb., 20 September 1939, col. 984.

"shattered the foundations of the complacent and leisurely British strategy . . . no German bankruptcy but instead the resources of a whole continent for Germany to exploit."[66]

With France out of the way, many British politicians swiftly reverted to their habitual isolationism, only now it was coupled with open contempt and even hostility toward the former ally. Lord Hankey, who had joined Chamberlain's war cabinet as minister without portfolio, complained to Sir John Simon, the chancellor of the exchequer, on 17 June that "the more I reflect on the events of the previous years, the more I realize that the French have been our evil genius from the Paris peace conference until today, inclusive."[67] He then wrote to Halifax, saying: "To my mind the French are more responsible for our troubles than anyone."[68] A British historian concludes: "The collapse of the Third Republic in the summer of 1940 provided British francophobes with all the evidence they needed to demonstrate the accuracy of their long-held opinion that France was rotten to the core and that Britain had made a disastrous error of judgment in allying itself with that country in 1939."[69] Actually, the most serious error of judgment was declaring war in the first place and dragging France into it. Not that Chamberlain had much choice; his hands were tied by the Polish guarantee. For anyone in Britain to accuse France of being rotten to the core, simply because it was defeated in battle and lacked a moat to keep the enemy at bay, is rank hypocrisy. France in September 1939 had a mass army, whereas Britain could muster only two ill-trained and ill-equipped divisions. Britain

---

[65] *The Ironside Diaries*, 313.

[66] Barnett, *Britain and Her Army*, 431.

[67] Michael Dockrill, "British Official Perceptions of France and the French, 1936-1940," Philippe Chassaigne and Michael Dockrill eds., *Anglo-French Relations, 1898-1998: From Fashoda to Jospin* (Basingstoke: Palgrave, 2002),106.

[68] Ludlow, "The Unwinding of Appeasement," 44.

[69] Dockrill, "British Official Perceptions of France and the French, 1936-1940," 107.

was in no position to declare war on Germany without French participation.

Throughout the Phoney War, Britain relied on France to contain Germany. It was this reliance, perhaps even more than ingrained francophobia, that explains why ordinary Britons were heard to exclaim. "No more bloody allies!" on learning of the French defeat. They had been led astray by their own government, which repeatedly proclaimed the French army to be "the strongest and best trained military force in the world."[70] The news media also helped maintain the illusion of French power. In November 1939, a leading conservative weekly published an article which began: "All along the line France is stronger today than twenty-five years ago." The author claimed that the iron ore deposits of Lorraine, now protected by the Maginot Line, were secure. France was economically self-reliant and did not depend on imports from beyond its empire for essential raw materials. The article concludes: "With her war chest full [sic], territory intact and industries mobilised, France, economically the best balanced of all the industrial countries of Europe, alongside Britain can face a major war of long duration confident of ultimate success."[71] The comforting falsehoods of British propaganda during the war of waiting inevitably contributed to widespread disillusionment among the public once the truth became known.

Less than a month after Marshal Pétain sued for an armistice, a British journalist named Gordon Waterfield dashed off a pamphlet in which he asserted that the French alone were responsible for their fate. Their individualism, political divisions and reliance on the Maginot Line, he claimed, left them incapable of resisting the German onslaught.[72] That France had a much smaller population and industrial base than Germany does not seem to have crossed his mind. But if

---

[70] Cf. *supra*, 137.

[71] V.S. Swaminathan, "The Strength of France," *The Spectator*, 24 November 1939, 737-8.

[72] Gordon Waterfield, *What Happened To France* (London: John Murray, 1940), *passim*.

Britain was to continue the fight, it could not accept responsibility for the recent fiasco, lest the public become demoralized. So France had to shoulder all the blame. The Maginot Line was in fact central to British strategy in the Phoney War.[73] Its very existence presumably excused Britain from having to raise a mass army. British politicians, from Chamberlain on down, had complete faith in France's wall of fortresses – more so than the French themselves. After Belgium announced its neutrality in 1936, several French politicians, including Daladier, proposed to extend the Maginot Line along the Belgian border. Gamelin opposed the idea. The French army needed room for manoeuvre. It also needed modern weapons, which could not be purchased if huge sums were spent on fortifications.

As it happened, French troops in the Maginot Line, which was never breached but taken from the rear, were the last to surrender – on 22 June, five days after Pétain gave the order.[74] They simply did not believe radio reports from Germany (nearby French stations had closed down) that France was defeated.[75] Since then, a myth has developed that France was in the grip of a "Maginot mentality." If anything, it was the British who had a Maginot mentality. In November 1939 Leslie Hore-Belisha, the war secretary, told the House of Commons that the Maginot Line gave "safe cover to our preparations" and added: "This is a fortress war . . . a war of endurance."[76] Even after his dismissal in January, British strategy remained fundamentally unchanged. Waterfield deals with the French defeat in a vacuum, ignoring Britain's role. Unfortunately, many historians follow his example. One would think that contemporary readers need the same encouragement to "keep calm and carry on" as the British civilians of 1940. They might refer to

---

[73] Brian Bond, *British Military Policy between the Two World Wars* (Oxford: Clarendon Press, 1980), 313.

[74] Smart and Black, *British Strategy and Politics during the Phony War*, 82, 93.

[75] Dorgelès, *La Drôle de Guerre*, 188-9.

[76] 355 H C Deb., 22 November 1939, cols. 1266-1267.

an official British publication of 1944 that states flatly: "In 1940 our two countries suffered a joint military disaster."[77]

Under the armistice terms, the Vichy regime retained control of the French navy, which was the fourth largest in the world after those of the United States, Britain and Japan; and most of its ships were of recent construction. The British government was naturally concerned that it might fall into German hands. On 25 June, Churchill received a brief message from George Bernard Shaw, which read: "Dear Prime Minister, Why not declare war on France and capture her fleet (which would gladly strike its colours to us) before A. H. recovers his breath? Surely that is the logic of the situation?"[78] Churchill did still better: he ordered the French fleet to be captured and, if necessary, sunk *without* declaring war. Admiral Darlan, the French naval commander, had given his word of honour that he would sink his own ships rather than turn them over to Germany, but he was not believed in Whitehall. British intelligence failed to intercept Darlan's signal of 24 June ordering all French warships to sail to the United States or be scuttled if there was any danger that they might be captured by Germany.[79] French vessels in British ports were taken with little loss of life; those in Alexandria struck their colours willingly.

At the Algerian port of Mers el-Kébir, the French commander, Admiral Gensoul, was given an ultimatum on 3 July to scuttle his fleet or relinquish control to the Royal Navy. When he refused, the French warships, lying at anchor, were fired upon. Only the battle cruiser *Strasbourg*, five destroyers and a seaplane tender managed to escape and find a safe harbour at Toulon. Some 1300 French seamen and officers, or roughly forty percent of the total American losses at Pearl Harbor, were killed. Churchill announced the results to Parliament the following day; and for the first time since becoming prime minister, he received a standing ovation from the Conservative benches.[80] In a radio

---

[77] *Instructions for British Servicemen in France 1944* (reprint, Oxford: Bodleian Library, 2005), 30.

[78] Colville, *The Fringes of Power*, 171.

[79] Hinsley, *British Intelligence in the Second World War*, 150.

address to the French people, de Gaulle approved the initiative. He could hardly do otherwise if he wished to retain British support, but he did note in his memoirs that voluntary enlistments in his newly created Free French organisation ceased altogether.[81] Worse, French seamen and naval officers in Britain, who had signed up to fight alongside de Gaulle, now asked to be repatriated.[82] For several months thereafter, he was left with an "army" of 7,000 men, and no navy. Anglo-French relations reached their nadir. In his report, the British commander at Mers el-Kébir, Admiral Somerville, referred to "enemy fire."[83] Darlan felt personally insulted at not being trusted, and he did keep his word. When the *Wehrmacht* occupied southern France in November 1942, he ordered the remaining warships at Toulon to be scuttled rather than fall into German hands. In an emotional message to Churchill dated 4 December, he recalled his earlier promise not to surrender the fleet, since that "would be contrary to our naval traditions and honour."[84] A British historian has characterized the operation at Mers el-Kébir as a "victory. . . of perceived political necessity over military reality."[85] The Roosevelt administration endorsed the action. Like Churchill, the president was concerned that the French fleet might be taken over by Germany.[86]

Mers el-Kébir did not end the Anglo-French alliance. It had already expired at Dunkirk, which the French viewed as a betrayal.[87] The successful evacuation convinced Churchill that Britain could hold

---

[80] Roberts, *Churchill: Embattled Hero*, 36-7; Azéma, *1940, l'année noire*, 243.

[81] De Gaulle, *Mémoires de guerre*: I, 98-100.

[82] David Brown, *The Road to Oran: Anglo-French Naval Relations, September 1939 – July 1940* (London: Frank Cass, 2003), pp. 198-204.

[83] Costello, *Ten Days That Saved the West*, 338.

[84] Winston Churchill, *The Second World War*, II *Their Finest Hour*, (London: The Reprint Society, 1951), 196-7.

[85] Brown, *The Road to Oran*, 204.

[86] Robert Dallek, *Franklin D. Roosevelt and American Foreign Policy, 1932-1945* (New York: Oxford University Press, 1979), 231.

[87] Bond, "Dunkirk: Myths and Lessons," 6.

out for at least three more months – not so much because the bulk of the B. E. F. had been repatriated. Having abandoned nearly all their weapons and equipment, the troops were in no condition wage war in the immediate future. Rather, the exploits of British fighter pilots, operating at the limit of their range, drew his admiration and encouraged him to believe – correctly – that they could successfully defend the island's airspace. In his speech of 4 June, he gave them fulsome praise. The ensuing battle of Britain did not unite the country quite as firmly as is depicted in film, but it did put an end to the sympathy expressed during the Phoney War by many well-meaning people, chiefly intellectuals, for the essentially good German citizen. Once the bombs began to fall on London and other cities, even pacifists like Vera Brittain had to seek shelter.[88] The Ministry of Information, which had previously sought to distinguish between the decent German people and their horrid dictator, now mounted an anger campaign against Germany as a whole. Henceforth, it made no distinction between a German and a Nazi. Nazism was now depicted as "but the latest and most virulent manifestation of the inherent wickedness of the German race."[89]

With France defeated and Britain on the defensive, Hitler once again addressed the Nazi Reichstag on 19 July to make another peace offer. "I see no reason why this war need go on," he said. In the days that followed, Germany made diplomatic representations through Sweden, the United States and the Vatican. A British historian very much opposed to Hitler has deemed this offer sincere. "For his part, he was perfectly willing to conclude an alliance with Great Britain and to recognize the continued existence of the British Empire, which (he told Rundstedt) must be looked on, together with the Catholic Church, as one of the cornerstones of Western civilization. England would have to return the German colonies and recognize Germany's dominant

---

[88] Vera Brittain, *Wartime Chronicle, 1939-1945* (London: Victor Gollancz, 1989), 51-3.
[89] Ian McLaine, *Ministry of Morale. Home Front Morale and the Ministry of Information in World War II* (London: George Allen & Unwin, 1979), 146.

position in Europe, but that was all."[90] The offer was quickly brushed aside. In his memoirs, Churchill did not impugn Hitler's sincerity; he simply refused "to accept the surrender by Britain of all she had entered the war to maintain."[91] Having promised victory at all costs, Churchill had to continue the war entered into by Chamberlain, or resign.

Even as the RAF scored victories over German warplanes, Britain was not yet out of danger. German surface raiders and U-boats took their toll of the British merchant fleet, whose losses were substantially greater than those of the armed services. During the autumn and winter of 1940-1941, nearly 580,000 gross tons of British commercial shipping were sent to the bottom by German warships and armed merchantmen; four times as many fell prey to submarines.[92] In a particularly animated session of Parliament on 15 October 1940, Churchill was asked by Labour MP Sidney Silverman to state the government's war aims once Britain attained victory. The prime minister, who was obviously rattled by this line of questioning, replied: "We are, among other things, fighting it [the war] in order to survive . . . ." When Silverman persisted in wanting to know what kind of better world Britain hoped to achieve, he was told, "I think there is great danger in making statements which are not of a very general character upon this subject. Take, for instance, the attitude which we adopt towards the enemy when he is defeated – you will find very different opinions prevailing about that."[93] As if to emphasize Churchill's point about survival, the debate was punctuated by the wail of air raid sirens, as bombs continued to fall on London.[94]

Despite the bombing and the privations caused by Germany's naval actions, Britain managed to survive; but it was nowhere near the victory to which Churchill had pledged himself. On the morning of 18

---

[90] Alan Bullock, *Hitler: A Study in Tyranny* (New York: Harper & Row, 1962), 589.

[91] Churchill, *Their Finest Hour*, 217.

[92] Todman, *Britain's War*, 499-500.

[93] 365 H C Deb., 15 October 1940, col. 596.

[94] *New York Times*, 16 October 1940.

May 1940, with the news from France increasingly bleak, his son Randolph found him in unusually good spirits. He was sure that Britain could defeat Germany. When Randolph asked how, Churchill replied simply: "I shall drag the United States in."[95] This represents a radical departure from the position of Chamberlain, who had written to his sister in January 1940: "Heaven knows I don't want the Americans to fight for us – we should have to pay too dearly for that if they had a right to be in on the peace terms. . . ."[96] Of course, the situation had changed radically, so that Chamberlain's earlier hopes for an easy victory without American support were now dashed. The chiefs of staff based their confidence that Britain would eventually prevail on the premise that "the United States of America is willing to give us full economic and financial assistance, *without which we do not think we could continue the war with any chance of success.*" [emphasis in the original.][97]

Churchill wanted more. He wanted full American participation; and to this end, he sent a sombrely worded telegram to Roosevelt on 20 May. While he, Churchill, and his cabinet would never consent to surrender, a successor government might negotiate a settlement with Germany, using the Royal Navy as its "sole remaining bargaining counter," if the United States left Britain to its fate. "Excuse me, Mr. President, putting this nightmare bluntly."[98] And a nightmare it surely was. In Hitler's hands, the Royal Navy would have posed a major threat to the United States. Even before Marshal Pétain took France out of the war, Roosevelt was genuinely concerned that Hitler might offer generous terms to Britain in exchange for its fleet.[99] Yet there is no

---

[95] Martin Gilbert, *Finest Hour: Winston S. Churchill, 1939-1941* (London: Heinemann, 1983), 358.

[96] Chamberlain to Ida, 27 January 1940, *The Neville Chamberlain Diary Letters*, 492.

[97] Moss, *Nineteen Weeks*, 127.

[98] Warren F. Kimball ed., *Churchill & Roosevelt: The Complete Correspondence* (Princeton, NJ: Princeton University Press, 1984), I, 40.

[99] Harold L. Ickes, *The Secret Diary of Harold L. Ickes*, III: *The Lowering Clouds* (New York: Simon and Schuster, 1954), 188.

indication that anyone in Britain, except perhaps the home-grown fascist Oswald Mosley, would have accepted such terms. Anticipating that possibility, Churchill had Mosley arrested on 23 May and interned in Brixton. Another 1,847 members of his British Union of Fascists, which had no representation in Parliament, were also put under arrest.[100] Lloyd George was a far more likely candidate for a compromise peace, and he was far too patriotic even to consider abandoning the Senior Service. Churchill might dangle the spectre of a British Quisling before Roosevelt; but privately he accepted the possibility that, in the event that Britain had to sue for peace, his likely successor would be Lloyd George or Halifax, neither of whom would commit such treason.[101]

Churchill had conjured up the same nightmare with Joseph Kennedy early in October 1939. "After all," he said, "if [the Germans] bombed us into a state of subjection, one of their terms of course would be to hand over the fleet; and if we attempted to scuttle the fleet their terms would be that much worse. And if they got the British fleet, they would have immediate superiority over the United States. . . ." So despite his brave rhetoric, Churchill seems to have realized from the start that without the support of the Soviet Union, the allies might not win. He had warned the Committee of Imperial Defence in 1925 that Britain and France would probably not be able to defeat Germany once it regained its strength.[102] Now that the British government had declared war, only the entry of the United States could help redress the balance. The U. S. ambassador concluded, in his usual forthright style: "If Germany does not break and throw Hitler out . . . they will spend every hour figuring how to get us in."[103]

---

[100] Lukacs, *The Duel*, 78.

[101] Paul Addison, "Lloyd George and Compromise Peace in the Second World War," A.J.P. Taylor ed., *Lloyd George: Twelve Essays* (London: Hamish Hamilton, 1971), 383.

[102] Stephen A. Schuker, *The End of French Predominance in Europe* (Chapel Hill, NC: The University of North Carolina Press, 1976), 388-9.

[103] Kennedy to Hull, FRUS I General, 2 October 1939, 500.

Here, Churchill was acting true to form. As first lord of the Admiralty, he had sought to drag the Americans into the First World War. In a letter of 30 April 1915 to Walter Runciman, the president of the Board of Trade, he wrote: "It is important to attract neutral shipping to our shores in the hope especially of embroiling the United States with Germany." Then, noting that seaborne commerce had been sharply reduced by the activity of German submarines, he added: "For our part we want the traffic - the more the better; and if some of it gets into trouble, better still."[104] A week later the *Lusitania*, the fastest and most luxurious liner afloat and the pride of the British merchant fleet, was torpedoed by a German submarine with the loss of 1197 passengers, including 128 Americans. There were two explosions: one of the torpedo itself, followed by another, of unknown origin. The *Lusitania* was a floating ammunition dump, transporting munitions manufactured in the United States for Britain; and the German embassy had put notices in 50 newspapers throughout the United States, warning American citizens not to board the liner, which was about to enter a war zone. There is no firm evidence that Churchill, who was in France at the time, had a hand in the disaster, but it did happen on his watch. The Admiralty, being responsible for the safety of British shipping in wartime, was clearly negligent in not sending two destroyers, then lying at anchor in a nearby port, to escort the vessel, which was ordered to reduce speed in an area where three ships had recently been sunk by enemy submarines. Nonetheless, the ultimate responsibility was German.

Americans generally were appalled at the loss of life but were not at all eager to make war on Germany. "We were sure," Churchill wrote later, "that [submarine warfare] would offend and perhaps embroil the United States,"[105] which it eventually did, but not just then. Commenting on President Wilson's war address to Congress nearly two

---

[104] Erik Larson, *Dead Wake: The Last Crossing of the Lusitania* (New York: Crown, 2015), 190.
[105] Walter Millis, *Road to War: America, 1914-1917* (New York: Houghton Mifflin, 1935), 137.

years later, he added: "What he did in April 1917 could have been done in May 1915."[106] So the sinking of the *Lusitania*, which was flying a British and not an American flag, was supposed to bring the United States into a European conflict after all. There seems to be no example in recorded history of one nation going to war with a second because it sank the ship of a third. But Churchill, whose mother was American, somehow expected that the United States, by virtue of cultural ties, would gladly help fight Britain's wars.

What is particularly distressing is Churchill's comment that the loss of 50 infants and children in the sinking would turn world public opinion against Germany. "In spite of all the horror," he wrote in 1937, "we must regard the sinking of the *Lusitania* as an event most favourable to the allies. . . . The poor babies who perished in the ocean struck a blow at German power more deadly than could have been achieved by the sacrifice of a hundred thousand fighting men."[107] Perhaps, but the "poor babies" were British subjects. Did Churchill want to put the lives of his compatriots at risk in order to embroil the United States? In September 1939, he confided to Dalton that the Americans were more likely to sympathize with Britain if the first civilian victims of aerial bombardment were British rather than German.[108] (He obviously gave little thought to the Poles.) In the summer of 1940, de Gaulle asked him: "Are you in such a hurry to see your cities and towns blown to bits?" Churchill replied, "You must understand that the bombing of Oxford, Coventry and Canterbury will provoke such a wave of indignation in the United States that the Americans will enter the war."[109]

Americans did, in fact, sympathize with British civilians caught in the bombing. The cover of *Life* magazine dated 23 September 1940

---

[106] Winston S. Churchill, *The World Crisis, 1916-1918*, New York: Scribner's, 1927), I, 237.

[107] Diana Preston, *Wilful Murder: The Sinking of the Lusitania* (London: Transworld, 2015), 5, 445.

[108] Cf. *supra*, 108-9.

[109] De Gaulle, *Mémoires de guerre,* I, 112.

bore the photograph of a pretty, bright-eyed little English girl, her head covered by a bandage, sitting upright in a hospital bed. The title read simply: "Air-raid Victim." The child was identified as Eileen Dunne, three years and nine months of age. A brief editorial explained: "A German bomber, whose crew had never met her, dropped a bomb on a North England village. A splinter from it hit Eileen." The feature article, entitled, "Hitler Tries to Destroy London," was illustrated with graphic images of the destruction taken by British photographer Cecil Beaton.[110] But however heart-rending the photographs may have been, the American people were still in no mood for war. Their attitude was remarkably similar to that of the British, who showed little interest in fighting even after their government declared war in September 1939. Not until Britain was directly threatened did its people gird themselves for battle. No one wanted a repeat of 1914-1918.

In the United States, war veterans and their families retained bitter memories of the First World War. The casualty figures of the Meuse-Argonne offensive in September and October of 1918 were the highest ever recorded by the U. S. Army in a similar period. The war's grim legacy was brought to public view by the march of 17,000 unemployed veterans who converged on Washington in July 1932 to demand immediate payment of their bonus due in 1945. The "Bonus Army" was first assaulted by the police with the death of two veterans. Then elements of the regular army, led by General Douglas MacArthur, dispersed the marchers forcibly and burned their shacks on the Anacostia Flats. The mood of the country once Britain and France declared war can be seen in the popularity of a gangster film released on 23 October 1939 by the Warner Brothers studio. "The Roaring Twenties" depicted the tribulations of a veteran, played by James Cagney, who returns home in 1919 after having done his patriotic duty on the battlefield, only to find that his job as an automobile mechanic has been taken. After trying to make a living as a taxi driver, he turns to bootlegging. His cellmate in prison, where he serves a brief sentence,

---

[110] *Life*, 23 September 1940, 21, 23-9.

is another veteran who likewise can no longer adjust to civil society. "I have seen too much blood, too much violence," he says.

Churchill's plan to drag the United States into the war was doomed from the start. The Americans were put off by the contraband lists and stoppages of their ships on the high seas that accompanied the British blockade. When the arms embargo was repealed on 2 November 1939 by a vote of 243 to 181 in the House of Representatives, Moffat wrote, "I cannot help feeling that the British may draw false conclusions from the size of the vote and think they have us in their pocket." They hadn't: the Americans were not in anyone's pocket. Among career diplomats in the State Department, the watchword was, "No help to Germany but no Dominion status for ourselves."[111] For the U. S. economy, arms sales to the allies were not an unmixed blessing. To pay for war matériel, Britain virtually ceased importing American automobiles, tobacco, canned vegetables and office equipment.[112]

With the defeat of France almost a certainty, Roosevelt firmly resisted allied efforts to involve the United States directly in the European conflict. On 10 June 1940, as the French government was preparing to leave Paris, Reynaud sent him an emotional appeal in which he pledged to continue the fight and added: "I beseech you to declare publicly that the United States will give the allies aid and material support by all means short of an expeditionary force. I beseech you to do this before it is too late."[113] The president's reply was non-committal: "The magnificent resistance of the French and British armies has profoundly impressed the American people."[114] Although the text offered little hope of American intervention, Churchill wanted to see it published immediately, in the hope of encouraging the French and drawing the United States closer to war. Roosevelt refused categorically. "My message to Reynaud is not to be published in any circumstances."[115] To avoid further misunderstanding, he informed

---

[111] *The Moffat Papers*, 276.

[112] *New York Times*, 3 November 1939.

[113] Dallek, *Franklin D. Roosevelt and American Foreign Policy*,229.

[114] *Roosevelt and Churchill: The Complete Correspondence*, 46.

Churchill that it "did not commit the [U. S.] government to military participation in support of allied governments." Only Congress, he reminded his British correspondent, has the authority to declare war.[116]

Roosevelt not only respected the constitution; he was an astute observer of public opinion. Once it became evident that France was about to be overrun, a group of thirty influential private American citizens released a communiqué to the press on 10 June 1940, urging the United States to declare war on Germany immediately. Their call was met with almost universal derision, and they were labelled "warhawks" by the *St. Louis Post-Dispatch* in an editorial which noted that most of the signatories were past military age.[117] Few Americans of military age had any taste for the army. At Roosevelt's behest, the first peacetime draft was voted into law on 14 September 1940 by wide margins in both houses of Congress. Service was to be for one year, but Army Chief of Staff General George C. Marshall appealed to Congress for an extension, which was duly approved on 12 August 1941. This time, however, the vote was much closer – 203 to 202 in the House of Representatives, whose members were deluged with messages from servicemen and their families, urging defeat of the measure.[118]

To assess the discontent, *Life* magazine sent a reporter to interview the draftees and their officers at an army base. He found training to be inadequate, as the soldiers were occupied more with close-order drill and chores such as mowing the grass than with preparation for battle. Most had never fired a trench mortar, and rifle practice was severely limited due to a shortage of bullets. With half a million Springfield rifles and 130 million rounds of 30-calibre ammunition going to Britain, this was hardly surprising. American small arms, being incompatible with the Lee-Enfield rifle which fired a

---

[115] Hull to Kennedy, 13 June 1940, FRUS, General (1940), I, 350.

[116] *Churchill & Roosevelt: The Complete Correspondence,* 48.

[117] Mark Lincoln Chadwin, *The Warhawks: American Interventionists before Pearl Harbor* (New York: Norton, 1968), 32-9.

[118] Lynne Olson, *Those Angry Days: Roosevelt, Lindbergh, and America's Fight over World War II, 1939-1941* (New York: Random House, 2013), 351.

303-calibre round, were destined primarily for the Home Guard, which was Britain's last line of defence in the event of invasion.[119] Since none occurred, they were never used.

Worse still, the Americans' morale was abysmally low. In latrines, on artillery pieces and on cars could be seen the letters O H I O, standing for "Over the hill in October." The conscripts seemed ready to desert if their tour of duty was extended. (In the event, very few did; nearly all preferred to avoid court-martial.) "The boys here hate the army," explained one private. "They have no fighting spirit, except among themselves when they get stinking drunk." Others complained of not being able to get their jobs back once they returned to civilian life. One draftee reported that a buddy requested leave to see his wife who had just given birth. When he was turned down, he went AWOL. "What would you do?" the soldier asked. No one saw much urgency in the international situation. "This country is in no danger," asserted one private. "The Germans can't cross the Channel. How can they get over here?" A lieutenant added: "All we do if we fight with England is lose a hell of a lot of money, and then England will say we profited from them."[120]

With the exception of some anglophiles in the north-eastern United States, Americans generally did not want their country to be dragged into war. They knew that Britain had not extended any help to Poland in 1939.[121] In September 1941, Captain Alec Cunningham-Reid, a Tory MP and air ace of the First World War, read to the House of Commons an excerpt from an article by a nationally syndicated American columnist (unnamed), who claimed that Britain "expects America . . . to drag her chestnuts out of the hot coals of the war she has declared and the diplomatic complications she has involved herself in." Cunningham-Reid then quoted John Martin, the war editor of *Life*, who observed that the Nazi invasion of the Soviet Union "has disunited American public opinion."[122] Most Americans hated Communism, and

---

[119] Todman, *Britain's War,* 417.

[120] "This is What Soldiers Complain About," *Life*, 18 August 1941, 17-18.

[121] Nicholas Bethell, *The War Hitler Won* (London: Allen Lane, 1972), 417.

even Roosevelt had reacted angrily to the Soviet aggression against Finland. "The Soviet Union," he declared on 10 February 1940, "is run by a dictatorship as absolute as any other dictatorship in the world. It has allied itself with another dictatorship, and it has invaded a neighbour so infinitesimally small that it could do no conceivable possible harm to the Soviet Union."[123] On learning that the Soviet Union had been invaded, Senator Harry S. Truman of Missouri stated publicly: "If we see that Germany is winning, we ought to help Russia, and if Russia is winning, we ought to help Germany . . . although I don't want to see Hitler victorious under any circumstances." Truman's views were widely shared throughout the country.[124]

Most Americans, indeed an overwhelming majority, did not want to see Hitler victorious and tended to sympathize with his enemies. For Churchill, however, obtaining military aid from the United States was no easy task. On 15 May 1940, just two days after taking office, he pleaded with Roosevelt to send Britain forty to fifty overage destroyers, as well as modern warplanes. This proud scion of the British Empire did not enjoy his role as supplicant. Having finished writing the message, he told his private secretary: "Here's a telegram for those bloody Yankees. Send it off tonight."[125] The allies had purchased few American arms during the Phoney War, relying on their own production; and in May 1940, the United States could hardly release any combat aircraft since it did not have enough for its own defence.[126] Britain eventually received the destroyers, but at a steep price: a 99-year lease to the United States of military bases in Newfoundland, Bermuda, British Guiana and the Caribbean. Most of these antiquated and poorly maintained vessels were useless. On Christmas day 1940, Churchill drafted a message to Roosevelt, which

---

[122] 374 H C Deb., 10 September 1941, cols. 271-2.

[123] Dallek, *Franklin D. Roosevelt and American Foreign Policy,* 212.

[124] David McCullough, *Truman* (New York: Simon & Schuster, 1992), 309.

[125] Colville, *The Fringes of Power,* 136.

[126] Dallek, *Franklin D. Roosevelt and American Foreign Policy,* 212, 222.

read in part: "We have of course been disappointed in the small number we have yet been able to get into service."[127] The draft was never sent.

Britain had been receiving weapons and the machine tools necessary for war production from the United States on a cash-and-carry basis. On 23 November 1940, Lothian warned assembled journalists at LaGuardia Airport that his country's currency reserves were running low and that it would need financial aid in 1941.[128] Churchill explained Britain's plight in a message to Roosevelt dated two weeks later, 7 December 1940. "The moment approaches," he wrote, "when we shall no longer be able to pay cash for shipping and other supplies." It would be morally wrong and mutually disadvantageous if "Great Britain were to be divested of all saleable assets" at the height of the struggle and "stripped to the bone."[129] In a radio address on 9 March 1941, which was re-transmitted by short-wave, he made a dramatic appeal to the Americans: "Give us the tools, and we will finish the job."[130]

Roosevelt had a better idea. He knew that neither Congress nor the American people would sanction an outright gift of war matériel to Britain. So he devised a subterfuge, which he called Lend-Lease. In a radio address or "Fireside Chat" to his fellow citizens on 17 December 1940, he proposed to lend weaponry and other items of immediate necessity to Britain. These would be returned at the war's end. The president would decide what the British needed and would allocate resources accordingly.[131] Most Republicans in Congress felt that Roosevelt was aggregating too much power for himself. They doubted that the goods would ever be returned. Senator Robert A. Taft of Ohio quipped: "Lending war equipment is a good deal like lending chewing

---

127 *Churchill & Roosevelt: The Complete Correspondence,* 119.

128 *New York Times,* 24 November 1940. The oft-quoted remark, "Well boys, Britain's broke. It's your money we want," was not reported in the press and is probably apocryphal.

129 *Churchill & Roosevelt: The Complete Correspondence,* 108.

130 Churchill, *War Speeches,* I, 352.

131 *New York Times,* 18 December 1940.

gum – you certainly don't want your old gum back."[132] Thanks to a strong Democratic majority in both houses, the Lend-Lease bill was voted into law on 11 March 1941. Before it could take effect, the Treasury Department insisted that Britain divest itself of the American Viscose Company, a subsidiary of the British textile conglomerate, Courtaulds. It was put on the block for $54.5 million, or about half its true worth.[133] The sale caused much resentment in London, but it had an important symbolic value by convincing the Americans that Britain's financial resources were by then well and truly depleted.

A steady flow of aid to Britain committed the United States to ensuring that it arrived safely. As German submarines took a growing toll of transatlantic shipping, American warships were sent on escort missions, and some were sunk. Roosevelt was genuinely concerned that Britain, which endured a long string of defeats – in Greece, Crete and North Africa – throughout 1941, might go under. In a radio address of 27 October, he announced that war matériel would henceforth be shipped to friendly nations in American merchant ships, escorted by the U. S. Navy.[134] Congress obliged him with a final revision of the Neutrality Act on 17 November. Lend-Lease had been extended to the Soviet Union ten days previously. Since the Soviet merchant fleet was small, the cargo was shipped almost entirely in American bottoms. The president was apparently convinced that the United States would be drawn into the fighting, but he told the cabinet on 23 May: "I am not willing to fire the first shot."[135] Churchill hoped he would. Addressing the House of Commons in late September, he belittled those "nations and individuals who take an easy and popular course or who are guided in defence matters by the shifting winds of well-meaning public opinion. Nothing is more dangerous is war-time than to live in the

---

[132] Clarence E. Wunderlin, ed., *The Papers of Robert A. Taft* (Kent, OH: Kent State University Press, 1997), II, 227.

[133] Charles P. Kindleberger, *A Financial History of Western Europe* (London: George Allen & Unwin, 1984), *425*.

[134] *New York Times*, 28 October 1941.

[135] Dallek, *Franklin D. Roosevelt and American Foreign Policy*, 265.

temperamental atmosphere of a Gallup Poll, always feeling one's pulse and taking one's temperature."[136]

Meanwhile, trouble was brewing in the Far East, as Japan rushed to fill the power vacuum left by Vichy France in Indo-China. In reprisal, the United States imposed an embargo on oil and scrap iron shipments to Japan. Bowing to American pressure, the Dutch government in exile agreed to suspend delivery of oil from the Netherlands East Indies. By July of 1941, Japan was left with an eighteen months' supply of oil. To recover its sources, Tokyo could either yield to the American ultimatum that it withdraw from China, or initiate war in the Pacific. It chose the latter course.

Churchill sensed intuitively that the Japanese were preparing for a war that would perforce involve the United States. In a speech at Mansion House on 10 November, he warned the Japanese government that "should the United Sates become involved in war with Japan, the British declaration will follow within the hour."[137] A war with Japan was the last thing Britain needed in 1941, but Churchill was so anxious to have the United States as a full-fledged military ally that he was willing to take the risk. Shortly before the Japanese attack on Pearl Harbor, he asked the newly appointed U. S. ambassador, John Gilbert Winant: "If they declare war on us, will you declare war on them?" Winant replied, "I can't answer that, Prime Minister. Only Congress has the right to declare war under the United States constitution." Churchill received this in stunned silence.[138]

The news of Japan's aggression filled Churchill with "the greatest joy. . . . So we had won after all!" he wrote.[139] Well no, not

---

[136] 374 H C Deb., 30 September 1941, col. 517; cf. Lynne Olson, *Citizens of London: The Americans Who Stood With Britain in Its Darkest and Finest Hour* (New York: Random House, 2010), 140.

[137] Churchill, *War Speeches,* II, 103.

[138] Max Hastings, *Winston's War, 1940-1945* (New York: Vintage Books, 2011), 180.

[139] Winston S. Churchill, *The Second World War*, III: *The Grand Alliance* (London: Cassell, 1955), 539.

necessarily. Roosevelt's brief and dramatic war address to Congress on 8 December called for hostilities against Japan alone and did not mention Germany or Italy. For three days, the United States had only one enemy; and some highly-placed Americans believed that their war was in the Pacific, while Britain and Russia would have to fight in Europe on their own. Had Hitler waited a few weeks before declaring war on the world's greatest industrial power, the United States would have been thoroughly absorbed in the struggle against Japan and could do little to help his enemies. Instead, he committed what, in retrospect, must be viewed as the greatest blunder of his political career.

On 11 December, the German foreign ministry handed the American chargé d'affaires in Berlin a diplomatically worded note recalling the many violations of neutrality committed by the United States since 3 September 1939. In particular, it alleged – correctly – that American warships had opened fire on German submarines without direct provocation. Hence, a state of war now existed between the two countries. This was followed the same day by an emotionally charged speech by Hitler to the Nazi Reichstag, in which the dictator compared himself, "the unknown soldier of the last war" (unfortunately not buried),[140] to the plutocrat in the White House. While he, Hitler, had to endure four years of trench warfare, Roosevelt enjoyed a cushy job in Washington as assistant secretary of the Navy. Since then, the Nazis, the party of the people in his words, had eliminated unemployment in Germany, while millions of Americans were still out of work. Surely, he proclaimed in conclusion, divine providence will crown the German nation with the victory it so rightly deserves.[141]

So it was Hitler, not Churchill, who dragged the United States into a European war.

---

[140] A.J.P. Taylor, *The Course of German History* (London: Hamish Hamilton, 1945), 206.

[141] Domarus, *Hitler, Speeches and Proclamations,* IV, 2531-2552.

Epilogue: Yalta and Beyond

A month after Britain declared war, Lloyd George was heard to say: "We are going to lose this war." He repeated this dire but unfortunately accurate prediction to a newspaper editor in January 1940. Liddell Hart concurred.[1] And lose it they did. Britain lost the Phoney War, the war that Neville Chamberlain declared pursuant to his ill-conceived guarantee of Poland's independence. Of course if one passes quickly over the period of September 1939 to May 1940, as do most historians, Britain emerges on the side of the victors; and history is written by the victors. A Canadian historian recalls: "War had also engendered a common spirit in the people, renewing British democracy," not to mention a decisive victory for the Labour Party.[2] British Conservatives (and like-minded Americans) could take comfort in Churchill's wartime leadership and his numerous photo-ops with Roosevelt. Sir Alexander Cadogan admitted that in 1939 "our own military capabilities were deplorably inadequate" and that "our guarantee could give no possible protection to Poland. . . . But it *did* bring us into the war [emphasis in the original]. And in the end we, with our allies, won it. Though of course the poor Poles cannot be expected to appreciate the result for them."[3]

And what about the peoples of Western Europe who had to endure Nazi occupation for more than four years?[4] Is this how Britain "saved" the West? After the war, Liddell Hart wrote that "the bright

---

[1] A. J. Sylvester, *Life with Lloyd George* (London: Macmillan, 1975), 238-9; Jackson, *The Fall of France*, 204-5.

[2] Stephen Brooke, *Labour's War: The Labour Party during the Second World War* (Oxford: Clarendon Press, 1992), 108.

[3] Cadogan *Diaries*, 166-7. "With our allies" speaks volumes.

[4] Prior, *When Britain Saved the West*, 263.

sunlight of 'victory' proved an illusion"[5] – which it certainly was for the vanquished of 1940, and perhaps also, for Britain itself. Hitler had not originally planned a war against Norway, the Low Countries and France. On 11 August 1939, he invited Carl J. Burckhardt, the League of Nations high commissioner for Danzig, to Berchtesgaden and told him flatly: "Everything I undertake is directed against Russia. If the West is too stupid and too blind to comprehend, I shall be forced to reach an understanding with the Russians, strike at the West, and then after their defeat turn back against the Soviet Union with all my collected strength. I need the Ukraine so that no one can starve us out as they did in the last war."[6] After meeting with Hitler, Burckhardt returned to his home in Basel and met with representatives from Britain (Roger Makins) and France (Pierre Arnal), to whom he conveyed Hitler's message, which was clearly intended to keep the two western democracies on the sidelines.

But it was too late to change policy. Although Chamberlain tried desperately until the last minute to avoid war, his guarantee to Poland left him with no choice. Daladier too shares responsibility for the ensuing disaster. On learning of the Nazi-Soviet pact, he realized that France was in a bind.[7] With the benefit of hindsight, it is clear that he should have avoided a war that France could not possibly win without the outside support it had enjoyed in 1918. Of course the British would have accused him of "ratting" and left France in the lurch. But that is what they did in any case. When Sumner Welles visited Paris as part of his peace mission in February and March of 1940, Daladier justified the current state of war by affirming that German agents in Alsace had tried to stir up the population much as they had done in the Sudetenland.[8]

---

[5] Liddell Hart, *Memoirs*, II, 256.

[6] Carl J. Burckhardt, *Meine Danziger Mission, 1937-1939* (Munich: Callwey, 1960), 348.

[7] Cf. *supra*, 175.

[8] Sumner Welles, *The Time for Decision* (New York: Harper, 1944), 123.

Hitler had publicly renounced all claims to Alsace and Lorraine. Addressing the Nazi Reichstag on 28 April 1939, he proclaimed that "the return of the Saar has removed from the face of the earth all territorial disputes between France and Germany in Europe."[9] In a message of 27 August, he tried to reassure Daladier that he and the German people were content to leave Alsace-Lorraine to France rather than risk another war.[10] Was he sincere? At that precise moment, he probably was. He was not interested in a war with the West – certainly not in 1939.[11] Hitler simply took up the challenge of war once it was declared on Germany. Any responsible statesman – Roosevelt, for example – would have done the same. If German agents were indeed at work in Alsace, it would have been wise to wait until the situation came to a head before declaring war – most likely a two-front war, with Hitler's forces primarily occupied in Russia. George Bernard Shaw was remarkably prescient in the fall of 1939: Neville Chamberlain's war had come too soon, as he himself recognized once the damage was done. "If only we had had another year of preparation, we should have been in a far stronger position, and so would the French."[12]

In Britain, France quickly became a convenient scapegoat for the débâcle of 1940. But to blame everything on the French is to forget that Britain, as noted by a British historian, had "inveigled" France into war.[13] Chamberlain needed a French declaration of war in order to remain in office; Churchill needed it in order to obtain a cabinet post. In 1939, according to A.J.P. Taylor, "Great Britain still ranked as a Great Power." Note the choice of words: it still *ranked* as a great power, which it certainly was – on the high seas. But without a land army of any consequence, it was not a great power on the continent of

---

[9] Domarus, *Hitler. Speeches and Proclamations*, III, 1562.
[10] *Le Livre jaune framçais*, 334.
[11] Norman Stone, *Hitler* (London: Coronet Books, 1982), 131.
[12] Chamberlain to Ida, 25 May 1940, *The Neville Chamberlain Diary Letters*, 533.
[13] Guy Chapman, *Why France Fell: The Defeat of the French Army in 1940* (New York: Holt, Rinehart and Winston, 1968), 334.

Europe. "The test of a great power," he writes, "is the test of strength for war."[14] The British Expeditionary Force in May 1940 was half the size of the Belgian army and only slightly larger than the Dutch. As for France, Taylor notes correctly that it "was almost over the edge into second-class status." Germany, on the other hand, was slightly stronger economically than Britain and France put together.[15] Churchill could, if he liked, thank God for the French army.[16] He never thanked God for the French economy – or the British.

So Britain went to war without a land army comparable to its expeditionary force of 1914 and with a declining power as its only ally – a frightful error of judgment for which it paid dearly. In January 1940, Ironside confided to his diary that he had nagging doubts about the French army, although "I saw nothing amiss with it on the surface." Would it hold? "I must say I don't know. But I say to myself that we must have confidence in the French army. . . . Our own army is just a little one, and we are dependent upon the French. We have not even the same fine army we had in 1914."[17] With or without the French, the British army did not give a particularly good account of itself. From Norway to Singapore and Tobruk, it suffered a string of defeats without parallel in its history. Britain managed to survive thanks to the Royal Navy and the Royal Air Force; but only American participation in the war could ensure victory, as Churchill well knew. Roosevelt was not eager to involve the United States in a war with Germany. American aid in 1940 and 1941 was designed to keep Britain in the fight and prevent Hitler from seizing the British fleet. It was not gratuitous, as was the help Britain received from the Dominions, especially Canada.[18] Of course the Dominions were already at war, having dutifully followed the mother country. The American people still wanted to keep

---

[14] A.J.P. Taylor, *The Struggle for Mastery in Europe, 1848-1918* (Oxford: Clarendon Press, 1954), xxiv.

[15] Taylor, *The Origins of the Second World War*, 218.

[16] 276 H C Deb., 23 March 1933, col.542.

[17] *The Ironside Diaries*, 10 January 1940, 203-4.

[18] Prior, *When Britain Saved the West*, 280.

out, and with some justification. Their president had not given a unilateral – and unfulfilled – guarantee to Poland.

Once Hitler dragged the United States into a European war, Britain was obliged to accept, however reluctantly, the American leadership that Chamberlain had sought to avoid.[19] The main bone of contention between the two allies was the opening of a second front in France. Churchill, as well as his military commanders, attempted to postpone such an operation until 1945 at the earliest.[20] They claimed that the British army might not be able hold a beachhead before then and would have to evacuate as it had done at Dunkirk. A second front in France also meant abandoning a project very dear to Churchill: an offensive in the Balkans to cut off the Soviet advance. His anti-Communism never wavered, not even in the heat of war against Nazi Germany. Chamberlain had sought to exclude Russia from European affairs altogether. With Britain's back to the wall in 1941, Churchill welcomed Soviet participation in the war but was determined to keep Russia out of Central Europe.

Postponing a second front would certainly have left Western Europe under Nazi occupation for at least another year and might well have opened up even more territory to the Soviet forces. We are all familiar with Churchill's "Iron Curtain" speech given at Fulton, Missouri on 5 March 1946. Let us try to imagine where the Iron Curtain would have been drawn had the Normandy landings not taken place in 1944: on the Rhine or perhaps even further west. Stalin's repeated pleas for an allied landing in France indicate that he was primarily concerned with defeating Germany. Propagating Communism would have to wait.

In 1942, Roosevelt yielded to the British on the question of a second front. He abandoned the plan of his own generals to tie down the Germans by sending eight American divisions to France. They were inadequately trained and would surely have been routed by a more experienced enemy. The president was more assertive at the Teheran

---

[19] Cf. *supra*, 228.

[20] Nigel Hamilton, *Commander in Chief: FDR's Battle with Churchill, 1943* (New York: Houghton Mifflin Harcourt, 2016), 217.

conference of November 1943. Overruling Churchill, he promised Stalin that the Western armies would land in France the following year. The Soviet Union was bearing the brunt of the fighting against Nazi Germany. An estimated 9 to 14 million Red Army soldiers were killed during the war; some 22 million were wounded; over 5 million were captured, of whom 3 million died in captivity. The offensives of the Western allies in North Africa and Italy could hardly constitute a second front.

Roosevelt and Stalin also agreed on a landing in southern France, called Operation Anvil (later renamed Dragoon). Churchill vehemently opposed the plan because it could draw German troops away from the eastern front and facilitate the Soviet advance. He had hoped to capture Vienna before the Russians got there and was adamant that all allied troops in Italy pursue their advance northward.[21] A landing in Provence necessitated diverting American and French forces from the Italian campaign. Anvil was originally supposed to precede, or at least coincide with, the Normandy landings and draw off German forces from the north, but was postponed until 15 August 1944 precisely because of allied difficulties in Italy. Even so, it was the most successful amphibious operation of the war, claiming the lives of only 95 Americans out of the 94,000 who went ashore on the first day. In Normandy, by contrast, 156,000 Americans landed on the first day, and some 2,000 perished. The Free French, whose army was still largely colonial, captured the ports of Marseille and Toulon on 28 August, a month ahead of schedule, giving the allies a new and more effective supply route. The Germans, having to fight on two fronts in France, beat a hasty retreat. Churchill was so upset at being overruled by Roosevelt and Eisenhower that he and the British chiefs of staff contemplated at one point breaking off all cooperation with the Americans in order to pursue their own Mediterranean strategy.[22]

---

[21] Andrew Roberts, *Masters and Commanders* (London: Penguin, 2009), 516-17.

[22] Cameron Zinsou, "The Forgotten Story of Operation Anvil," *New York Times*, 15 August 2019.

When Roosevelt attended the Yalta conference in February 1945, he often dealt directly with Stalin, bypassing Churchill on most crucial issues, in particular the war against Japan. (Without consulting Roosevelt, Churchill had hurried off to Moscow in October 1944, where he made a separate deal with Stalin to define British and Soviet spheres of interest in the Balkans. Roosevelt was merely repaying him in kind.[23]) American military planners desperately wanted Soviet help against the Japanese, and Stalin promised to engage his forces ninety days after Germany's surrender. The American delegation left Yalta fully satisfied with the result. General Marshall was positively exultant. Getting Stalin to commit Soviet troops to the Pacific war, he said, was well worth the long journey and the inconveniences (bedbugs, inadequate sanitation facilities etc.) that the westerners had to endure.[24]

Stalin kept his word. A Soviet force of over 1.5 million battle-hardened veterans of the European theatre, 3,704 tanks, 1,852 self-propelled guns and 3,721 aircraft attacked the Japanese in Manchuria at midnight, 9 August 1945, exactly ninety days after the war in Europe had ended. Transferring ground and air forces from Central Europe to the Far East was a remarkable feat of logistics – all the more so because troop movements on a single-track railway had to be concealed from the enemy. His commitment to an allied victory in the Pacific was hardly altruistic. At Yalta, he demanded, and received, Port Arthur, the southern half of the Sakhalin peninsula and (much to the dismay of the Chinese Communists) control over the Manchurian railways, all of which Tsarist Russia had ceded to Japan in 1905, plus the Kurile Islands.

Soviet intervention was decisive in convincing the Japanese government to surrender. The atomic bomb alone did not tip the balance since Japanese military leaders, who at first knew only about the blast and not the long-term effects of radiation, simply assumed that it was just another, more powerful weapon. They had not been cowed into submission by the fire-bombing of Tokyo, which had taken

---

[23] S. M. Plokhy, *Yalta, the Price of Peace* (New York: Penguin, 2011), 395.
[24] Reynolds, *Summits*, 127.

100,000 Japanese lives in a single night.[25] On 10 August, an inspection team sent by the Japanese government to Hiroshima filed a report giving full details of the devastation, but even then a panel of experts in Tokyo minimized the danger in the mistaken belief that white clothing could protect the wearer from radiation.[26] Japanese military leaders tended to dismiss the Nagasaki bomb, which was less destructive than that of Hiroshima, and claimed that the army had "countermeasures."[27] After the first bomb was dropped on Hiroshima, Senator Richard Russell of Georgia urged Truman to plaster the Japanese with nuclear weapons. The president, who replied on 9 August, the day of the Nagasaki explosion, did not think this was necessary. "It is my opinion that after the Russians enter the war, the Japanese will very shortly fold up."[28] And so they did, officially accepting the surrender terms on 14 August. The following day, Truman ordered all military operations against Japan to cease.

But not Stalin. The Red Army continued its offensive for two more weeks, seeking to capture all the territory promised at Yalta.[29] Acting in its own interest, the Soviet Union actually facilitated the American military occupation of the Japanese home islands. There was no resistance. Emperor Hirohito did not mention the atomic bomb in convincing die-hard soldiers and sailors to surrender; he spoke only of Soviet participation in the war.[30] Japanese civilians, including schoolchildren who a few weeks earlier had been trained to make suicidal rushes on the allied invasion force with awls and bamboo

---

[25] Tsuyoshi Hasegawa, "The Atomic Bombs and the Soviet Invasion," Tsuyoshi Hasegawa ed., *The End of the Pacific War: Reappraisals* (Stanford, CA: Stanford University Press, 2007), 120.

[26] Robert J.C. Butow, *Japan's Decision to Surrender* (Stanford, CA: Stanford University Press, 1954), 152.

[27] Alvin D. Coox, "The Pacific War," Peter Duus ed., *The Cambridge History of Japan* (Cambridge: Cambridge University Press, 1988), VI, 375.

[28] Tsuyoshi Hasegawa, *Racing the Enemy: Stalin, Truman, and the Surrender of Japan* (Cambridge, MA: Belknap Press, 2005), 202.

[29] *Ibid.*, 251-5.

[30] Hasegawa, "The Atomic Bomb and the Soviet Invasion," 139.

spears dipped in manure,[31] accepted their conquerors' presence without qualm. General MacArthur ensured that the Soviet Union did not participate in the occupation. The Japanese political class and business interests were quite content to deal with the Americans alone. The United States, they knew, respected private property and private enterprise, whereas a Soviet military presence could bring Communism to Japan. In February 1945, Prince Konoye had warned the emperor that the strain of war gave renewed impetus to Communist-inspired revolutionists.[32]

Most importantly, Soviet intervention eliminated the need for an invasion of Japan, the mere prospect of which filled General Marshall with horror. Thanks to their code breakers, the American high command could follow day by day the enemy's military preparations for the defence of Kyushu, the southernmost island of the Japanese archipelago, where the invasion was to begin. These included suicidal air and sea assaults, which Japanese strategists predicted would destroy 30 to 50 percent of the invasion force. A first wave of more than 400,000 American troops, plus sizeable contingents from Britain and the Dominions, was slated to face a force of 525,000 defenders, who were ordered to fight to the death. American military leaders estimated that at least one million of their soldiers and marines would be needed to subdue Japan and that the casualty rate would be 25 percent.[33] They were so dismayed at this eventuality that they considered using atomic bombs as tactical weapons on the beaches.[34] In that event, not only Japanese, but allied soldiers as well would have succumbed to radiation sickness. So Stalin's engagement in the Far East, carried out in pure self-interest, saved countless Western and Japanese lives.

---

[31] Richard B. Frank, "Japanese Political and Military Strategy in 1945," Hasegawa, ed., *The End of the Pacific War*, 77.

[32] The United States Strategic Bombing Survey, *Japan's Struggle to End the War* (Washington: United States Government Printing Office, 1946), 21.

[33] Hasegawa, *Racing the Enemy*, 181.

[34] Edward J. Drea, *In the Service of the Emperor: Essays on the Imperial Japanese Army* (Lincoln, NE: University of Nebraska Press, 1998), 149-64.

In Europe it was the Soviet Union, more than any other power, that ensured the defeat of Nazi Germany. True, the Russians were fighting to save their own country. Among the Western allies, only the French were in a similar position. The American, British and Canadian soldiers who landed in France risked their lives to liberate Western Europe, not their home territory. Their courage under fire is all the more commendable. Nor should aid from Britain, Canada and the United States to the Soviet Union go unnoticed. As Khrushchev recalled, "The English helped us tenaciously and at great peril to themselves. They shipped cargo to Murmansk and suffered huge losses."[35] Soviet pilots were especially fond of the American P-63 Kingcobra fighter, with its 37 millimetre cannon. Many of the famous Soviet T-34 tanks were built with American steel. More than 400,000 American-built Jeeps and trucks were shipped to the Soviet Union, often in perilous conditions.[36] The trucks allowed the Red Army to move troops quickly from one sector of the front to another. Still, the fact remains that at least three-quarters of all German casualties throughout the war occurred on the eastern front. For this, the Russians paid a disproportionate share of the blood tax.

The rapid succession of Soviet victories in Eastern Europe greatly alarmed Winston Churchill. He urged Eisenhower to take Berlin before the Russians got there. The latter not only refused; he informed Stalin of his refusal.[37] At Yalta, Berlin had been placed in the Soviet zone of occupation, and Eisenhower saw no reason to squander the lives of his soldiers in a frontal assault on the German capital, only to relinquish it to the Red Army. American troops did, in fact, take Leipzig, which was well within the proposed Soviet zone, and advanced as far as Torgau on the Elbe, where they met up with the Russians. They later evacuated the conquered territory beyond what

---

[35] *Khrushchev Remembers*, 225.

[36] ru.usembassy.gov/world-war-ii-allies-u-s-lend-lease-to-the-soviet-union-1941-1945/

[37] Walter Reid, *Churchill 1940-1945: Under Friendly Fire* (Edinburgh: Birlinn, 2009), 339.

was allotted to them, in keeping with the Yalta accords. When a U. S. force under General Patton liberated Pilsen, many Czechs urged them to push on to Prague. Eisenhower ordered Patton to halt and let the Red Army take the rest of Czechoslovakia. Not to do so could prompt Stalin to withhold Soviet support in the war against Japan. Patton's force withdrew to the American zone of Germany in November.

Churchill was incensed. He protested to Truman against the transfer of American troops from Europe to the Pacific, but was ignored. In desperation, he ordered the British chiefs of staff to prepare a contingency plan for war with the Soviet Union, to commence on 1 July 1945. The chiefs dutifully produced a hypothetical proposal on 22 May, two weeks after the fighting in Europe had ended, which they named, most aptly, "Operation Unthinkable." They explained that the undertaking, which assumed that British and American soldiers were willing to fight the Russians and that both armies could draw on Polish and German (!) manpower, required "the full support of public opinion in the British Empire and the United States." Even then, the Soviet forces would have a three-to-one numerical advantage. To win a war with Russia, the chiefs concluded, "would take us a very long time," and the Russians could resume hostilities whenever they wished.[38]

In the hysteria of the Cold War, the Yalta conference was commonly viewed as a defeat for the West – and it still is, in some circles.[39] Poland, in particular, was deemed a great loss. The Polish government based in London was brushed aside by Moscow in favour of hand-picked Polish Communists who assumed power in a rigged election. Stalin knew that pre-war Poland had been more anti-Russian than anti-German, and he could not tolerate a Polish regime that might be hostile to the Soviet Union. Moreover, there were facts on the

---

[38] CAB 120/691; cf. Jonathan Walker, *Churchill's Third World War: British Plans to Attack the Soviet Empire, 1945* (London: The History Press, 2017), 13, 69, 114 *et passim*.

[39] Diana Preston, *Eight Days at Yalta: How Churchill, Roosevelt and Stalin Shaped the Post-war World* (New York: Atlantic Monthly Press, 2019), 3-4 *et passim*.

ground to consider. When the "Big Three" (actually the big two-and-a-half) met at Yalta in February 1945, the Red Army was already in Poland. It was a foregone conclusion that the Soviet Union would push its western frontier back to the Curzon line established by the allied powers in 1919.[40] As a moral issue, Poland often intruded on negotiations with Stalin, but Britain had effectively abandoned that country in 1939. While not quite the "economic impossibility" denounced by Keynes, it was certainly no prize. Nor were the other countries absorbed into the Soviet bloc immediately after the war. The oil fields of Romania were virtually depleted, and even the Soviet zone of Germany had little economic value. The bulk of German industry was situated in the western zones of occupation, especially the British. The western continental powers themselves – France, Belgium, the Netherlands, and Italy – had far greater economic strength and potential than the subordinate nations of the Soviet bloc.

There remained Czechoslovakia, whose eastern frontier was now contiguous with the recently expanded Soviet Union. In his speech at Fulton, Churchill put Prague, along with Vienna, behind the Iron Curtain, and Czechoslovak Foreign Minister Jan Masaryk felt compelled to disagree publicly.[41] Czechoslovakia in 1946 was still a functioning democracy. In free elections held on 26 May, the Communists won 30 percent of the vote in Slovakia, but 42 percent in Bohemia and Moravia. They owed much of their support to the general disillusionment with the West that was felt by the electorate after Munich.[42] With 114 seats in parliament out of 300, the Communists had to govern with parties of the democratic Left, whose members held several positions, such as foreign affairs and foreign trade, in the new cabinet. Like Churchill, however, the Americans had already written

---

[40] Plokhy, *Yalta, the Price of Peace*, 154-5.

[41] Sylvia F. Crane and John O. Crane, *Czechoslovakia: Anvil of the Cold War* (New York: Praeger, 1991), 274.

[42] George F. Kennan, *From Prague after Munich: Diplomatic Papers, 1938-1940* (Princeton, NJ: Princeton University Press, 1971), 7; cf. Lukes, *Czechoslovakia Between Stalin and Hitler*, 260.

off Czechoslovakia. Secretary of State Marshall wrote that "a seizure of power by the Communist party in Czechoslovakia would not materially alter . . . the situation which has existed in the last three years. . . . Czechoslovakia has faithfully followed the Soviet line . . . and the establishment of a Communist regime would merely crystallize and confirm for the future previous Czech policy."[43] This self-fulfilling prophesy conceded to the Soviet Union at least one satellite with a dynamic economy.

On balance, then, the post-war settlement favoured the West over the Communist bloc. The United States emerged from the conflict more powerful and more prosperous than ever; it dominated the United Nations Organization, which Roosevelt had persuaded Stalin to join. Thus was confirmed the prediction of Henry R. Luce in his essay, "The American Century," published in February 1941. Whether they liked it or not, he wrote, the American people were already at war, "a war to defend and even to promote, encourage and incite so-called democratic principles throughout the world." The United States must not repeat the mistake of 1919, when it retreated into isolation. It must accept "the opportunities of leadership" that the war in Europe offered. Luce was confident that the British would gladly yield their former position of dominance to the Americans, who "must undertake now to be the Good Samaritan of the entire world."[44] In his mind, the United States was the role model which all other nations wished to emulate.

Not all Americans agreed. Senator Taft doubted whether an "American Raj," as he called it, would be any more successful than the British one. He was not encouraged by the abysmal record of the United States territorial administration in Puerto Rico, "where we have been for forty-five years without relieving poverty or improving anyone's condition."[45] In his radio address of 15 September 1939 (two years before he went off on a tangent and accused American Jews of

---

[43] Benn Steil, "Who Lost Czechoslovakia?" *History Today*, 9 May 2018.

[44] "The American Century," *Life,* 17 February 1941, 61-5.

[45] Clarence E. Wunderlin, *Robert A. Taft: Ideas, Tradition and Party in U. S. Foreign Policy* (Oxford: Rowman & Littlefield, 2004), 78.

pushing for war), Charles A. Lindbergh warned his compatriots: "If we enter [the war] fighting for democracy abroad, we may end by losing it at home."[46] Although premature, his words were eerily prophetic.

Pearl Harbor and the subsequent German declaration of war sounded the death knell of American isolationism. The interventionists were redeemed; and since then, the United States has been intervening practically everywhere, with meagre and often negative results. Increasingly, Americans seem to be having second thoughts about their country's global mission. The July/August 2019 issue of the prestigious journal *Foreign Affairs* raised the question, "What happened to the American century?" Of the six contributors to the discussion, only one proposed that the United States should promote democracy throughout the world.[47] The others concentrated on internal problems, both political and economic, that threaten to undermine American democracy itself. An essay in the same issue confirmed Senator Taft's earlier contention that the United States has neglected Puerto Rico.[48]

As for Britain, its intervention in the affairs of continental Europe during the inter-war period achieved nothing except to ensure German domination. Chamberlain enabled, nay encouraged, Hitler to crush Czechoslovakia in order to give Nazi Germany a free hand in the east. He then turned around and guaranteed Poland's independence in the hope of deterring Hitler from actually going to war. The deterrent failed utterly. By declaring war without an army of its own, Britain handed the leading democracies of Western Europe to Hitler on a silver platter. Germany acquired the iron mines of Lorraine and Normandy, whose reserves were greater than those of Sweden. French, Dutch and Belgian railways provided Germany with 4,260 locomotives and

---

[46] Wayne S, Cole, *Charles A, Lindbergh and the Battle against American Intervention in World War II* (New York: Harcourt Brace and Jovanovich, 1974), 88.

[47] Larry Diamond, "Democracy Demolition: How the Freedom Agenda Fell Apart," *Foreign Affairs*, June-July 2019, 17-25.

[48] Antonio Weiss and Brad Setser, "America's Forgotten Colony: Ending Puerto Rico's Perpetual Crisis," *Ibid.*, 158-68.

140,000 freight cars. Germany also captured 81,000 tons of copper, plus vast quantities of tin, nickel and motor fuel.[49] Hitler may have wanted the Ukraine so that his people would not be reduced to starvation, but it was French agriculture that became Germany's prime foreign source of food; its supplies equalled those of all his eastern conquests put together. Dutch and Danish farms also helped to keep German civilians and soldiers well fed. The occupied countries of Western Europe furnished their captors with industrial production, forced labour and even volunteers for the German army.[50] Eventually, the Russians repulsed the German invaders, but they might have done so earlier if Germany had not been able to exploit the human and economic resources of the defeated nations. The Jewish population of France, Belgium, and the Netherlands was decimated under the Nazis.

As he surveyed Germany's conquests in 1940, Ismay wrote: "If, in August 1939, the chiefs of staff had reason to think that this was going to be the situation after less than twelve months of hostilities, I believe that they would have unhesitatingly warned the cabinet that to go to war would be to invite overwhelming disaster."[51] Their failure to recognize the danger may be attributed to an almost dogmatic belief in the superiority of defence. All things being equal, an offensive force was presumed to require a three-to-one superiority in men and matériel in order to prevail. Even though Germany had more than twice as many young men of military age as France, its numerical superiority was considered insufficient. Taking the British Expeditionary Force plus the Dutch and Belgian armies into account, it was considered a mathematical certainty that the Germans could not win.

But all things were not equal. Hitler's *Wehrmacht* was the finest military machine of modern times. It was a homogeneous force under a unified command; the armies facing it were not.[52] To overcome

---

[49] Tooze, *The Wages of Destruction*, 385.

[50] Brian Bond, *War and Society in Europe, 1870-1970* (Montreal: McGill–Queen's University Press, 1998), 179-80.

[51] Ismay, *Memoirs*, 153.

[52] Michel, *La Drôle de Guerre*, 302.

Nazi Germany in the final phase of the war, the allies, including the Soviet Union, needed not three, but *five* times as many men and weapons.[53] In 1940, Germany took the offensive and defeated the Western powers through superior strategy, weapons, and training. It nearly defeated the Soviet Union a year later. Only a country with a strong defence line and a well-trained and well-equipped army could have held out against Germany in a short war. That country was Czechoslovakia. With Czechoslovakia as an ally, Britain and France, whose military posture was essentially defensive, had a far better chance of containing Hitler than with Poland. But British strategists had already written off the Czechoslovak army; and in 1938, Chamberlain was not anti-Nazi.

Having abandoned the second most important military power in Central Europe, Britain and France were at a military disadvantage when they had to face Nazi Germany. A French historian has recognized that the war began at "a most inopportune time" for the democracies.[54] If they had postponed a declaration of war until Hitler was engaged against both the Soviet Union and the United States, it is doubtful that most, or even part, of Western, democratic Europe would have had to endure four years and more of Nazi occupation. Given Chamberlain's guarantee to Poland, however, the allies were honour-bound to act immediately (or almost immediately). His policy was based on the nineteenth-century belief that Britain was somehow the arbiter of European affairs. When he wrote to Hitler in August 1939, warning him that Britain would stand by Poland, he expected to be taken seriously. Failing that, he declared war reluctantly and, in the months that followed, publicly exuded confidence in an inevitable allied victory. His confidence was misplaced. The Phoney War was a disaster waiting to happen.

In the preface to the first volume of his memoirs, Churchill refers to the European conflict of 1939-1945 (he seems to ignore the

---

[53] Alexandroff and Rosecrance, "Deterrence in 1939," 406.

[54] Guy Rossi-Landi. *La Drôle de Guerre. La vie politique en France, 2 septembre 1939 – 10 mai 1940* (Paris: Armand Colin, 1971), 26.

Far East) as "the unnecessary war." He claims that "there was never a war more easy to stop."[55] In his "Iron Curtain" speech he recalled with pride: "Last time I saw it all coming and cried aloud to my fellow countrymen and to the world, but no one paid any attention." The horrific bloodshed could have been prevented by "timely action."[56] Just show Hitler that you mean business, and he'll back down – or be overthrown by his military leaders. This is exactly what Chamberlain did in guaranteeing the independence of Poland, but Hitler did not back down; and it is doubtful that he would have backed down earlier. Churchill never proposed actually going to war for Czechoslovakia, and he assumed that Britain could rely on the French army to do any fighting on land that might occur. As he later admitted to the House of Commons, "At the outbreak of war our army was an insignificant factor in the conflict."[57] It certainly did not impress Hitler. Nor, at the outbreak of war, did Britain's prime minister, whose measure Hitler had taken in 1938. "Our enemies are little worms (*kleine Würmchen*)," he told his generals. "I came to know them in Munich."[58] For Daladier, who had been a front-line solider in the First World War, he had some respect; but Chamberlain was just "that silly old man [who] comes interfering . . . with his umbrella."[59] The arch-appeaser of 1938 did not stop being an appeaser simply because Parliament had goaded him into declaring war.

Neville Chamberlain's war was a war of appeasement. By declaring war, he sought to appease Germany – not Hitler's Germany of course, but the good Germany, the Germany that nearly everyone in Britain knew existed somewhere. He was convinced that he had Hitler on the ropes and that "if we can hold firm, he is done."[60] Faced with "the magnificent soldiers of France," presumably invincible in defence,

[55] Churchill, *The Gathering Storm*, xiv.
[56] *New York Times*, 6 March 1946.
[57] 374 H C Deb., 30 September1941, col. 516.
[58] Domarus, *Hitler, Speeches and Proclamations*, III, 1667.
[59] Ivone Kirkpatrick, *The Inner Circle* (London: Macmillan, 1959), 135.
[60] Cf. *supra*, 139.

and the ever-tightening British naval blockade, the good German people, "for whom we have no bitter feeling," would surely realize that they could not possibly win. They would then depose Hitler and replace him with a regime that Britain could do business with. Georges Mandel, France's extremely able and lucid minister for colonies, was less sanguine. He told Harold Nicolson in March 1940, "We are at present trying to conduct a war of appeasement, which means that Hitler may win."[61] Chamberlain continually entertained the possibility of a negotiated peace with the good Germany.

It was not to be. "Chamberlain's flaws," writes a British historian who seems to have a favourable view of him as war leader, "made [the allied] defeat inevitable."[62] So what exactly, after six years of war – phoney at first, real later on – did Britain gain? A zone of occupation in Germany and a permanent seat on the U. N. Security Council. In return, it lost its empire and became subordinate to the United States.

The Anglo-French alliance was *un marché de dupes* – a suckers' deal. The British government expected the French army to hold, no matter what. The French government expected Britain to provide sufficient military support, as it had in 1914-1918, to keep Germany from overrunning Europe. Neither supposition proved correct. The Phoney War itself was a mug's game. By declaring war over Poland, both democracies sought to preserve their status as great powers. Chamberlain trashed Czechoslovakia in order to exclude the Soviet Union from Europe. Instead, Russia extended its power westward. Against Germany, he expected to win an easy and economical victory. Instead, Britain was bled white by the Second World War. In 1939, the British government and people saw themselves at war with Hitler, not the good Germans. Subsequently, the area bombings by the RAF of Cologne and Hamburg, two cities with strong anti-Nazi majorities, caused immense suffering to German civilians and actually strengthened Hitler's hold on his subjects, since

---

[61] Nicolson, *Diaries and Letters*, II, 62.
[62] Maiolo, "To Gamble All on a Single Throw," 227.

all air-raid victims depended on the Nazis for food, shelter, and medical care. Daladier went to war saying, "Today, France is in command." He sought to free his country from British tutelage. Instead, France had to endure four years of Nazi occupation. The British people, from the King on down, were happy in the spring of 1940 to be relieved of their French ally. They got the Americans ("overpaid, oversexed and over here") instead.

A British historian notes that his country's continental commitment came too late "to create a genuine western alliance in either political or strategic terms."[63] Britain and France were engaged in two different wars, with very different aims – the British against Hitler, the French against Germany. But even if they had managed to forge a real alliance, it is doubtful that they could have defeated, or even contained, Nazi Germany in 1940. "For a successful foreign policy," wrote Harold Macmillan, "there must be sufficient force of arms."[64] This applies to the Munich accords and, *a fortiori*, to the Phoney War. Even if one assumes that there exists sufficient force of arms (which Britain and France had not), a war avoided is usually preferable to a war won and always preferable to a war lost.

The final word on the subject belongs to Macaulay, who wrote a century earlier: "If there be any truth established by the universal experience of nations, it is this: that to carry the spirit of peace into war is a weak and cruel policy. The time of negotiation is the time for deliberation and delay. But when an extreme case calls for that remedy which is in its own nature most violent, and which, on such cases, is a remedy only because it is violent, it is idle to think of mitigating and diluting. Languid war can do nothing which negotiation or submission will not do better; and to act on any other principle is not to save blood and money, but to squander them."[65]

---

[63] Bond, *British Military Policy between the Two World Wars*, 339.
[64] Macmillan, *Winds of Change*, 382.
[65] Thomas Babington Macaulay, *Critical and Historical Essays* (London: Longmans, 1848), 171.

Bibliography

Public Documents

British Parliamentary Debates (abbreviated as H C Deb. and H L Deb.).
Journal Officiel de la République Française, Débats parlementaires, Chambre des Députés (abbreviated as J O C débats).
Documents Diplomatiques Français (abbreviated as DDF).
Documents on British Foreign Policy (abbreviated as DBFP).
Documents on German Foreign Policy (abbreviated as DGFP).
Foreign Relations of the United States (abbreviated as FRUS).
Le Livre jaune français.

Books and Articles

Adamthwaite, Anthony P. *France and the Coming of the Second World War, 1936-1939*. London: Frank Cass, 1977.
_____. *The Making of the Second World War*. London: George Allen & Unwin, 1977.
_____. "The British Government and the Media, 1937-1938," *Journal of Contemporary History*, April 1983, 281-297.
Addison, Paul. "Lloyd George and Compromise Peace in the Second World War," A.J.P. Taylor, ed. *Lloyd George: Twelve Essays*. London: Hamish Hamilton, 1971, 361-84.
Addison, Paul and Angus Calder, eds. *Time to Kill: The Soldier's Experience in the West, 1939-1945*. London: Pimlico, 1997.
Alexander, Martin S. "'Fighting to the Last Frenchman'? Reflections on the BEF Deployment to France and the Strains in the Franco-British Alliance," *Historical Reflections/Réflexions Historiques*, Winter 1996, 235-262.

_____. *The Republic in Danger: Maurice Gamelin and the Politics of French Defence, 1933-1940.* Cambridge: Cambridge University Press, 1992.

Alexandroff, Alan and Richard Rosecrance. "Deterrence in 1939," *World Politics,* April 1977, 404-24.

Allport, Alan. *Britain at Bay: The Epic Story of the Second World War, 1938-1941.* New York: Knopf, 2020.

Amery, Leopold S. *My Political Life,* III: *The Unforgiving Years, 1929-1939.* London: Hutchinson, 1953.

Angell, Norman. *For What Do We Fight?* London: Hamish Hamilton, 1939.

Artaud, Denise. "Reparations and War Debts: The Restoration of French Financial Power, 1919-1929," Robert Boyce, ed. *French Foreign and Defense Policy: The Decline and Fall of a Great Power.* London: Routledge, 1998, 88-105.

Aster, Sidney. *1939: The Making of the Second World War.* London: André Deutsch, 1973.

Atkin, Ronald. *Pillar of Fire: Dunkirk 1940.* Edinburgh: Birlinn, 2000.

Attlee, C.R. *et al. Labour's Aims in War and Peace.* London: Lincolns-Prager, n.d. [1940].

Azeau, Henri. *La guerre franco-italienne.* Paris: Presses de la Cité, 1967

Azéma, Jean-Pierre. *1940, l'année noire.* Paris: Fayard, 2010.

Baldwin, Hanson W. *The Crucial Years, 1938-1941.* New York: Harper & Row, 1976.

Barnett, Correlli. *Britain and Her Army, 1509-1970.* London: Allen Lane, 1970.

_____. *The Collapse of British Power.* London: Eyre Methuen 1972

Bauer, Major Eddy. *La guerre des blindés,* I. Paris: Payot, 1962.

Baughen, Greg. *The Rise and Fall of the French Air Force: French Air Operations and Strategy, 1919-1940.* London: Fonthill, 2018.

Bédarida, François. "La 'gouvernante anglaise'," René Rémond and Janine Bourdin, eds. *Édouard Daladier, chef de gouvernement.* Paris: Presses de la Fondation Nationale des Sciences Politiques, 1977.

_____. "La rupture franco-britannique de 1940. Le Conseil Suprême Interallié, de l'invasion à la défaite de la France," *Vingtième Siècle. Revue d'histoire*, January-March 1990, 37-48.

_____. *La stratégie secrète de la Drôle de Guerre. Le Conseil Suprême Interallié.* Paris: Presses de la Fondation Nationale des Sciences Politiques, 1979.

Bell, Philip. "'Thank God for the French Army': Churchill, France and the Alternative to Appeasement in the 1930s," Christopher Baxter, Michael L. Dockrill and Keith Hamilton, eds. *Britain in Global Politics*, I: *From Gladstone to Churchill.* London: Palgrave Macmillan, 2013, 175-89.

Bell, P.M.H. *France and Britain, 1900-1940: Entente and Estrangement.* London: Longman, 1996.

Benoist-Méchin, Jacques. *Sixty Days that Shook the West: The Fall of France, 1940*, trans. Peter Wiles. New York: Putnam's, 1963.

Bethell, Nicholas. *The War Hitler Won.* London: Allen Lane, 1972.

Bloch, Marc. *L'étrange défaite.* Paris: Albin Michel, 1951.

Bond, Brian. *British Military Policy between the Two World Wars.* Oxford: Clarendon Press, 1980.

_____. "The Calm before the Storm: Britain and the 'Phoney War' 1939-40," *The RUSI Journal,* Spring 1990, 61-67.

_____. "Dunkirk: Myths and Lessons," *The RUSI Journal,* September 1982, 3-8.

_____. *France and Belgium, 1939-1940.* Newark, DE: University of Delaware Press, 1979.

_____. *War and Society on Europe, 1870-1970.* Montreal: McGill-Queen's University Press, 1998.

Bond, Brian, ed. *Chief of Staff: The Diaries of Lieutenant-General Sir Henry Pownall*, I: *1933-1940.* London: Leo Cooper, 1972.

Bonnet, Georges. *Défense de la paix. De Munich à la guerre.* Paris: Plon, 1967.

Boothby, Robert. *I Fight to Live.* London: Victor Gollanz, 1947.

Bouverie, Tim. *Appeasement: Chamberlain, Hitler, Churchill and the Road to War.* New York: Tim Duggan Books, 2019.

Bowyer, Chaz. *History of the RAF.* London: Bison Books, 1986.

Boyce, Robert, ed. *French Foreign and Defense Policy: The Decline and Fall of a Great Power.* London: Routledge, 1998.

Brailsford, Henry Noel. *After the Peace.* London: Leonard Parsons, 1920.

Brittain, Vera. *Wartime Chronicle, 1939-1945.* London: Victor Gollancz, 1989.

Brogan, Denis W. *The Development of Modern France.* London: Hamish Hamilton, 1940.

Brooke, Stephen. *Labour's War: The Labour Party during the Second World War.* Oxford: Clarendon Press, 1992.

Brown, David. *The Road to Oran: Anglo-French Naval Relations, September 1939–July1940.* London: Frank Cass, 2003.

Bruegel, J. W. *Czechoslovakia before Munich: The German Minority Problem and British Appeasement Policy.* Cambridge: Cambridge University Press, 1973.

Bryant, Arthur. *English Saga, 1840-1940.* London: Fontana, 1940.

_____. *Unfinished Victory.* London: Macmillan, 1940.

Bullitt, Orvill H., ed. *For the President, Personal and Secret: Correspondence between Franklin D. Roosevelt and William C. Bullitt.* London: André Deutsch, 1972.

Bullock, Alan. *Hitler: A Study in Tyranny.* New York: Harper & Row, 1962.

_____."Hitler and the Origins of the Second World War," Esmonde M. Robertson, ed. *The Origins of the Second World War.* London: Macmillan, 1971, 189-224.

Burckhardt, Carl. J. *Meine Danziger Mission, 1937-1939.* Munich: Callwey, 1960.

Butler, J.R.M. *Grand Strategy,* II. London: H. M. Stationary Office, 1948.

Butow, Robert J.C. *Japan's Decision to Surrender.* Stanford, CA: Stanford University Press, 1954.

Caquet, P.E. The *Bell of Treason: The 1938 Munich Agreement in Czechoslovakia.* London: Profile Books, 2018.

Carley, Michael Jabara. *The Alliance that Never Was and the Coming of World War II.* London: House of Stratus, 2000.

263

_____. "'A Situation of Delicacy and Danger,' Anglo-Soviet Relations, August 1939 – March 1940," *Central European History*, July 1999, 175-208.

Chadwin, Mark Lincoln. *The Warhawks: American Interventionists before Pearl Harbor*. New York: Norton, 1968.

Chamberlain, Neville. *In Search of Peace*. New York: Putnam's, 1939.

Channon, Sir Henry. *Chips: The Diaries of Sir Henry Channon*, ed. Robert Rhodes James. London: Weidenfeld & Nicolson, 1967.

Chapman, Guy. *Why France Fell: The Defeat of the French Army in 1940*. New York: Holt, Rinehart and Winston, 1968.

Charman, Terry. *Outbreak 1939: The World Goes to War*. London: Virgin Books, 2009.

Charmley, John. *Chamberlain and the Lost Peace*. London: Hodder & Stoughton, 1989.

Charpentier, Pierre-Frédéric. *La Drôle de Guerre des intellectuels français, 1939-1940*. Paris: Lavauzelle, 2008.

Churchill, Winston S. *Step by Step, 1936-1939*. London: Thornton Butterworth, 1939.

_____. *The Second World War*, I: *The Gathering Storm*; II: *Their Finest Hour*, III: *The Grand Alliance*. London: Penguin, 1985

Ciano, Galeazzo. *The Ciano Diaries, 1939-1943*, ed. Hugh Gibson. New York: Howard Fertig, 1973.

Citno, Robert M. *The Path to Blitzkrieg: Doctrine and Training in the German Army, 1920-1929*. Boulder, CO: Lynne Rienner, 1999. 1939.

Clews, Graham T. *Churchill's Phoney War: A Study in Folly and Frustration*. Annapolis, MD: Naval Institute Press, 2019.

Cole, G.D.H. *War Aims* London: New Statesman and Nation, 1939.

Cole, Wayne S. *Charles A. Lindbergh and the Battle against American Intervention in World War II*. New York: Harcourt Brace and Jovanovich, 1974.

Collier, Richard. *1940, the World in Flames*. London: Hamish Hamilton, 1979.

Colville, John. *The Fringes of Power: Downing Street Diaries. 1939-1955*. New York: Norton, 1985.

Colvin, Ian. *The Chamberlain Cabinet.* New York: Taplinger, 1971.

Coox, Alvin D. "The Pacific War," Peter Duus, ed. *The Cambridge History of Japan,* VI Cambridge: Cambridge University Press, 1988, 315-382.

Corrigan, Gordon. *Blood, Sweat and Arrogance, and the Myths of Churchill's War.* London: Phoenix, 2007.

Costello, John. *Ten Days That Saved the West.* London: Bantam Press, 1991.

Cot, Pierre. *Triumph of Treason.* Chicago: Ziff-Davis, 1944.

Coulondre, Robert. *De Staline à Hitler. Souvenirs de deux ambassades.* Paris: Hachette, 1950.

Cowling, Maurice. *The Impact of Hitler: British Politics and British Policy, 1933-1939.* Cambridge: Cambridge University Press, 1975.

Crane, Sylvia F. and John O. Crane, *Czechoslovakia: Anvil of the Cold War.* New York: Praeger, 1991.

Crankshaw, Edward, ed. *Khrushchev Remembers.* Boston: Little, Brown, 1970.

Crémieux-Brilhac, Jean-Louis. *Les Français de l'an 40,* I: *La guerre oui ou non,* II: *Ouvriers et soldats.* Paris: Gallimard, 1990.

Crowe, Sybil Eyre. "Sir Eyre Crowe and the Locarno Pact," *English Historical Review,* January 1972, 49-71.

Daladier, Édouard. *Défense du pays.* Paris: Flammarion, 1939.

Dallek, Robert. *Franklin D. Roosevelt and Foreign Policy, 1932-1945.* New York: Oxford University Press, 1995.

Dalton, Hugh. *The Fateful Years: Memoirs, 1931-1945.* London: Friedrich Muller, 1957.

_____. *Hitler's War, Before and After.* London: Penguin, 1940.

Daridan, Jean. *Le chemin de la défaite, 1938-1940.* Paris: Plon, 1980.

Davies, Norman. *Europe at War, 1939-1945: No Simple Victory.* London: Macmillan, 2006.

Debski, Slawomir. "Polish Perceptions of the Strategic Situation on the Eve of the Second World War," Michael H. Clemmesen and Marcus S. Faulkner, eds. *Northern European Overture to War, 1939-1941.* Leiden: Brill, 2013, 189-208.

Deighton, Len. *Blood, Tears and Folly*. London: Vintage Books, 2007.

Delbos, Yvon. *L'expérience rouge*. Paris: Au Sans Pareil, 1933.

Deroo, Eric and Pierre de Taillac. *Carnets de déroute, 1939-1940. Lettres et récits inédits*. Paris: Tallandier, 2010.

Dilks, David, ed. *The Diaries of Sir Alexander Cadogan, O. M., 1938-1945*. London: Cassell, 1971.

_____. "The Twilight War and the Fall of France: Chamberlain and Churchill in 1940," *Transactions of the Royal Historical Society*, 1978, 61-86.

Dockrill, Michael. *British Establishment Perspectives on France, 1936-1940*. London: Macmillan, 1999.

_____."British Official Perceptions of France and the French, 1936-1940," in Chassaigne, Philippe and Michael Dockrill, eds. *Anglo-French Relations 1898-1998: From Fashoda to Jospin*, New York: Palgrave, 2002, 94-108.

_____. "The Foreign Office and France during the Phoney War, September 1939 – May 1940," Michael Dockrill and Brian McKercher, eds. *Diplomacy and World Power: Studies in British Foreign Policy, 1890-1950*. Cambridge: Cambridge University Press, 1996, 171-96.

Domarus, Max, ed. *Hitler: Speeches and Proclamations, 1932-1945*, trans. Chris Wilcox. New York: Bolchazy-Carducci, 1997.

Dorgelès, Roland, *La Drôle de Guerre, 1939-1940*. Paris: Albin Michel, 1957.

Doughty, Brigadier-General. Robert A. *The Breaking Point: Sedan and the Fall of France, 1940*. New York: Archon Books, 1990.

Douglas, Roy. *The Advent of War, 1939-1940*. New York: St. Martin's Press, 1974.

_____. *In the Year of Munich*. London: Macmillan, 1977.

Drea, Edward J. *In the Service of the Emperor: Essays on the Imperial Japanese Army*. Lincoln, NE: University of Nebraska Press, 1998.

Duff Cooper, Alfred. *Old Men Forget*. New York: Dutton, 1954.

Duroselle, Jean-Baptiste. *L'abîme, 1939-1945*. Paris: Imprimerie Nationale, 1982.

_____. *La décadence, 1933-1939.* Paris: Imprimerie Nationale, 1979.

Eade, Charles, ed. *The War Speeches of the Rt. Hon. Winston S. Churchill.* 3 vol., London: Cassell, 1951.

Edgerton, David. *Britain's War Machine: Weapons Resources, and Experts in the Second World War.* New York: Oxford University Press, 2011.

Esnouf, Guy Nicolas. "British Government War Aims and Attitudes towards a Negotiated Peace, September 1939 to July 1940," unpublished Ph.D. thesis, Kings College, London, 1988.

Eubank, Keith. *The Origins of World War II.* Wheeling, IL: Harlan Davidson, 2004.

Faber, David. *Munich 1938: Appeasement and World War II.* New York: Simon and Schuster, 2009.

Fabre-Luce, Alfred. *Journal de la France, 1940-1944.* Geneva: Éditions du Cheval Ailé, 1946.

Feiling, Keith. *The Life of Neville Chamberlain.* London: Macmillan, 1946.

Finkel, Alvin and Clement Leibovitz, *The Chamberlain-Hitler Collusion.* Halifax, NS: James Lorimer, 1997.

Fischer, Fritz. *Germany's Aims in the First World War.* New York: Norton, 1967.

Flynn, George O. *Conscription and Democracy: The Draft in France, Great Britain and the United States.* Westport, CT: Greenwood Press, 2002.

Frank, Richard B. "Japanese Political and Military Strategy in 1945," Tsuyoshi Hasegawa, ed. *The End of the Pacific War: Reappraisals.* Stanford, CA: Stanford University Press, 2007, 65-94.

Frankenstein, Robert. *Le prix du réarmament français, 1935-1939.* Paris: Publications de la Sorbonne, 1982.

French, David. *Raising Churchill's Army: The British Army and the War against Germany* .New York: Oxford University Press, 2000.

Frieser, Karl-Heinz with John T. Greenwood. *The Blitzkrieg Legend: The 1940 Campaign in the West.* Annapolis, MD: Naval Institute Press, 2012.

Fuller, Major-General J.F.C. *The Second World War, 1939-1945.* London: Eyre and Spottiswoode, 1948.

Gamelin, General Maurice. *Servir.* 3 vol., Paris: Plon, 1947.

Gardiner, Juliet. *Wartime Britain, 1939-1945.* London: Headline Book Publishing, 2004.

Gates, Eleanor M. *End of the Affair: The Collapse of the Anglo-French Alliance, 1939-1940.* London: George Allen & Unwin, 1981.

Gatzke, Hans W. *Stresemann and the Rearmament of Germany.* Baltimore, MD: Johns Hopkins Press, 1954.

Gaulle, Charles de. *Mémoires de guerre,* I: *L'appel, 1940-1942.* Paris: Plon, 1954.

Gedye, G.E.R., *Fallen Bastions: The Central European Tragedy.* London: Victor Gollancz, 1939.

Gilbert, Martin. *Finest Hour: Winston S. Churchill, 1939-1941* London: Heinemann, 1983.

Goebbels, Joseph. *The Goebbels Diaries, 1939-1941,* ed. and trans. Fred Taylor. New York: Putnam's, 1983.

Goldstein, Erik. "Neville Chamberlain, the British Official Mind and the Munich Crisis," *Diplomacy and Statecraft,* vol. 10, issue 2-3, 276-292.

Gooch, George Peabody. *Franco-German Relations, 1871-1914.* London: Longmans, 1923.

Gorodetsky, Gabriel. "Les dessous du pacte germano-soviétique," *Le Monde diplomatique,* July 1997, 22-3.

Gorodetsky, Gabriel, ed., *The Maisky Diaries,* trans. Tatania Sorokina and Oliver Ready (New Haven, CT: Yale University Press, 2015.

Goutard, Colonel Alphonse. *The Battle of France, 1940,* trans. A.R.P. Burgess. New York: Ives Washburn, 1959.

Graves, Robert. *Goodbye to All That.* London: Penguin, 1960.

Great Britain, Ministry of Information. *The Assurance of Victory.* London: H. M. Stationary Office, 1939.

Greenwood, Arthur. *Why We Fight, Labour's Case*. London: Routledge, 1940.

Grenard, Fabrice. *La Drôle de Guerre. L'entrée en guerre des Français*. Paris: Belin, 2015.

Griffiths, Richard. *What Did You Do During the War? The Last Throes of the British pro-Nazi Right, 1940-1945*. London: Routledge, 2017.

Gunther, John. *Inside Europe*. New York: Harper, 1940

Haarr, Geirr H. *The Battle for Norway: April – June 1940*. Annapolis, MD: Naval Institute Press, 2010.

Hajek, Milos and Josef Novotny, "Munich. Politique et armée tchécoslovaques," *Revue d'histoire de la Deuxième Guerre mondiale*, October 1963, 1-20.

Hamilton, Nigel. *Commander in Chief: FDR's Battle with Churchill, 1943*. New York: Houghton Mifflin Harcourt, 2016.

Hancock, W.K. and M. Gowing. *British War Economy*. London: H. M. Stationary Office, 1949.

Harman, Nicholas. *Dunkirk: The Patriotic Myth* (New York: Simon and Schuster, 1980.

Harrison, Tom and Charles Madge, eds. *War Begins at Home, by Mass Observation*. London: Chatto & Windus, 1940.

Harvey, John, ed., *The Diplomatic Diaries of Oliver Harvey*. London: Collins, 1970.

Hasegawa, Tsuyoshi. "The Atomic Bomb and the Soviet Invasion," *The End of the Pacific War: Reappraisals*, 113-44.

_____. *Racing the Enemy: Stalin, Truman, and the Surrender of Japan*. Cambridge, MA: Belknap Press, 2005.

Hastings, Max, *Winston's War, 1940-1945*. New York: Vintage Books, 2011.

Hauner, Milan. "Czechoslovakia as a Military Factor in British Considerations of 1938," *Journal of Strategic Studies*, 1978, 194-228.

Hayes, Nick. "An 'English War', Wartime Culture and 'Millions Like Us'," Nick Hayes and Jeff Hill, eds. *"Millions Like Us"?*

British Culture in the Second World War. Liverpool: Liverpool University Press, 1999 1-32.

Henderson, Sir Nicholas. "A Fatal Guarantee: Poland, 1939," *History Today*, October 1997, 19-25.

Herman, John. *The Paris Embassy of Sur Eric Phipps: Anglo-French Relations and the Foreign Office.* Brighton: Sussex Academic Press, 1998.

Hillgruber, Andreas. *Germany and the Two World Wars*, trans. William C. Kirby. Cambridge, MA: Harvard University Press, 1981.

Hinsley, F.H. *British Intelligence in the Second World War*, I. London: H. M. Stationary Office, 1979.

Hooker, Nancy Harvison, ed. *The Moffat Papers. 1919-1943.* Cambridge, MA: Harvard University Press, 1956.

Ickes, Harold L. *The Secret Diary of Harold Ickes*, II: *The Inside Struggle, 1936-1939*; III: *The Lowering Clouds, 1939-1941.* New York: Simon and Schuster, 1954.

Imlay, Talbot C. *Facing the Second World War: Strategy, Politics and Economics in Britain and France, 1938-1940.* Oxford: Oxford University Press, 2003.

_____. "France and the Phoney War, 1939-1940," Boyce. *French Foreign and Defense Policy,* 261-82.

_____. "Paul Reynaud and France's Response to Nazi Germany, 1938-1940," *French Historical Studies*, Summer 2003, 497-538.

Ironside, General Sir Edmund. *Time Unguarded: The Ironside Diaries, 1937-1940*, ed. Roderick MacLeod and Denis Kelly. New York: D. McKay, 1963.

Irvine, William D."Domestic Politics and the Fall of France in 1940," Joel Blatt, ed. *The French Defeat of 1940: Reassessments.* Providence, RI: Berghahn Books, 1998, 85-99.

Ismay, General Hastings. *The Memoirs of General the Lord Ismay.* London: Heinemann, 1960.

Jackson, Julian. *The Fall of France: The Nazi Invasion of 1940.* Oxford: Oxford University Press, 2003.

Jackson, Peter. *France and the Nazi Menace: Intelligence and Policy Making, 1933-1939*. Oxford: Oxford University Press, 2000.

James, Robert Rhodes. "The Politician," A.J.P. Taylor ed., *Churchill Revised*, 63-129.

Jedrzejewicz, Waclaw, ed. *Diplomat in Berlin,1933-1939: Papers and Memoirs of Jozef Lipski, Ambassador of Poland*. New York: Columbia University Press, 1968.

Jessop. T.E. *The Treaty of Versailles, Was It Just?* London: Nelson, 1942.

Johnson, Paul. *Modern Times: The World from the Twenties to the Eighties*. New York: Harper & Row, 1983.

Kennan, George F. *From Prague after Munich: Diplomatic Papers*. Princeton, NJ: Princeton University Press, 1971.

Kennedy, Paul. *The Realities behind Diplomacy: Background Influences to British External Policy, 1865-1980*. London: Fontana, 1980.

_____. *The Rise and Fall of the Great Powers*. London: Unwin Hyman, 1988.

Kershaw, Ian. *Hitler*, I: *1889-1936, Hubris*. London: Penguin, 1999.

Keynes, John Maynard. *The Economic Consequences of the Peace*. New York: Harcourt, Brace and Howe, 1920.

_____. *A Revision of the Treaty*. London: Macmillan, 1922.

Kimball, Warren F., ed. *Churchill & Roosevelt: The Complete Correspondence*, I. Princeton, NJ: Princeton University Press, 1984.

Kindleberger, Charles P. *A Financial History of Western Europe*. London: George Allen & Unwin, 1984.

King, Cecil H. *With Malice Toward None: A War Diary*. London: Sedgwick & Jackson, 1970.

Kirkpatrick, Sir Ivone. *The Inner Circle*. London: Macmillan, 1959.

Knight, Nigel. *Churchill: The Greatest Briton Unmasked*. Cincinnati, OH: David and Charles, 2008.

Kochan, Lionel. *The Struggle for Germany, 1914-1945*. Edinburgh: University Press, 1963.

Kotkin, Stephen. *Stalin: Waiting for Hitler, 1929-1941*. New York: Penguin, 2017.

ILamb, Richard. *Churchill as War Leader*. New York: Carroll & Graf, 1991.

_____. *The Drift to War, 1922-1939*. London: Bloomsbury, 1991.

Liddell Hart, Sir Basil H. *The British Way in Warfare*. London: Faber & Faber, 1932.

_____. *The Defence of Britain*. London: Faber & Faber, 1939.

_____. *Europe in Arms*. London: Faber & Faber, 1939.

_____. *History of the Second World War*. London: Macmillan, 1997.

_____. *The Memoirs of Captain Liddell Hart*. London: Cassell, 1965.

_____. "The Military Strategist," A.J.P. Taylor, ed. *Churchill Revised: A Critical Assessment*. New York: Dial Press, 1969, 173-225.

_____. *The Real War, 1914-1918*. Boston: Little, Brown, 1930.

Liss, Colonel Ulrich. *Westfront 1939/40: Erinnerung des Feldarbeiters im OKH*. Neckargemünd: Vowinkel, 1959.

Lloyd George, David. *The Truth about Reparations and War Debts*. London: Heinemann, 1932.

Lloyd of Dolobran, Lord. *The British Case*. London: Eyre & Spottiswoode, 1939.

Lockhart, R.H. Bruce. *Comes the Reckoning*. London: Putnam, 1947.

Ludlow, Peter, "Le débat sur les buts de paix en Grande-Bretagne durant l'hiver 1939-1940,"
Comité d'histoire de la Deuxième Guerre mondiale, *Français et Britanniques dans la Drôle de Guerre*. Paris: Éditions du Centre National de la Recherche Scientifique, 1979, 93-122.

_____. "The Unwinding of Appeasement," Lothar Kettenacker, ed. *Das "Andere Deutschland" im Zweiten Weltkrieg*. Stuttgart: Ernst Klett Verlag, 1977.

Lukacs, John. *The Duel, 10 May – 31 July 1940: The Eighty-Day Struggle Between Churchill and Hitler*. New York: Ticknor & Fields, 1991.

Lukes, Igor. "The Czechoslovak Partial Mobilization in May 1938: A Mystery (almost) Solved," *Journal of Contemporary History*, October 1996, 699-720.

_____. *Czechoslovakia between Stalin and Hitler: The Diplomacy of Eduard Benes in the 1930s*. New York: Oxford University Press, 1996.

Lukes, Igor and Erik Goldstein, eds. *The Munich Crisis, 1938: Prelude to World War II*. London: Frank Cass, 1999.

Macleod, Iain. *Neville Chamberlain*. London: Frederick Muller, 1961.

Macmillan, Harold. *Winds of Change, 1914-1939*. London: Macmillan, 1966.

Maiolo, Joe. "'To Gamble All on a Single Throw': Neville Chamberlain and the Strategy of the Phoney War," *Britain in Global Politics*, I, 220-41.

Marks, Sally. *The Ebbing of European Ascendancy*. London: Hodder Arnold, 2002.

_____. "The Myths of Reparations," *Central European History*, September 1978, 231-55.

Massock, Richard G. *Italy from Within*. New York: Macmillan, 1943.

May, Ernest R. *Strange Victory: Hitler's Conquest of France*. New York: Hill and Wang, 2000.

Mayer, Arno J. *Politics and Diplomacy of Peacemaking: Containment and Counterrevolution at Versailles, 1918-1919*. New York: Knopf, 1967.

McCullough, David. *Truman*. New York: Simon and Schuster, 1992.

McElwee, William. *Britain's Locust Years, 1918-1940*. London: Faber & Faber, 1962.

McLaine, Ian. *Ministry of Morale: Home Front Morale and the Ministry of Information in World War II*. London: George Allen & Unwin, 1979.

Mee, Richard Charles. "The Foreign Policy of the Chamberlain Wartime Administration, September 1939 – May 1940." Unpublished Ph.D. thesis, University of Birmingham, 1998.

Michel, Henri. *La défaite de la France*. Paris: Presses Universitaires de France, 1980.

_____. *La Drôle de Guerre*. Paris: Hachette, 1971.

Montgomery, General Bernard. *The Memoirs of Field-Marshal the Viscount Montgomery of El Alamein, K. G.* London: Collins, 1958.

Morley, Joel. "The Memory of the Great War and Morale during Britain's Phoney War," *The Historical Journal*, March 2020, 437-67.

Mosier, John. *The Blitzkrieg Myth: How Hitler and the Allies Misread the Strategic Realities of World War II*. New York: HarperCollins, 2003.

Mosley, Leonard. *On Borrowed Time: How World War II Began*. London: Pan Books, 1971.

Moss, Norman. *Nineteen Weeks: America, Britain, and the Fateful Summer of 1940*. Boston: Houghton Mifflin, 2003.

Müller, Rolf-Dieter, *Enemy in the East: Hitler's Secret Plans to Invade the Soviet Union*, trans. Alexander Starritt. London: Tauris, 2015.

Munch-Petersen, Thomas. *The Strategy of Phoney War: Britain, Sweden and the Iron Ore Question, 1939-1940*. Stockholm: Militarhistoriska Förlaget, 1081

Murray, Williamson. *The Change in the European Balance of Power, 1938-1939*. Princeton, NJ: Princeton University Press, 1984.

_____."The Strategy of the 'Phoney War': a Re-evaluation," *Military Affairs*, February 1981, 13-17.

_____. *A War to Be Won: Fighting the Second World War*. Cambridge, MA: Belknap Press, 2000.

Naegelen, Marcel-Edmond. *L'attente sous les armes ou la Drôle de Guerre*. Paris: Jérôme Martineau, 1970.

Namier, Sir Lewis. *Diplomatic Prelude, 1938-1939*. London: Macmillan, 1948.

_____. *Europe in Decay: A Study in Disintegration, 1936-1940*. New York: Macmillan, 1950.

_____. *In the Nazi Era*. London: Macmillan, 1952.

Newman, Scott. *Profits of Peace: The Political Economy of Anglo-German Appeasement*. Oxford: Clarendon Press, 1996.

Newman, Simon. *March 1939: The British Guarantee to Poland.* Oxford: Clarendon Press, 1976.

Nicolson, Harold. *Why Britain is at War.* London: Penguin, 1939.

Nicolson, Nigel, ed. *Harold Nicolson Diaries and Letters,* I: *1930-1939*; II: *The War Years, 1939-1945.* New York: Atheneum, 1967.

Nord, Philip. *France 1940: Defending the Republic.* New Haven, CT: Yale University Press, 2015.

Olson, Lynne. *Those Angry Days: Roosevelt, Lindbergh, and America's Fight over World War II, 1939-1941.* New York: Random House, 2013.

Osborn, Patrick R. *Operation Pike: Britain versus the Soviet Union.* Westport, CT: Greenwood Press, 2000.

Ovendale, Ritchie. *"Appeasement" and the English Speaking World.* Cardiff: University of Wales Press, 1975.

Overy, Richard. *The Air War, 1939-1945.* London: Europa, 1980.

_____. *1939: Countdown to War.* London: Allen Lane, 2009.

_____. *The Origins of the Second World War.* Abington: Routledge, 2008.

Overy, Richard and Andrew Wheatcroft. *The Road to War.* London: Macmillan, 1989.

Panter-Downes, Mollie. *London War Notes, 1939-1945.* New York: Farrar, Strauss and Giroux, 1971.

Parker, R.A.C. *Chamberlain and Appeasement: British Policy and the Coming of the Second World War.* New York: St. Martin's Press, 1993.

Peden, G.C., "Sir Horace Wilson and Appeasement," *The Historical Journal,* December 2010. 983-1014.

Pertinax (André Géraud). *Les fossoyeurs.* New York: Éditions de la Maison Française, 1943.

Phillips, Adrian. *Fighting Churchill, Appeasing Hitler: Neville Chamberlain, Sir Horace Wilson, & Britain's Plight of Appeasement,* New York: Pegasus Books, 2019.

Pimlott, Ben, ed. *The Political Diary of Hugh Dalton, 1918-1940, 1945-1960.* London: Jonathan Cape, 1986.

Plokhy, S.M. *Yalta, the Price of Peace*. New York: Penguin, 2010.

Ponting, Clive. *1940, Myth and Reality*. London: Sphere Books, 1990.

Prior, Robin. *When Britain Saved the West: The Story of 1940*. New Haven, CT: Yale University Press, 2015.

Ragsdale, Hugh. *The Soviets, the Munich Crisis, and the Coming of World War II*. Cambridge: Cambridge University Press, 2004.

Réau, Élisabeth du. *Édouard Daladier, 1884-1970*. Paris: Fayard, 1993.

_____. "Édouard Daladier: The Conduct of the War and the Beginnings of Defeat," Blatt, *The French Defeat of 1940*, 100-25.

Reid, Walter. *Churchill 1940-1945: Under Friendly Fire*. Edinburgh: Birlinn, 2008.

Reynaud, Paul. *Au coeur de la mêlée, 1930-1945*. Paris: Flammarion, 1951.

Reynolds, David. *The Creation of the Anglo-American Alliance, 1937-41*. Chapel Hill, NC: University if North Carolina Press, 1982.

_____. *Summits: Six Meetings that Shaped the Twentieth Century*. New York: Basic Books, 2007.

Roberts, Andrew. *Churchill: Embattled Hero*. London: Phoenix, 1995.

_____. *Eminent Churchillians*. London: Weidenfeld & Nicolson, 1994.

_____. *"The Holy Fox," a Biography of Lord Halifax*. London: Weidenfeld and Nicolson, 1991.

_____. *Masters and Commanders*. London: Penguin, 2009.

Robbins, Keith. *Appeasement*. Oxford: Blackwell, 1980.

Rochat, Georgio. "La campagne italienne de juin 1940 dans les Alpes occidentales," *Revue historique des armées*, 250 (2008), 77-84.

Rocolle, Pierre. *La guerre de 1940*, I: *Les illusions, novembre 1918 – mai 1940*. Paris: Armand Colin, 1990.

Rosecrance, Richard and Zara Steiner. "British Grand Strategy and the Origins of World War II," Richard Roserance and Arthur A. Stein, eds. *The Domestic Bases of Grand Strategy*. Ithaca, NY: Cornell University Press, 1993, 124-153.

Rossi-Landi, Guy. *La Drôle de Guerre; la vie politique en France, 2 septembre 1939 – 10 mai 1940*. Paris: Armand Colin, 1971.

Rowse, A.L. *Appeasement: a Study in Political Decline, 1933-1939.* New York: Norton, 1961.

Salerno, Reynolds M. *Vital Crossroads: Mediterranean Origins of the Second World War.* Ithaca, NY: Cornell University Press, 2002.

Schuker, Stephen A. *American "Reparations" to Germany, 1919-1933: Implications for the Third-World Debt Crisis.* Princeton, NJ: International Finance Section, Department of Economics, 1988.

_____. *The End of French Predominance in Europe.* Chapel Hill, NC: The University of North Carolina Press, 1976.

_____. "France and the Remilitarization of the Rhineland, 1936," *French Historical Studies*, Spring 1986, 299-338.

_____. "Seeking a Scapegoat. Intelligence and Grand Strategy in France, 1939-1940," Haslam, Jonathan and Karina Urbach, *Secret Intelligence in the European States System, 1918-1989*, Stanford, CA: Stanford University Press, 2014, 81-127.

Schwoerer, Lois G. "Lord Halifax's Visit to Germany: November 1937," *The Historian*, May 1970, 353-75.

Seager, Frederic. "Les buts de guerre alliés devant l'opinion, 1939-1940," *Revue d'histoire moderne et contemporaine*, October-December 1985, 617-38.

Seaman, L.C.B. *Post-Victorian Britain, 1902-1951.* London: Routledge, 1991.

Self, Robert. *Neville Chamberlain, a Biography.* Aldershot: Ashgate, 2006.

_____, ed. *The Neville Chamberlain Diary Letters, IV: The Downing Street Years, 1934-1940.* Aldershot: Ashgate, 2005.

Shachtman, Tom. *The Phony War, 1939-1940.* New York: Harper & Row, 1982.

Shaw, Louise Grace. "Attitudes of the British Political Elite towards the Soviet Union," *Diplomacy and Statecraft*, vol. 13, issue 1 (2002), 55-74.

Shirer, William L. *Berlin Diary: The Journal of a Foreign Correspondent, 1934-1941.* New York: Knopf, 1941.

_____. *The Collapse of the Third Republic: An Inquiry into the Fall of France in 1940.* New York: Simon and Schuster, 1969.

Shlaim, Avi. "Prelude to Downfall: The British Offer of Union to France, June 1940," *Journal of Contemporary History*, July 1974, 27-63.

Smalley, Edward. *The British Expeditionary Force, 1939-40.* London: Palgrave Macmillan, 2015.

Smart, Nick and Jeremy Black. *British Strategy and Politics during the Phony War: Before the Balloon Went Up.* Westport, CT: Praeger, 2003.

Spears, General Sir Edward. *Assignment to Catastrophe.* 2 vol., London: Heinemann, 1954.

Stargardt, Nicholas, *The German War: A Nation Under Arms, 1939-1945.* New York: Basic Books, 2015.

Stedman Andrew David. *Alternatives to Appeasement: Neville Chamberlain and Hitler's Germany.* London: Tauris, 2011.

Steed, Henry Wickham. *Our War Aims.* London: Secker and Warburg, 1939.

Steiner, Zara. *The Triumph of the Dark: European International History, 1933-1939.* New York: Oxford University Press, 2011.

Stewart, Graham. *Burying Caesar: Churchill, Chamberlain and the Battle for the Tory Party.* London: Weidenfeld and Nicolson, 1999.

Stone, Norman. *Hitler.* London: Coronet Books, 1982.

Strang, Lord William. *Home and Abroad.* London: André Deutsch, 1956.

Sylvester. A.J. *Life with Lloyd George.* London: Macmillan, 1975.

Taylor, A.J.P. *English History, 1914-1945.* Oxford: Clarendon Press, 1965.

_____. *The Origins of the Second World War.* London: Hamish Hamilton, 1961.

_____. *The Second World War: An Illustrated History.* London: Hamish Hamilton, 1975.

Taylor, Edmund. *The Strategy of Terror: Europe's Inner Front.* Boston: Houghton Mifflin, 1940.

Taylor, Telford. *The March of Conquest: The German Victories in Western Europe, 1940.* London: Edward Hulton, 1959.

_____. *Munich, the Price of Peace*. New York: Doubleday, 1979.

Terraine, John. *The First World War, 1914-1918*. London: Macmillan, 1965.

Thorne, Christopher. *The Approach of War, 1938-1939*. London: Macmillan, 1967.

Todman, Daniel. *Britain's War: Into Battle, 1937-1941*. London: Penguin, 2017.

Tombs, Robert and Isabelle, *That Sweet Enemy: The French and the British from the Sun King to the Present*. New York: Knopf, 2007.

Tooze, Adam. *The Wages of Destruction: The Making and Breaking of the Nazi War Economy*. London: Penguin, 2006.

Trevor-Roper, H.R. *Hitler's War Directives, 1939-1945*. London: Sidgwick and Jackson, 1964.

Turner, Barry. *Waiting for War: Britain 1939-1940*. London: Icon Books, 2019.

Turner, E.L. *The Phoney War on the Home Front*. London: Michael Joseph, 1961.

Upton, Anthony F. *Finland, 1939-1940*. Newark, DE: University of Delaware Press, 1974.

Villelume, Paul de. *Journal d'une défaite, 26 août 1939 - 16 juin 1940*. Paris: Fayard, 1970.

Vital, David. "Czechoslovakia and the Powers, September 1938," *Journal of Contemporary History*, October 1966, 37-67.

Waites, Neville, ed. *Troubled Neighbours: Franco-British Relations in the Twentieth Century*. London: Weidenfeld and Nicolson, 1971.

Walker, Jonathan, *Churchill's Third World War: British Plans to Attack the Soviet Empire, 1945*. London: The History Press, 2017.

Wark, Wesley K. *The Ultimate Enemy: British Intelligence and Nazi Germany, 1933-1939*. London: Tauris, 1985.

Watt, Donald Cameron. "German Plans for the Reoccupation of the Rhineland: A Note," *Journal of Contemporary History*, October 1966, 193-99.

_____. *How War Came: The Immediate Origins of the Second World War, 1938-1939*. New York: Pantheon Books, 1989.

Weight, Richard. *Patriots: National Identity in Britain, 1940-2000*. London: Macmillan, 2002.

Weinberg, Gerhard L. *Hitler's Foreign Policy, 1933-1939: The Road to World War II*. New York: Enigma Books, 2010.

Welles, Sumner. *The Time for Decision*. New York: Harper, 1944.

Werth, Alexander and Denis W. Brogan, *The Twilight of France, 1933-1940*. New York: Harper, 1942.

Wheeler-Bennett, John W. *King George VI, His Life and Reign*. London: Macmillan, 1958.

_____. *Munich, Prologue to Tragedy*. New York: Duell, Sloan and Pearce, 1962.

_____. *The Nemesis of Power: The German Army in Politics, 1918-1945*. New York: St. Martin's Press, 1954.

Williams, Maude and Bernard Wilkin. *French Soldiers' Morale in the Phoney War, 1939-1940*. London: Routledge, 2019.

Woodward, Sir Llewellyn. *British Foreign Policy in the Second World War*. London: H. M. Stationary Office, 1962.

Wuorinen, John H., ed. *Finland and World War II, 1939-1944*. New York: Ronald Press, 1948.

Young, Robert J. *In Command of France: French Foreign Policy and Military Planning, 1933-1940*. Cambridge, MA: Harvard University Press, 1978.

Zévaès, Alexandre. *Histoire de six ans, 1938-1944*. Paris: Éditions de la Nouvelle Revue Critique, 1944.

Zinsou, Cameron, "The Forgotten Story of Operation Anvil," *New York Times*, 15 August 2019.

INDEX

Admiral Graf Spee, 133.
Alsace-Lorraine, 16-17, 35, 102, 112-113, 130, 146, 242-243.
Amery, Leopold, 110, 134-135, 184, 191.
Angell, Norman, 157.
Attlee, Clement, 57, 64, 72, 105, 121, 191, 208.
Austria, 14, 32, 35, 39-42, 44-45, 47, 80, 112.
Australia, 9, 125, 161.
Baldwin, Stanley, 34, 68.
Bastid, Paul, 159-160.
Belgium, 14-15, 21-22, 24, 27, 33, 66, 76, 120, 146, 193-194, 209, 213, 223.
Beck, Jozef, 84, 88, 92-93.
Benes, Edvard, 45-46, 60.
Blockade, 9, 116, 130, 137-138, 140, 153, 171, 173, 178, 180, 182, 186.
Blum, Léon, 52, 160, 202.
Bolshevism, 24, 39-41, 84, 138, 152, 159, 177.
Bonnet, Georges, 63, 60, 85, 110-111, 114.
Brest-Litovsk, treaty, 19-20, 146.
British Expeditionary Force, 15, 123, 134, 139, 196, 202-203, 210-212, 226, 244, 256.
Brittain, Vera, 158, 227.
Bryant, Arthur, 98, 155-156, 212.
Buchanan, George, 158.
Bullitt, William, 175.
Burckhardt, Carl J., 242.
Butler, R.A., 148.
Cadogan, Alexander, 50, 83, 111, 142.
Canada, 9, 109, 125-126, 132, 161-162, 165, 244, 250.
Chamberlain, Anne, 212.
Chamberlain, Arthur, 139.
Chamberlain, Austen, 29.

Churchill, Winston, 7-10, 13, 15, 19, 24, 29-31, 47-48, 52, 67-68, 80, 83, 86, 90, 96, 106-110, 121-122, 128, 136, 147, 155, 157, 171-172, 176, 178, 183, 189-190, 192, 198-199, 202, 206, 208-217, 220, 224-225, 22-231, 233-234, 236-240, 244-247, 250-252, 256-257.

Ciano. Galeazzo, 70, 108, 143.

Clemenceau, Georges, 23-25.

Cole, G.D.H., 138, 151.

Colville, John, 128, 159, 184, 216.

Corbin, Charles, 106, 160, 172.

Coulondre, Robert, 61-62, 88, 101.

Cripps, Stafford, 131, 155.

Czechoslovakia, 8, 23, 37-39, 41-57, 59-69, 71, 74, 76-80, 84, 90-91, 96, 105, 107, 110, 112, 114, 155, 162, 155, 169, 178, 215, 252-254, 256-258.

Daladier, Édouard, 13, 48-50, 52, 57-59, 62-64, 68, 70-71, 73, 76, 78, 85-86, 101-102, 105-106, 110-111, 121, 123, 131-132, 134, 160-161, 170, 175, 177-178, 189, 182, 186, 219, 223, 242-243, 257, 259.

Dalton, Hugh, 106, 108, 155, 166.

Danzig, 82, 89-92, 94, 96.

Darlan, François, 225-226.

Dawson, W.H., 151.

Delbos, Yvon, 45.

Duff Cooper, Alfred, 66-67, 107.

Eden, Anthony, 33, 39, 48, 68, 96.

Eisenhower, Dwight D., 250-251.

Faucher, Louis-Eugène, 64.

Finland, 104, 183-187.

Fisher, H.A.L., 168.

Gamelin, Maurice, 54, 56, 119-122, 159. 173, 183, 186, 201, 207, 216, 223.

Gaulle, Charles de, 19, 61-62, 187, 196, 225, 231.

George VI, King, 109, 219.

Goebbels, Joseph, 189, 202.

Göring, Hermann, 38, 40, 91, 143, 151.

Gort, John Vereker Viscount, 202.

Greenwood, Arthur, 105, 112, 154, 208, 220.

Halifax, Edward Frederick Lindley Wood 1st Earl, 38-39, 41, 46, 52-54, 58, 62, 64, 68-69, 72-73, 77-78, 80-81, 88, 96-97, 103, 105, 116, 129, 132, 138, 141-143, 152, 154-155, 162-63 177-178, 184, 208, 214, 217, 220-221, 229.

Hankey, Maurice, 1st baron, 221.

Harvey, Oliver, 103, 141, 209.

Henderson, Nevile, 38, 56, 90, 94-95, 116.

Henlein, Konrad, 48-49.

Hitler, Adolf, 7-13, 25, 27, 29-33, 35-37, 41-43, 45-46, 48-55, 57-58, 63, 65-70, 72-74, 76-98, 100-105, 112, 116-118, 121, 125, 127, 133, 136, 139, 142, 145, 147-148, 163, 166, 170-171, 175, 180, 185, 188-189, 191, 199, 205, 207, 215, 227-228, 229-230, 233, 237, 241, 243-245, 255-257.

Hoare, Samuel, 46, 107.

Hore-Belisha, Leslie, 171, 223.

Inskip, Thomas, 43, 55, 64-65, 78.

Ironside, Edmund Baron, 79, 122, 184, 220, 244.0.

Ismay, Hastings 1st Baron, 167, 214, 256.

Italy, 11, 70, 73, 85, 129, 138, 173, 183, 204, 240, 246, 252.

Japan. 10, 130, 239-240, 249, 251.

Jews, 49, 69, 89, 91, 150, 169.

Kennedy, Joseph, 83, 96, 100, 140, 152, 229.

Keynes, John Maynard, 20, 23, 25-27, 30, 36, 218, 252.

King-Hall, Stephen, 170, 217.

Léger, Alexis, 94, 175.

Liddell Hart, Basil, 18-19, 89, 93, 103, 115, 122, 124, 137-138, 173-174, 201, 241.

Lloyd George, David, 24, 28, 31, 47, 87, 137, 158, 212, 229, 241.

Lloyd of Dolobran, George Ambrose Baron, 58, 149.

Locarno treaty, 30-31, 69.

Luce, Henry R., 174, 254.

Mackenzie King, W.L., 109, 126, 132.

Maginot Line, 9, 81, 102, 137, 170, 172-173, 202, 222-223.

Maisky, Ivan, 41, 58, 83.

Masaryk, Jan, 78, 253.

Mers el-Kébir, 224-225.

Moffat, Jay Pierrepont, 51, 96, 233.

Montgomery, Bernard Viscount, 189, 211.

Morrison, Herbert, 110.

Mosley, Oswald, 229.

Munich conference, 8, 25, 44, 54, 57-58, 113, 121, 155, 174, 176, 178, 257, 259.

Mussolini, Benito, 12, 73, 76, 105, 110, 129.

Namier, Lewis, 35, 62.

Nazi-Soviet pact, 100, 109, 114, 149, 175-176, 242.

Netherlands, 80, 120, 192, 210, 255.

New Zealand, 125, 161.

Newton, Basil, 50, 56, 77.

Norman, Montagu, 40.

Norway, 11, 104, 170, 187, 190-191, 199.

Operation Pike, 188-189.

Operation Unthinkable, 251.

Paul-Boncour, Joseph, 63, 67.

Peace Front, 68, 93-94.

Pétain, Philippe, 206, 216, 222-223.

Phipps, Eric, 54, 64, 102, 111, 162-163.

Poincaré, Raymond, 26-27, 127, 166.

Poland, 8-9, 11-13, 20, 53, 55-57, 60-61, 67, 80-96, 98-105, 108-110, 112-113, 115, 117, 119-121, 124, 127-131, , 133-134, 143-145, 147, 150, 152, 161, 169, 175, 186, 204, 214, 221, 252-253, 256-258

Pownall, Henry, 32, 211.

Rathbone, Eleanor, 147.

Reparations, 20-21, 23-24, 26-28, 34, 159, 178.

Reynaud, Paul, 45, 170, 176, 178-182, 186, 190, 201, 206, 209-210, 212, 217, 220, 233.

Rhineland, 30-34, 117, 156.

Ribbentrop, Joachim, 89, 91-92, 100, 139.

Roosevelt, Franklin D., 8, 58, 74-75, 96, 115, 126, 129-130, 141, 215, 228-229, 233-234, 236-237, 240-241, 244-247, 253.

Royal Air Force, 80, 117, 123, 127, 187, 194-195, 244, 258.

Royal Navy, 18, 80, 188, 190-191, 224, 228, 244.

Ruhr, 25, 27, 34, 120, 127-128, 164, 195.

Runciman, Walter 1st Viscount, 49-50, 73, 230.

Saar, 101, 119, 244.

Schliffen-Moltke plan, 14, 17, 193.

Shaw, George Bernard, 129, 157, 225, 243.

Siegfried Line, 54, 120.

Sinclair, Archibald, 29, 57, 188.

Snell, Henry 1st Baron, 77, 155.

Soviet Union, 10-11, 46, 50, 55, 57, 61, 84, 86-88, 92, 129-130, 136, 138, 142, 145, 165, 167, 175, 185-187, 230, 239, 243, 247, 249-254, 258.

Spears, Edward, 73, 202, 216.

Stalin, Joseph, 46, 55-56, 68, 85, 88, 99-100, 129, 145, 185, 248, 250-252.

Steed, Henry Wickham, 143.

Stresemann, Gustav, 26-27, 89.

Stronge. H.C.T., 44, 53-54.

Sudetenland, 47-49, 53, 59, 64, 66, 70, 80, 90, 96-97, 143, 242.

Supreme Inter-allied War Council, 123.

Taft, Robert A., 239, 254.

Taylor, A.J.P., 11, 145, 156, 243-244.

Toynbee, Arnold, 48, 134.

Truman, Harry S., 236, 248, 251.

Ukraine, 80, 243, 255.

United States, 9, 18-19, 23, 26-27, 36, 42, 51, 74-75, 81, 97, 104, 107, 109, 126, 130, 132, 134, 141, 144, 147, 165, 179, 216-217, 224, 226, 228-234, 236-237, 239, 246, 254-255, 257, 259.

Versailles treaty, 19, 21, 24-27, 30, 34-36, 39, 64-65, 90, 92, 101, 127-128, 131, 142, 144, 160-161, 162, 164.

Waterfield, Gordon, 222-223.

Watt, Donald Cameron, 168.
Welles, Sumner, 95, 242.
Weygand, Maxime, 216.
Wilson, Horace, 41, 58, 90.
Wilson, Woodrow, 16, 19-20, 42, 230.
Winant, John Gilbert, 239.
Yalta conference, 247, 251-252.